The General Aviation
Industry in America

The General Aviation Industry in America

A History

Second Edition

Donald M. Pattillo

McFarland & Company, Inc., Publishers
Jefferson, North Carolina

LIBRARY OF CONGRESS CATALOGUING-IN-PUBLICATION DATA

Names: Pattillo, Donald M., 1940– author.
Title: The general aviation industry in America : a history / Donald M. Pattillo.
Other titles: Pushing the envelope.
Description: Second Edition. | Jefferson : McFarland & Company, Inc., Publishers, 2020. | Revised edition of the author's Pushing the envelope, 1998. | Includes bibliographical references and index.
Identifiers: LCCN 2020000984 | ISBN 9781476677217 (paperback : acid free paper) ∞ ISBN 9781476638256 (ebook)
Subjects: LCSH: Aircraft industry—United States—History. | Aerospace industries—United States—History.
Classification: LCC HD9711.U6 P37 2020 | DDC 338.4/7629133340973—dc23
LC record available at https://lccn.loc.gov/2020000984

BRITISH LIBRARY CATALOGUING DATA ARE AVAILABLE

ISBN (print) 978-1-4766-7721-7
ISBN (ebook) 978-1-4766-3825-6

© 2020 Donald M. Pattillo. All rights reserved

No part of this book may be reproduced or transmitted in any form or by any means, electronic or mechanical, including photocopying or recording, or by any information storage and retrieval system, without permission in writing from the publisher.

On the cover: Front cover images © 2020 Shutterstock

Printed in the United States of America

McFarland & Company, Inc., Publishers
   Box 611, Jefferson, North Carolina 28640
      www.mcfarlandpub.com

To my family

Table of Contents

Acknowledgments viii
Preface to the Second Edition 1
Preface to the First Edition 3

1—Origins of Personal Aviation 5
2—Growth from the Lindbergh Boom 19
3—Market Expansion and War Production 34
4—The Postwar Era, 1946–1954 53
5—General Aviation Matures, 1954–1967 77
6—The Modern Era, 1967–1979 105
7—The General Aviation Crisis 127
8—The Path to Recovery 153
9—The Industry Enters the New Millennium 172
10—Again, Crisis and Recovery 196

Chapter Notes 223
Bibliography 231
Index 237

Acknowledgments

Several years ago, I decided to undertake an expanded, revised, and updated history of the American general aviation manufacturing industry. My original edition was published in 1998, and many transformative events had occurred in the industry since then. While I regard my knowledge and understanding of the industry to be extensive, I still needed to acquire additional insights. Accordingly, I sought added information and insights from a variety of sources.

In no particular order, I wish to acknowledge the assistance of Tom Crouch of the Aeronautics Department, National Air & Space Museum, and more recently of Jonathan Sweatman of Cirrus Aircraft. Many individuals at the Experimental Aircraft Association in Oshkosh, Wisconsin, also helped. Also, there were those in the industry who were generous in supplying me with illustrations from their firms for inclusion in the new edition.

I especially wish to acknowledge the assistance of my friend and neighbor, Ellie Gratz of Atlanta, for her computer expertise, which bailed me out more than once.

I greatly appreciate the support, attention, and prompt responses of David Alff of McFarland & Company, and the staff. Their advice and assistance served to make this book a higher quality production than it would have been otherwise.

Formally, those I acknowledged in the publication of my first edition, but who are too numerous to mention here, still merit my thanks.

As always, I have endeavored to be factually accurate and to present sound interpretations of industry conditions and events. But as an author, the responsibility for any factual errors, or any flaws or omissions in analysis or inference, is mine and mine alone.

Preface to the Second Edition

There have been developments of wide-ranging significance in the general aviation industry since the first edition of this work appeared more than two decades ago. In addition, new information has become available on many of the companies and developments covered in the earlier years of the industry. Further, little has been published over that same period specifically dealing with general aviation history. Accordingly, I determined that a new edition of my history of the general aviation industry was overdue, and was especially timely as general aviation closes in on a century of existence.

In addition to some rewriting of the earlier chapters of the first edition, both to clarify and expand coverage, I incorporated new developments in the industry, bringing the history up to the present. I developed two further chapters specifically dealing with those recent developments, along with updated statistical tables to support the narrative. Of special note has been the coverage of the impact of the terrorism threat on general aviation, of new and amended regulations that influence general aviation operations, and especially of the impact of globalization on general aviation manufacturing.

In addition, expanded coverage of the homebuilt, rotary wing, and agricultural aviation segments resulted in a major expansion from the earlier work. Perhaps most important is updated and expanded coverage of the business jet field, which has continued to grow through the national security and economic upheavals of the early years of the 21st century, and more than ever dominates the industry in dollar volume of output. As before, attention is paid to technological innovation and development of new general aviation roles, which have continued even during a deep economic recession and political upheavals, and to the challenges to affordability of general aviation, given increasing fuel costs, environmental restrictions, and relentless increases in aircraft prices.

It is the author's hope that this revised and updated edition will serve to enhance the understanding of general aviation, not only within the business community, but with the general public.

Preface to the First Edition

Aviation history is a highly developed field. Numerous works cover specific periods such as the Golden Age of 1919–1939; famous aircraft and major aircraft classes, such as fighters; histories of such major firms as Boeing, Lockheed, and McDonnell Douglas; and biographies of such leading personalities as the Wright brothers, Lindbergh, and Earhart. There are also histories of major aeronautical developments such as the jet engine and the helicopter, of record-breaking flights, and of other aeronautical feats. In addition, there are scholarly studies of the societal and economic impact of aviation and of its technical development. No aspect of aviation has been ignored by scholars or aviation professionals.

A conspicuous gap in the literature, however, is a comprehensive, balanced history of the general aviation manufacturing sector of what is now the aerospace industry. There are, of course, numerous books on private flying and published histories of such companies as Piper, Beech, Cessna, Taylorcraft, and Luscombe, but there has been no overall survey history of general aviation aircraft manufacture. This gap stands in marked contrast to the extensive literature on the large military and commercial aircraft sectors.

Yet the general aviation sector predates both, extending from the beginnings of powered flight, and has been particularly characterized by a spirit of entrepreneurship. General aviation also differs from the much larger military, commercial, and space sectors in that it more closely approaches a consumer products industry, marketing a range of aircraft to single customers, rather than sales of scores or hundreds of a single type to a large airline or military service. General aviation dominates in such important measures as numbers of active aircraft, airfields, pilots, and flying hours, yet is the least understood sector of the industry. A major reason is a lack of historical perspective.

This work bridges that gap in both aviation and business history. Yet defining which firms should be included in a history of the general aviation sector was not always clear. Leading companies such as Beech and Cessna have important military operations, and indeed would not have been likely to survive without that strong military base. Conversely, many large military-commercial firms have been involved in general aviation as well. Most general aviation helicopters have been developed, in fact, by primarily military firms. Their activities in civil helicopters have been allotted extensive coverage in this work.

An overlap in civil and military design has always existed, as business and personal aircraft have been adapted for military training and utility use, while certain military and commercial designs have been adapted as executive transports, firefighting aircraft, and for other civil roles. That overlap is particularly evident in smaller helicopters. Accordingly, certain determinations were necessary as to which firms and operations were included. Further, given the numerous attempts at designing, building, and selling light aircraft, only those firms judged to have been significant, either in production or innovation, have been included. Thus many readers may find an obscure or short-lived firm of their knowledge missing.

Maintaining a manageable focus also presented a challenge. In more recent years the homebuilt or kit industry has gained in significance, largely succeeding the factory-built small trainer aircraft segment. Several firms now offer innovative, successful kit designs. Accordingly, that segment has given substantive treatment. But ultralight/microlight sport aircraft, sailplanes, racing aircraft, and experimental prototypes generally are excluded. While undoubtedly significant to many, these activities are very narrow segments of general aviation, which is primarily oriented toward business flying and other revenue-generating activities. Moreover, microlights do not require FAA certification or pilot licensing. Also generally excluded are modification and conversion firms, as they do not involve original design and production.

The general aviation industry has experienced a turbulent history with a very high failure rate. But general aviation is indeed a national resource with a significant impact on the economy. It remains an underappreciated aspect of the national aviation heritage. It is the author's hope that this work will be a step toward fuller understanding.

1

Origins of Personal Aviation

In the early years of powered flight, as aircraft first began to be produced in series, almost all aviation activity was encompassed within what would later be defined as general aviation. There were no well-defined roles for military aircraft and no scheduled commercial services. Thus the market for aircraft was largely limited to training and to sport and exhibition flying by and for a wealthy few. But World War I saw military applications developed and implemented, and the military sector dominated aviation and aircraft production. Then with the return of peace, many saw the potential for a large civil sportplane market, building on wartime technical progress and on the increased public awareness of aviation. Other aircraft categories and roles that would later become included in general aviation were not then foreseen and thus had not evolved. But as this opening chapter illustrates, many developments important to the future of aviation, and to personal aviation specifically, occurred during the 1920s.

The Light Aircraft Market

Efforts to fill the anticipated peacetime market for sport flying and new sport aircraft were made on both coasts. The young inventor Lawrence Sperry of New York and the Loughead (later Lockheed) brothers of California were among the first to develop small sportplanes. The Loughead S-1 monoplane of 1919, designed by John Northrop, had many advanced features, as did the Sperry M-1A Messenger, a single-seat biplane. Both were worthy designs but did not sell, given the glut of surplus wartime models on the small civil market, although the Army procured 20 Messengers in 1921 as communications aircraft. Sperry, tragically, died in a crash on December 12, 1923, at age 31, ending his company's prospects. The Loughead firm suffered bankruptcy in 1921.

While a substantial market for new private aircraft did not develop in the early 1920s, wartime aeronautical progress still conveyed major benefits to private aviation: the number of pilots had increased rapidly, and there had been major advances in aircraft production techniques. The open-cockpit biplane of wood and fabric construction still dominated, but the abundance of wartime surplus trainers, especially the ubiquitous Curtiss JN-4D Jenny, enabled many to learn to fly relatively cheaply. Interest in private flying was further stimulated in the early 1920s by the barnstorming era and by the popular military-sponsored air races. Barnstormers, or "flying gypsies," traveled from place to place conducting flying exhibitions in the Jenny and comparable aircraft. But barnstorming, while undoubtedly promoting interest in aviation, declined after the mid–1920s. Further, flying was still publicly regarded, not inaccurately, as dangerous. Yet the groundwork had been laid for a sustainable private aviation sector.

Development of scheduled airline service began roughly concurrently with growth of the private aviation sector. But development of efficient, safe, and comfortable passenger-carrying aircraft was painfully slow. Sustained scheduled passenger services in fact lagged air mail, the first commercial growth area, by several years.

All commercial and private aviation, or civil aviation, began to be encompassed within a somewhat nebulous sector under the name aerial service. While lacking precise definition, aerial service involved much more than sport or exhibition flying. Among the first to envision broader roles for light aircraft was Sherman Fairchild of New York, who pioneered not only aerial photography but also development of specialized photographic planes. The State Experiment Station of Ohio first tested airplanes for agricultural use in August 1921. Lieutenant J. A. Macready of McCook Field, a recording-breaking Air Service pilot, conducted the experiments. A new firm, Huff Daland Airplanes of Ogdensburg, New York, first adapted an airplane for aerial cropdusting in 1924. The company thereupon founded Huff Daland Dusters in Macon, Georgia, as the first aerial cropdusting service. The present-day Delta Air Lines sprang from that service. Huff Daland also experimented with, but did not produce, personal aircraft.

Despite innovation and development, the market for new airplanes remained depressed. Public concerns about flying safety further inhibited market growth. The government had done little to develop civil aviation policy and airways development, and there was a lack of licensing and training standards. Then-active aero clubs, led by the New York Aero Club, developed and administered their own standards and regulations. Further, the light aircraft manufacturing sector was too small to exert political influence. Both the Manufacturers Aircraft Association (MAA) and the Aeronautical Chamber of Commerce (ACC) focused chiefly on military aviation and commercial, primarily air mail, operations. The National Advisory Committee for Aeronautics (NACA), the government agency conducting research and experimentation in aviation, did little specifically to advance personal aviation or light aircraft development.

Another deterrent to those potentially attracted to the field was that light aircraft design generally overlapped technically with military aircraft. Military-oriented firms could and did serve both the military and civil sectors. Curtiss, for example, while a leading military firm, was also active in light personal aircraft. Accordingly, a firm wishing to specialize in light civil aircraft could find itself at a disadvantage in resources.

In the midst of dismal financial and market prospects faced by all aircraft manufacturers in the 1920s, the President's Aircraft Board, popularly known as the Morrow Board and established in response to Billy Mitchell's charges of official neglect of air power, carried an impact. The Morrow Board report at the end of 1925, while emphasizing military needs, spurred passage of the Air Commerce Act of 1926. Signed into law by President Coolidge and implemented by Secretary of Commerce Herbert Hoover, the Act benefited all civil aeronautics, including personal flying and other aerial service activities. Aircraft safety and airfield development advanced, and the first federal pilot's licenses were issued in 1927. William P. MacCracken, head of the MIT aeronautical engineering program, was named first chief of the new Aeronautics Branch, and was issued license No. 1 on April 6, 1927. The Act also enabled reliable statistics to be compiled on flying and pilots for the first time. The letter N for U.S.-registered aircraft was adopted on September 1, 1929.

The aerial service sector concurrently gained more precise definition, to include industrial roles such as crop dusting, aerial photography and survey, forest fire patrol and wildlife management, as well as air taxi service and flying instruction.[1] Air mail service continued to grow, as did sport or recreational flying as the number of pilots increased. Skywriting, oil and timber survey, and emergency medical transport roles also appeared. Another new aerial service function was that of news coverage, as aircraft could reach the site of a news event or disaster faster than other means of transport. Scheduled passenger service, while embryonic, was also considered as falling under aerial service, as the personal and commercial sectors did not become largely separate until the early 1930s. The number of airfields increased, and fixed-base operators, primarily involved with training, service, and maintenance, were established from 1920. Such operators facilitated growth of the sector, especially cross-country flying. Partially reflecting the rather primitive aviation technology of the day, however, was that personal aircraft still used automobile gasoline. Specially refined aviation gasoline had not yet appeared.

One private aviation function, little discussed at the time or for years afterward, was the transportation of illegal liquor during Prohibition. The pilot Ben O. Howard, later to gain fame in air racing and as a designer, admitted years after to having participated in aerial bootlegging during the 1920s.[2]

Another civil aircraft role beginning in the 1920s, which was to attain near-legendary status in decades to come, was that of bush flying. The term *bush*, originally referring to the scrublands of South Africa, was extended to include all remote or wilderness regions. Originating in western Canada, Alaska, and wilderness areas of the Pacific Northwest, bush flying eventually included the Australian outback, New Guinea, Mexico, and South America. Functions not only included transportation of hunters, fishermen, and prospectors but aerial mapping, transportation of vital food and medical supplies, and emergency evacuations from sites unreachable by land or water. Float- and ski-landing gear largely developed from bush flying.

Business flying, however, still was very rare; only the largest corporations and a few wealthy businessmen used personal aircraft. But executive aviation began to develop from the mid–1920s, and the Loening Air Yacht, a comfortable enclosed-cabin design powered by a pusher Liberty engine, was a popular business amphibian. The Douglas Dolphin of 1929, with six to eight seats and twin engines, also was a successful business amphibian, and was ordered by the Army, Navy, and Coast Guard as well. President Roosevelt used a Dolphin during the 1930s on official travel. Keystone Aircraft (formerly Huff Daland), after acquiring Loening in 1928, also produced an Air Yacht, although unrelated to the earlier Loening design.

Personal Aircraft Industry Entrants

Despite the virtually nonexistent market for new personal aircraft the early 1920s, production ventures, based more on optimism for the future rather than in response to current demand, were formed. Among the earliest light aircraft firms was that of the barnstormer George E. "Buck" Weaver, who had experience with the pioneer East Coast firms L-W-F and Aeromarine, and his brother-in-law Charles W. Meyers. The partners first located in Lorain, Ohio, late in 1919 to test Weaver's design. The partnership was dissolved in 1920, but a successor Weaver Aircraft Company emerged in 1921 in Medina, Ohio. Weaver brought in two associates, Clayton J. Brukner, with experience at Curtiss and other East Coast aircraft firms, and his friend Elwood James "Sam" Junkin, as investors. Both contributed to design and production. After financial struggles Weaver was reorganized as Advance Aircraft Company on February 26, 1923, in Troy, Ohio, with further backing from the wealthy Alden Sampson II. Junkin became president. Buck Weaver departed the company and died in July 1924, but Advance Aircraft, trading under the acronym WACO, continued his designs and became one of the most successful producers of open-cockpit biplanes.

Sampson later withdrew his interest, then Junkin, who had married

Weaver's widow, died on November 1, 1926. But the company progressed during the late 1920s under Brukner as majority owner, and by avoiding debt was able to survive the Depression. In June 1929 it floated a public stock offering as WACO Aircraft Corporation, and was numerically the largest producer in the industry. From 1930 all designs were given letter designations, and the product line included cabin monoplanes as well as biplanes.[3]

Emil Matthew "Matty" Laird, a young aviator and businessman from Chicago and a friend of Buck Weaver, located in Wichita, Kansas, in the summer of 1919 to produce personal aircraft. This marked the first such manufacturing venture in the city that was to become the light aircraft or general aviation capital. Wichita, enjoying an oil boom at the time, had investors available, and Laird attracted support from local businessmen W. A. "Billy" Burke and Jacob Moellendick of $15,000 each, while he contributed designs, materials, and experience. The group purchased Moellendick's Wichita Aircraft Company, formed only in July, in December 1919. The E. M. Laird Company was formed in May 1920, and Wichita Aircraft Company was dissolved.

The Laird Swallow biplane, designed with the assistance of Buck Weaver, was tested in April 1920 and attracted immediate orders. A new factory was completed in late 1921. Matty Laird was soon joined by his brother Charles, and then by two former military aviators who were later to become prominent figures in the industry: Lloyd Stearman and Walter Beech. Weaver continued to help Laird even as his own firm was floundering, but was fired by Moellendick late in 1921. Laird produced the Swallow until September 1923 when, after conflicts with Moellendick over expansion plans, he sold his interest and returned to Chicago.[4] Then on January 22, 1924, Moellendick formed Swallow Airplane Manufacturing Company, named after its major product, and continued production. The improved New Swallow, designed by Lloyd Stearman, was also employed on airmail services from 1926.

Swallow suffered a major setback when its entry into the California-Hawaii air race was lost, and declared bankruptcy on August 12, 1927, ruining Moellendick financially. The firm was reorganized as Swallow Airplane Company on November 15, 1927, after Moellendick sold rights to Lincoln, Nebraska, investors led by Victor Roos.[5] Swallow sales recovered. Charles Laird established concurrently a separate Laird Aircraft Corporation with himself as president. The firm traded as Whipporwill in order to avoid confusion with the new E. M. Laird Company in Chicago, which Matty Laird had organized in 1926.[6] Whipporwill found little market success with its design, however, and succumbed to the Depression and bankruptcy on December 31, 1930. Swallow survived as a firm, but exited aircraft production during the Depression.

Although Moellendick is a largely forgotten figure in aviation and appears to have been rather difficult as a business associate, he probably deserves more credit than any other individual for establishing Wichita as the center of the light aircraft industry. While he grew wealthy during the oil boom, Moellendick suffered from alcoholism as well as business reverses, and died penniless in 1940. But city support, topography, climate and a trained and experienced labor force enabled Wichita to attract and retain numerous light aircraft firms. The later success of Beech and Cessna in particular secured its claim as the aviation capital. Stearman, a manufacturing division of Boeing after Boeing became independent of United Aircraft in 1934, later led Wichita into military aircraft production as well.

To have an enduring impact on personal aviation was the Travel Air Corporation, formed late in 1924 and incorporated on February 4, 1925. Walter H. Beech, the former Army Air Service pilot and barnstormer, founded the firm with several associates including Stearman, and served as general manager. While with Laird, Beech and Stearman had favored steel airframes for the new Swallow, which Moellendick opposed, and both departed early in 1924. Beech capitalized on numerous aviation contacts extending from his wartime service in organizing the new venture.

Businessman Walter P. Innes, Jr., owner of Wichita's largest department store, arranged financial backing for Travel Air from the investment firm Hayden, Stone and Co., and served as president. Innes in fact suggested the name Travel Air. Clyde V. Cessna, a pioneer pilot, designer, and builder, joined as vice president. Successful in farming in Oklahoma at the time, Cessna also became a major Travel Air investor. Mac Short, an MIT engineering graduate and, like Stearman, a native Kansan, joined, and Charles Yankey, another Wichita native, prominent attorney, and friend of Beech, was an original investor.[7] Beech, while neither a designer nor engineer, was the driving force in management. Joining the small staff as company secretary and bookkeeper was 21-year-old Olive Ann Mellor. In 1930 she became Mrs. Walter H. Beech.

The Travel Air 2000/3000/4000 series of open-cockpit biplanes was one of the most successful of the period. They were later joined by the 5000/6000 series of six-seat cabin monoplanes, which Clyde Cessna helped design. The Model 6000 was also offered with Edo floats, as floatplane operation expanded in the 1920s. (Earl D. Osborn patented aircraft float gear. He incorporated his Edo firm on Long Island on October 29, 1925, and began production in 1926.)

Walter Beech became president of Travel Air on February 15, 1927, and was firmly in control of the company. By that time Stearman had left to form his company, and Cessna soon followed. In 1929 Travel Air sold a total of 547 aircraft and was the largest producer in Wichita.[8] The factory had expanded to 116,000 square feet. R. K. Beech, younger brother of Walter, joined the firm in 1928. In the aviation boom Beech sold Travel Air to Wright Aeronautical Corporation, also financed by Hayden, Stone, and soon to merge to become Curtiss-Wright in June 1929, providing stockholders with a major profit.[9] The

1—Origins of Personal Aviation 11

timing was sheer luck, as the stock market crash soon thereafter would have largely destroyed Travel Air's value.

The entrepreneur J. Don Alexander moved to Englewood, Colorado, a Denver suburb, where he established Alexander Industries, principally for production of motion picture film. He became determined to build an airplane as good as the Laird Swallow, and which would perform well at higher elevations. He thereupon formed Alexander Aircraft Corporation in August

Walter Beech, early 1920s (Wichita State University, Special Collections and University Archives).

Travel Air biplane, late 1920s (Wichita State University, Special Collections and University Archives).

1925 as a subsidiary of Alexander Industries. Alexander employed the youthful Al Mooney as a designer. Mooney gave up a chance to study engineering for the opportunity. Mooney designed the successful Eaglerock two-seat biplane and went on the design the advanced Bullet cabin monoplane. Alexander moved production to a new factory in Colorado Springs in April 1928, and became a leading light aircraft manufacturer in the expanding market of the late 1920s. The Bullet won substantial orders, but experienced stability problems and few were delivered. Alexander also became a victim of the Depression and went bankrupt in August 1932. Al Mooney had left earlier, in May 1929, to form his own firm in Wichita. He tested his M-4 design later that year, but the Depression ended his efforts in 1931.

Lloyd Stearman, formerly a naval aviator, experienced a varied career in Wichita with Laird, Swallow, and Travel Air. But Stearman, in common with many others in those early years, aspired to run his own company, and departed Travel Air in October 1926.

He founded Stearman Aircraft, Inc., in Venice, California, by taking over the West Coast distributor from Travel Air.[10] Mac Short joined him. Stearman's first design, the C-1 three-place biplane, powered by the old OX-5 engine, won favorable attention. He entered production with the successor C-2 but soon encountered financial difficulties. Attracted again to Wichita with financial assistance from Walter Innes, he established Stearman Aircraft Corporation on September 27, 1927. Mac Short followed, joining him as vice president, and a new factory was built. Production of the C-3 series of biplanes built up rapidly in the late 1920s.[11]

The young Boston investment banker Robert Gross first met Stearman in 1928 while evaluating his firm as a financing client. Given his first airplane ride by Stearman, Gross was motivated to cast his future in aviation and became a financial adviser to Stearman. On August 15, 1929, Stearman Aircraft joined other firms as a component of the new giant, United Aircraft and Transport Corporation (UATC). The transaction was in the form of a stock swap, however, and with the crash Stearman was left with only his salary from UATC.

Alfred V. Verville, a major designer and innovator from World War I period to the 1930s, enjoyed a richly varied career as a designer and manufacturer. He began with Glenn Curtiss in 1914, then went briefly to the Thomas Brothers firm in 1915. He formed his General Aviation Company in April 1915, but the venture lasted only two years. He worked for Fisher Body during the war period, then for the Air Service Engineering Division helping

Stearman C-3R sales brochure photograph, circa 1927 (National Air and Space Museum, Smithsonian Institution).

with pursuit and racing aircraft development. He also collaborated with Lawrence Sperry on the Messenger and other postwar designs. Verville resigned from the Engineering Division in February 1925 and joined Lawrence D. Buhl to form the Buhl-Verville Aircraft Company in Michigan. The company enjoyed some success with the Airster cabin monoplane design, but in 1927 Verville sold his interest to Buhl, who continued development.

Forming a new Verville Aircraft Company, he achieved a notable success with the Air Coach cabin monoplane. In 1930 Verville entered and won the army trainer competition with his PT-10, adapted from a civil design. But he could not arrange financing to fulfill the order and became another bankruptcy victim in 1931.[12] While never a major manufacturer, Verville's design abilities nonetheless won him a place in aviation history.

Edward A. "Eddie" Stinson, who learned to fly with the Wright brothers in 1911, earned renown as an instructor, stunt flyer, and record-breaking pilot. He established a flight school with his sisters in December 1915. He formed the Stinson Airplane Company in 1920 in Dayton, but his major activity would be in Detroit, Michigan. The Aviation Committee of the Detroit Board of Commerce backed Stinson in forming the Stinson Airplane Syndicate, which located in suburban Wayne in 1925. Many of his backers later were involved in the ill-fated Detroit Aircraft Corporation.

Stinson was provided with $25,000 to develop an inherently stable cabin monoplane. His design, the six-seat S.M. 1 Detroiter, first flew on January 25, 1926. The Detroiter was advanced for its time, with a quiet, fully enclosed heated cabin, engine starter, and wheel brakes. During its career the Detroiter broke or established numerous flight records. With his new design a success, Stinson formed the Stinson Aircraft Corporation on May 4, 1926, with public capital of $150,000.[13] Stinson by then was earning $100,000 a year as a stunt pilot. The company sold ten Detroiters in 1926 and pursued further development of the basic design.

Including exports, Stinson delivered 121 airplanes in 1929, and in September of that year the automobile magnate E. L. Cord, increasingly involved in aviation, acquired 60 percent of the stock. With Cord's support, the Stinson 6000 trimotor airliner, originally the Corman 3000, achieved some success and also underpriced the successful Ford trimotor. (Corman Aircraft, Inc., of Dayton, was a venture of E. L. Cord and Lucius P. Manning, hence the name.) Cord employed the trimotor in his airline services. Stinson next developed the S. M. 2 Junior, a smaller version of the Detroiter, in 1929. Stinson's sales held up better than most in the Depression, and by 1930 he offered six models, ranging from the four-seat Junior to the trimotor airliner. Successive designs were produced well into the 1940s under later owners Aviation Corporation and Consolidated Vultee. Stinson did not live to see the later success of his company, however, as he died in an air crash at Chicago on January 26,

1932, while on a sales trip. Only 38, he had accumulated some 16,000 flying hours, more than any other pilot to that time.

Sherman Fairchild determined to develop a specialized airplane for aerial photography. In that pursuit, and with the benefit of family wealth, he formed Fairchild Airplane Manufacturing Corporation in 1925 in New York. This was a separate undertaking from his other interests. Fairchild's FC-1 (for Fairchild cabin model) photographic airplane, designed with the assistance of Igor Sikorsky, first flew on June 14, 1926. The FC-1 and successive variants became popular for bush flying as well. Fairchild also acquired the Caminez Engine Company of Ohio in 1925 as the Fairchild Engine Company.

Fairchild Aviation grew to hold two manufacturing arms, the airplane corporation in Farmingdale, Long Island (in the old Sperry factory), and early in 1929 Kreider-Reisner Aircraft Company of Hagerstown, Maryland.[14] Kreider-Reisner had been incorporated on September 5, 1925, by Ammon H. Kreider and Lewis Reisner as the East Coast distributor for Waco but soon began producing their developments of Waco open-cockpit designs. Fairchild purchased a majority of Kreider-Reisner stock on April 1, 1929, but Kreider remained as president and the Hagerstown factory was expanded.[15]

Fairchild enjoyed strong aerial mapping business, and with overall growth consolidated aviation operations under a reorganized Fairchild Aviation Corporation, incorporated in Delaware in 1927, thereby becoming a somewhat vertically integrated holding company in aviation.[16] Acquisition of K-R enabled Fairchild to broaden his product line and to increase overall aircraft production. Kreider was killed in a mid-air collision on April 13, 1929, however, and Reisner departed soon thereafter, but the K-R designs remained under the Fairchild nameplate. The Kreider-Reisner Challenger C-6 light biplane, modified from the Waco Model 9, became the Fairchild KR-21.

Ultimately to become one of the most successful light aircraft manufacturers was Clyde V. Cessna. Cessna had first flown in 1911, and he established a small shop in Wichita in 1916 to construct his own design.[17] His Comet monoplane of 1917, the first airplane ever built in Wichita, held promise, but Cessna failed to sell the design to the War Department and subsequently returned to farming at his Oklahoma home for some years.[18] Reentering the industry in 1924 with Travel Air, Cessna eventually differed with Walter Beech, who emphasized biplanes, while Cessna was determined to develop fully cantilevered monoplanes. Cessna was primarily motivated by a desire to start his own company, however, and he and Beech remained on good terms. Leaving in April 1927, Cessna sold his Travel Air stock to outside investors and incorporated his firm on September 8, 1927, in Wichita.[19] Cessna was the major stockholder, but the second largest investor was Victor Roos. Another original stockholder was Clement Keys, president of Curtiss. The firm was briefly named Cessna-Roos, but Roos resigned in November 1927 after taking

Travel Air production workshop, 1929 (Wichita State University, Special Collections and University Archives).

control of Swallow and becoming general manager, and the new firm became Cessna Aircraft Company on December 31, 1927.

Cessna began his A-series of high-wing monoplanes in 1928, producing 50 of the model AW, followed by 117 of the later model AA, excellent business for a new firm. A significant further development was the CW-6 (for third series, Wright power, and six seats), which flew in November 1928, followed by the more refined DC-6 with a Curtiss Challenger engine, which cost in the $11,000 range.

There were numerous short-lived private aircraft ventures during the 1920s, although details of their organization and operations were often obscure. The Buffalo firm of G. Elias and Brothers, Inc., established in 1881, entered aircraft manufacturing in 1919. It produced sporadically a series of biplane military trainers and civil cabin airplane through the 1920s. It was succeeded by an autonomous Elias Aircraft and Manufacturing Company in 1929, but the firm disappeared in the Depression.

The Gates-Day Aircraft Corporation was chartered on October 17, 1927, in Paterson, New Jersey, to manufacture an updated version of the wartime

1—Origins of Personal Aviation

Travel Air Factory, circa 1930 (Wichita State University, Special Collections and University Archives).

Standard J-1 trainer for the civil market. Ivan Gates, owner of the Gates Flying Circus and a successful exhibition flyer, was president, and Charles H. Day, a wartime engineer for Standard, was chief engineer. The four-seat Gates-Day D-23 was followed by the GD-23 and GD-24 versions, all open-cockpit biplanes. After policy differences occurred, Gates withdrew in April 1928 and Charles L. Augur came in as president, bringing stronger financial backing. The company name was changed to the New Standard Aircraft Company on December 28, 1928, still marketing developments of the J-1.[20] Over 60 of the improved D-25 model were built, but the Great Crash weakened the company. A few naval NT-1 trainers were delivered in 1930 but could not assure the company a future. Day became president in 1930, but he sold his interest in April 1931. New Standard, along with many others, went bankrupt later in 1931. Day and his wife then won acclaim for their around-the-world trip, which they completed in December 1931 in a New Standard Model A airplane.

The Aerial Service Corporation was founded in Hammondsport, New York, in 1920, It produced a series of light aircraft under the Mercury nameplate and was later renamed Mercury Aircraft. Small-scale production extended into the 1930s. The Cox-Klemin Aircraft Corporation was founded at College Point, Long Island, in 1921. A collaboration of Charles Cox and Professor Alexander Klemin of New York University, who was an early graduate of Dr. Jerome Hunsaker's aeronautics program at MIT, the firm produced biplane army trainers and scout floatplanes for the Navy. It also developed an experimental two-place amphibian design. Cox-Klemin took over the wartime Ordnance/Baldwin plant on Long Island in 1924, but Klemin soon resigned. Unable to sustain production, the business faded in 1925.

One short-lived venture, that nonetheless attained near-legendary status, was Heath Aircraft Company of Chicago, founded in 1926 by Edward A. Heath. Beginning just when the supply of cheap wartime surplus trainers was drying up, Heath believed he could offer a reliable aircraft with a price low enough to sell in the limited market. His Heath Parasol, a small single-seater somewhat similar to later ultralight aircraft, and powered by a 27 hp motorcycle engine, first flew in 1926. It represented one of the earliest entries into what eventually became known as the homebuilt field. (Aircraft plans for home construction had been offered from the earliest days of flight, but home construction had never attained a sustained market. It could even be said that the Wright brothers were the first homebuilders of aircraft.) The Parasol was produced both fully assembled and in kit form from 1927 to 1931. Complete aircraft at a flyaway cost of $795, and kits, with a base price of $199, enjoyed brisk sales. Ed Heath did not live to see the later growth of the field, however, as he was killed in a crash in February 1931, and his company succumbed to the Depression.

Most who founded light aircraft firms were classic entrepreneurs, and most were youthful when forming their ventures. Early manufacturers were geographically dispersed from the East Coast to Colorado, and those in the East tended to be isolated from those farther West. There were numerous personal associations, however, which led to business collaborations. But disputes, even among friends, were not uncommon, and many ventures broke up over such disputes. One factor very much in the small industry's factor was that even during the Depression it was recognized that the United States was the only nation in the world with the potential for a mass market in light aircraft, and consequently for a viable light aircraft industry. Thus new ventures continued to appear even in the face of unpromising economic conditions.

2

Growth from the Lindbergh Boom

Government support for aviation development remained extremely limited through the 1920s, but private support for civil aviation began to grow. Among the most important private sources was the Daniel Guggenheim Fund for the Promotion of Aeronautics. Established in 1925 with a bequest of $2.5 million, the Guggenheim Fund granted support to many aspects of aeronautics and acted as a spur to private flying and to the industry.[1] Daniel Guggenheim believed, correctly, that public acceptance for aviation and market prospects were strongly linked to flying safety, and the Guggenheim Fund accordingly announced a national Safe Airplane Competition in 1927. The objective was a new design making real advances in flying safety.

In part due to several withdrawals of original entrants, the competition and its $100,000 prize was won by the Curtiss Tanager. A small single-engined cabin model based on the successful Robin, the Tanager was a high-lift biplane employing full-span upper wing slots. It was one of the first short takeoff-and-landing (STOL) aircraft. Despite its merits, the Tanager proved rather expensive for its time and thus was not practical for production. Also, the prototype was destroyed in 1930 in an airfield grass fire, ending development. The Safe Airplane Competition undoubtedly enhanced design and increased safety awareness, but its measurable impact on the industry was rather minor. The Guggenheim Fund continued to exert an important influence on several other aspects of aviation, however, particularly in aeronautical education.

The event that did carry an immediate and major impact was the epochal solo flight of Charles A. Lindbergh from New York to Paris May 20–21, 1927, in his Ryan single-engined monoplane. No event to that point had raised awareness of the potential of aviation than Lindbergh's feat. Demand for aircraft increased, thousands wished to learn to fly, investors were attracted to aircraft manufacturing, and aviation quickly became regarded as the next growth industry in what was then a booming economy. While new aircraft firms had appeared with regularity to that point, the so-called "Lindbergh Boom," with an expanding market and optimism for its continued growth,

New York Aeronautical Salon, May 1930 (National Air and Space Museum, Smithsonian Institution).

attracted scores of light aircraft production ventures. Many firms specialized in racing aircraft, as the popular air races became exclusively civil after 1929, although racers were not candidates for series production. Established firms, including Travel Air with its low-wing Mystery S of 1929, also entered racing.

Personal aircraft market growth in the latter half of the 1920s was sufficient for major manufacturers to employ distributors. In addition, 42 firms used business aircraft by 1928, and business use grew steadily.[2] The importance of aircraft to business was well established by 1930, but business usually required aircraft that were faster and longer-ranged than was typical, leading to larger cabin models such as the Detroiter. Such aircraft could cost up to $12,000, as compared to the $2,000 to $3,000 for small open-cockpit models. Continued growth of fixed base operations provided operational support for business aircraft as well.[3] Ford Motor Company was a major business aircraft user, as were most large oil companies, where executives found the speed and flexibility of aircraft valuable in traveling to widely dispersed oil fields. Lieutenant James H. "Jimmy" Doolittle resigned from the Air Corps in 1930 to accept a position as pilot with Shell Oil Company in St. Louis. Other famed pilots of that era included Frank Hawks at Texaco, Al Williams at Gulf, and

Roscoe Turner at Gilmore. Certain corporate-owned aircraft became especially noteworthy in racing.

New Personal Aircraft Entrants

Postwar aircraft production had rebounded from the low of 263 in 1922, of which only 37 were civil, to 6,123 in 1929, of which 5,516 were civil. Sales of new civil aircraft in 1928 exceeded those of military aircraft for the first time since 1916.[4] Market prospects led the formation of new personal aircraft ventures to peak in 1928 and 1929, although few were to be of long duration. Identified manufacturers dropped from a peak of 132 in 1929 to 48 by 1934.

One noteworthy entrant was the Sicilian immigrant Giuseppe M. Bellanca, one of the most innovative designers of the period. Among the earliest experimenters, Bellanca built his first airplane in 1911, and from 1917 to 1920 was an engineer with the Maryland Pressed Steel Company. By 1919 he had risen to chief engineer and produced his own designs for the company's aviation section, but the company failed after the war.[5] Bellanca then met the investor Victor Roos and moved to Omaha, Nebraska, where his Roos-Bellanca cabin monoplane, financed by Roos, won wide attention.[6] The Roos-Bellanca Company, or Omaha Aircraft Company, was active only in 1922 and 1923, however. In 1924, after failing to establish his own form, Bellanca took a position with Wright Aeronautical Corporation. There he designed the record-breaking Wright-Bellanca, incidentally the last aircraft to be produced by an independent Wright Aeronautical.

In early 1927 Bellanca was invited to become president of the new Columbia Aircraft Corporation, founded by the wealthy enthusiast Charles Levine. Columbia had purchased the rights to the Wright-Bellanca from Wright Aeronautical and was interested in building air mail planes. Levine, incidentally, earned the distinction of being the first transatlantic air passenger, on a flight from New York to Germany soon after Lindbergh's. Soon tiring of conflicts with the mercurial Levine, Bellanca left to establish his Bellanca Aircraft Corporation of America on Staten Island, New York, in June 1927. Then the Du Pont family, always interested in aviation, offered to back an aviation venture, and Bellanca won their support to form a new company in New Castle, Delaware.[7] The new Bellanca Aircraft Corporation was established on December 30, 1927, with 51 percent of the stock owned by Du Pont. The Du Pont family soon experienced policy conflicts with Bellanca, however, and sold its interest.[8] From that point Bellanca designed and produced both military designs and a series of business aircraft, beginning with the six-seat CH-300 Pacemaker of 1929, followed by the larger Skyrocket in 1930. The CH-300 Pacemaker became a popular bush aircraft as well. While his designs were respected and modestly successful, Bellanca never won the prestige and fame of others of that era. He also faced periodic challenges from outside investors over his control, although he remained in control of the board.

The Aeronautical Corporation of America (Aeronca) of Cincinnati, Ohio, began operations on November 11, 1928. The Lunkin family of Cincinnati, who owned the local airfield, incorporated the new firm and moved into the factory vacated by the defunct Metal Aircraft Corporation. The new firm counted among its directors Robert A. Taft, and enjoyed financial support from the politically prominent family. It was the firm to develop a truly successful light airplane and was to become a major producer of light aircraft.[9] The original C-2 model, designed by Jean A. Roche, who sold the rights to Aeronca, first flew in the summer of 1929. It featured the trademark "bathtub" fuselage and was powered by a small two-cylinder engine also built by Aeronca.[10] The C-2, priced at only $1,495, also brought the cost of flying to a more reasonable level, important for the future growth of the field.[11] The Model C-2 was followed by the more powerful C-3 in 1931, which became a popular model through the next decade.[12] The C-3 was also license-produced in Great Britain during the 1930s. The unrelated C-4 model was designed by company general manager Conrad Dietz, who was killed in an aerial demonstration on September 12, 1931.

In 1927 the brothers C. Gilbert and Gordon Taylor founded Taylor Brothers Aircraft Corporation in Rochester, New York, to produce and sell a small high-wing monoplane, named the Chummy, that Gilbert Taylor had designed the previous year. Gilbert Taylor, in common with many aviation contemporaries, was not formally educated but was an instinctive designer. The new firm relocated to Bradford, Pennsylvania, in 1928 in response to economic inducements by that community, and it began operations in February 1929. The Taylor Brothers name was retained even though Gordon Taylor had been killed in a crash.

In its relocation to Bradford the company attracted the attention and investment interest of several local businessmen, including the oilman William T. Piper, who purchased $400 in Taylor stock and became company treasurer. Although a worthy design, only six Chummy models were sold in the Depression-curtailed market, and the company soon faced insolvency. On Piper's recommendation the company filed for voluntary bankruptcy, after which he purchased the firm's assets for only $761 (incidentally the only bid), but he still gave Gilbert Taylor a half interest. The reorganized Taylor Aircraft Corporation emerged in March 1931, with Taylor still president but with Piper effectively in control as treasurer. Piper abandoned his oil business and devoted himself entirely to aviation.

Piper was convinced that a small firm manufacturing simple, low-cost

Taylor Factory, Bradford Pennsylvania, circa 1930 (National Air and Space Museum, Smithsonian Institution).

private airplanes could survive even in the Depression. Working under that premise, Taylor designed and tested an improved model, the E-2 Cub, which first flew in February 1931. Piper felt that the E-2 was a superior aircraft to the Aeronca C-2, and to be competitive set the initial price at only $1,325. Late in 1932 the firm attracted the 19-year-old aspiring designer Walter Jamouneau of New Jersey. Joining the firm in January 1933, initially without salary, Jamouneau refined the Cub design. Gilbert Taylor, who had been on sick leave at the time, was displeased over the redesign, and fired Jamouneau. William Piper promptly rehired him. The improved Cub was designated J-2, continuing the alphabetical sequence used by Taylor models, but widely regarded as being in Jamouneau's honor. Piper's support for Jamouneau as well as his desire to develop a mass market for the Cub as a trainer for flying schools led his relationship with Taylor, never easy, to deteriorate.[13]

The firm struggled from 1931 through 1935, and Piper sank a major portion of his personal funds into the venture to keep it afloat. But in the latter year the Cub's popularity was such that 228 were sold, constituting almost a quarter of the country's civil aircraft output.[14] More important, the company was approaching profitability after years of losses. Both the Piper and Taylor names were to endure in the field.

A typical short-lived venture of the period was the American Eagle Aircraft Company. Formed originally in 1926 by Edward E. "Ed" Porterfield, a war veteran, in Kansas City, Kansas, it was then incorporated in Delaware in

September 1928. Porterfield designed the light, two-seat high-wing American Eaglet sportplane, similar to the Heath Parasol in presaging later ultralights, to sell for under $1,000. American Eagle built about 500 airplanes, the majority being the A-129 model on which Giuseppe Bellanca assisted, but the company suffered bankruptcy in 1931. Its operations were merged with the Lincoln-Page Aircraft Company of Lincoln, Nebraska, on May 15, 1931, which consolidated operations in Kansas City, Missouri. Ed Porterfield remained as sales manager, but left in 1932 to pursue a new venture. Victor Roos, having left Swallow in December 1928 but continuing his involvement with aviation, was president of American Eagle-Lincoln. Unfortunately, this venture also did not endure. Roos later formed the Victor H. Roos Aircraft Company to continue the American Eaglet, but few were produced. Although cost was the limiting factor in personal aviation, the market still did not favor those aircraft at the smallest, lightest end of the scale.

Aircraft Mechanics, Inc., of Colorado was begun in 1932 by former Alexander employees to succeed the bankrupt Alexander Aircraft Corporation. It attempted to continue the Alexander line, but failed in 1934. Matty Laird remained active in the 1930s in racing planes rather than series production.

The Central States Aero Corporation of Davenport, Iowa, was founded in 1926. The young designer Don A. Luscombe designed the Monocoupe Model 60 cabin monoplane, which first flew on April 1, 1927, for Central States. Luscombe strongly believe the enclosed cabin represented the future of light aircraft. The firm was succeeded by Mono Aircraft, Inc., in 1929, but Mono Aircraft went into receivership in 1931, and was in turn succeeded by the Monocoupe Corporation with Luscombe as president. The refined Monocoupe Model 90 two-seat cabin monoplane was a successful design that was the have a long production life; more than 500 of the basic design were produced. Monocoupe was taken over by new owners in 1933 as Lambert Aircraft Corporation in St. Louis, which continued the Model 90. Luscombe resigned in October 1933 to organize a new company under his own name in New Jersey.

R. A. Rearwin, already a successful lumber dealer and investor in Salina, Kansas, became interested in aircraft manufacturing after the Lindbergh flight. On a trip to Wichita in 1927 he took his first flight in a Travel Air biplane. Rearwin observed that most manufacturers were pilots, not businessmen, and he felt that by applying sound management principles he could be more successful than most. He formed Rearwin Airplanes, Inc., in May 1929, hiring Fred Landgraf, with experience at Alexander, to design and engineer his first airplane. His design, named the Ken-Royce after his two sons, first flew on February 24, 1929. Rearwin also produced small aircraft engines under the Ken-Royce nameplate. Rearwin soon moved operations to Kansas City, Kansas, adjacent to the American Eagle factory. Needing some

$300,000 to build a factory and start production, he formed a 50–50 venture with the wealthy Bert Jones of A. R. Jones Oil Company, and incorporated as Rearwin Airplanes, Inc., of Delaware. Struggling in the Depression, the firm entered air races for business promotion, began a flight school, and also developed the small Rearwin Junior, competitive with the American Eagle Eaglet. Although losing money steadily, both Rearwin and Jones were determined to keep going. A new design, the Speedster, did not sell well, but the next model, the Sportster, enjoyed steady sales until stopped by World War II. In the meantime, the Rearwin-Jones partnership ended in 1937, and with it Rearwin Airplanes, Inc., to be succeeded by Rearwin Aircraft Company. The flight school continued. Rearwin then purchased the established LeBlond engine concern of Cincinnati on January 9, 1938, and moved it to Kansas City. By 1939 he formed a new corporation, Rearwin Aircraft and Engines, Inc.[15] Although profits were still elusive, Rearwin persisted.

Willis C. Brown, a pioneer experimenter and designer and World War I pilot, aspired to enter the business with an airplane that could replace the aging Jennys and Standards then being widely used. In partnership with Waldo D. Emory, another pilot, they established the Mid-Continent Aircraft Company in Emory's native Tulsa. Their first design, the Spartan C-3 biplane, was tested in October 1926. In November 1927, during what became the Lindbergh Boom, the company was incorporated with a capital of $100,000. They hoped that a successful design would attract investors from Tulsa's booming oil industry at the time, which in fact occurred. On January 17, 1928, the oilman W. G. "Bill" Skelly of Skelly Oil Company, took control, invested large sums, and renamed the firm Spartan. Brown remained as president, and a new plant was constructed.[16] The Spartan C-3 began to find modest success as a trainer and sportplane. The company also established the Spartan School of Aeronautics as well as pursuing further aircraft development and production. The C-3 was followed by the C3–255 and C2–60 and C2–65 monoplanes. The larger C-4 and C-5 cabin monoplanes were predecessors of the later Executive.

The Cunningham-Hall Aircraft Corporation was organized in Rochester, New York, in 1928 by former associates of the early military firm Thomas-Morse (Including Randolph Hall) in association with the automobile firm James Cunningham Son and Co. William T. Thomas, a founder of Thomas-Morse, served as a director and consultant. Cunningham-Hall was an unsuccessful entrant into the Safe Airplane Competition, and market prospects for its promising PT-6 six-passenger all-metal business model disappeared in the Depression.[17] The company produced a variety of all-metal sportplanes in the mid–1930s but never became a market leader, and turned exclusively to subcontracting during the Second World War.

It was also from the late–1920s boom period that a more distinct light aircraft engine industry sector developed. Many light aircraft to that time were powered by converted automobile or motorcycle engines. Several aircraft firms continued to build engines, but specialized engine firms became more prominent. Among the most successful was Continental Motors Corporation of Michigan, founded in 1905, which first built an aircraft engine in 1928. Its flat four, or horizontally opposed, configuration became a standard for small engines. The Lycoming Manufacturing Company of Pennsylvania, founded in 1910, developed its first aircraft engine also in 1928. Production began in 1931, and it also became a leader in the field. The aircraft engine operation, after being acquired by E. L. Cord, became the Lycoming Division of the Cord-controlled Aviation Corporation in a reorganization effective January 1, 1936.

The Jacobs Aircraft Engine Company of Pottstown, Pennsylvania, founded in 1929 by Philadelphia businessmen backing the engineer Al Jacobs, specialized in small radial engines. The Warner Aircraft Corporation of Detroit first tested the small Scarab engine in 1927 and developed it and the larger Super Scarab into the 1930s. Fairchild's Ranger Aircraft Engine Division, extending from its purchase of Caminez in 1925, was brought within the new Fairchild Engine and Airplane Corporation organized in 1936. Ranger specialized in the in-line configuration, and it pioneered a series of personal aircraft and military trainers. Kinner Motors, Inc., of Glendale, California, was organized in 1939 after the bankruptcy of the older Kinner Airplane and Motor Corporation in 1938, and it became the largest engine manufacturer on the West Coast. The Aircooled Motors Corporation took over the works of the old Franklin Automobile Corporation and continued to develop Franklin aircraft engines, which entered service in 1938. Somewhat larger radial engines widely used on business aircraft were the Pratt & Whitney R-985, developed from the original Wasp, of 450–600 hp, and the Wright Whirlwind, of 300–450 hp.

The Autogiro

One approach to the quest for an airplane for everyman was the autogiro, combining certain conventional fixed-wing aircraft characteristics with vertical takeoff, rotary-wing features. The autogiro involved a free-turning rotor for lift and a conventional tractor engine and propeller for forward thrust. The combination of ease of operation, safety, and freedom from long runways made the autogiro the potential solution to mass-market aerial transportation.

The autogiro in the United States will always be linked to Harold Pitcairn. Pitcairn, an aviation enthusiast and scion of a wealthy Philadelphia family, began his Pitcairn Aviation flying school and passenger service on

November 2, 1924, and expanded into aircraft construction in 1926.[18] Pitcairn possessed extensive industry experience prior to his involvement with the autogiro, having first worked as an apprentice to Curtiss in 1914. He met Agnew E. Larsen, later a close associate, at flight school in 1916.[19] Initially Pitcairn was interest in producing aircraft only for his own needs, as he expanded into air mail in addition to passenger service. He placed the engineer Larsen, with previous experience at Thomas-Morse, in charge of his Pitcairn Aircraft subsidiary on June 17, 1927. He achieved success first with sportplanes and then with mailplanes, culminating in the famous Pitcairn Mailwing later in 1927. He had received his first air mail contract on January 28, 1927.

The Spanish designer Juan de la Cierva, working in England, had discovered the autorotation principle, essential to autogiro operation and also valuable later in helicopter development. The term *autogiro* (or autogyro) originally was proprietary to Cierva but became generic. Pitcairn and Larsen first made contact with Cierva in 1925, and by the late 1920s the potential of the autogiro had attracted widespread interest. Pitcairn passionately believed in its promise of becoming the affordable, easy-to-fly, mass-market aircraft.

Pitcairn transformed his manufacturing arm into Pitcairn Aircraft Company in 1928, continuing in mailplanes as well as holding the U.S. license for the autogiro. He developed the Cierva C-8 model and tested it successfully on December 19, 1928. He then organized the Pitcairn-Cierva Autogiro Company of America in February 1929 to hold the Cierva license and to control the patents. Although suffering a factory fire in November 1929, Pitcairn still completed his first PCA-1 autogiro the next month. He moved to his new Willow Grove factory in suburban Philadelphia in 1930, and by that time was the leading proponent of the autogiro in the country. He improved the original Cierva concept by angling propeller thrust toward the rotorblades, enabling the autogiro to attain nearly vertical takeoff and hovering capability.

Pitcairn-Cierva Autogiro Company became the Autogiro Company of America (ACA) in January 1931. The company aggressively developed and marketed autogiros, including demonstrations by Amelia Earhart, who in fact set an autogiro altitude record of 18,415 feet on March 6, 1931, at Willow Grove. Pitcairn Aircraft Company remained as the operating company under ACA. Despite winning the Collier Trophy in 1930 for his accomplishment with the autogiro, Pitcairn models never succeeded in gaining wide market acceptance or practical application.

Pitcairn still produced mailplanes, but their day was rapidly drawing to an end. He also produced the PA-7S three-seat sportplane version of the Mailwing from 1930, but still regarded the autogiro as the mass-market that might even begin to replace the automobile. The PA-18 Tandem two-seat open-cockpit model of 1932, at a base price of $5,000, was marketed as the Model T of the air, but orders were few. The enclosed cabin model PA-32 and the still larger 4–5 place PA-19 cabin model also appeared in 1932. Another problem was that the autogiro was never as safe as originally claimed, with mishaps and damage occurring frequently. Although Pitcairn fell short of his mass-market goal, his efforts aided the later development of practical helicopters. The name of the original manufacturing arm, Pitcairn Aircraft, was changed to Pitcairn Autogiro Company in January 1933, after Mailwing production had ended.[20]

Kellett Autogiro Company, also in the Philadelphia area, was the second American licensee, purchasing the license from ACA. Formed by the brothers W. Wallace and Rodney G. Kellett, the firm followed Pitcairn in developing and seeking practical applications for autogiros, and Wallace Kellett and Harold Pitcairn were longtime friends. Also participating in the firm were the Ludington brothers, involved in air mail operations, and Elliott Daland, a founder of Huff Daland Airplanes. The Englishman W. Lawrence LePage served as chief engineer. Kellett models were generally wingless, while Pitcairn models were configured with short wings. A few examples of the Kellett autogiro were sold to the Army, but commercial sales proved disappointing, and the company later turned to helicopter development.

Depression Era Struggles

Another outgrowth of the Lindbergh Boom, beyond the broad aircraft market expansion, was the formation of large aviation holding companies, principally through mergers of existing firms. While primarily oriented toward the military and commercial markets, the holding companies also had some involvement in private aviation. With the Depression the Lindbergh Boom proved to be a bubble, however, and most large firms abandoned their personal aviation interests.

The first aviation holding company effort, the Detroit Aircraft Corporation of 1927, acquired the well-known Ryan and Lockheed firms, plus several others primarily in private aviation, but went bankrupt and disappeared in the 1931 Depression. United Aircraft and Transport Corporation (UATC) of Connecticut, organized in February 1929, gained an involvement in personal aircraft, although of rather brief duration, through its acquisition of Stearman. Lloyd Stearman, while an outstanding pilot, designer, and engineer, was less effective as an executive, and soon encountering differences with UATC management, resigned in December 1930. UATC phased out production of his designs in 1931 with the market decline. The Stearman Division of Boeing, formed in 1934 from the UATC Stearman operations, had no managerial or design participation by Lloyd Stearman.

The Aviation Corporation (AVCO) also became involved with personal aviation, first with Fairchild and from 1933 with Stinson. Shortly after its organization in 1929, largely by Wall Street interests, AVCO acquired 55 percent of Fairchild Aviation Corporation stock, bringing with it Fairchild's Farmingdale factory. Sherman Fairchild became a vice president of AVCO. He withdrew on April 1, 1931, however, in disenchantment with AVCO management, leaving his aircraft operations but regaining his 55 percent stock holding. Then, when E. L. Cord gained complete control of the Aviation Corporation in March 1933, he brought it under his Cord Corporation, and with it the Vultee and Stinson aircraft operations and Lycoming engine operations. The manufacturing divisions remained at their existing locations as they were combined under the subsidiary Aviation Manufacturing Corporation, headquartered in Chicago, in 1934. The former Fairchild aircraft models were phased out.

Curtiss Aeroplane and Motor, later Curtiss-Wright, built a substantial and long-term private aviation involvement. Particularly noteworthy was its association with Robertson Aircraft Corporation of St. Louis, formed on July 1, 1923, primarily as a mail carrier by the brothers Frank H. and Major William B. Robertson, a wartime aviator.[21] Among the firm's air mail pilots was Charles A. Lindbergh. William Robertson's contract with Curtiss concerning his interest in small aircraft resulted in the three-to four-seat Robin high-wing cabin monoplane, a Curtiss-Robertson collaboration built in the Curtiss factory at Garden City, Long Island. A Curtiss-Robertson Manufacturing Corporation, 50 percent owned by Curtiss, was formed on November 9, 1927, with capital of $500,000.

The Robin first flew in the spring of 1928, but Curtiss's heavy military aircraft commitment at the time made Robin production uneconomical. The company adopted Robertson's suggestion to produce the Robin in St. Louis, and a new factory was constructed. Entering production on August 7, 1928, initially powered by the 90 hp Curtiss OX-5 engine and later with the 170 hp Curtiss Challenger, the Robin became one of the most successful light aircraft of the time, with a total of 769 produced and with many-breaking flights to its credit.[22] Other Curtiss-Robertson designs included the Thrush and the Kingbird, a twin-engine light transport, but neither was produced in quantity. The Robertson Aircraft Corporation remained a separate entity.

The merger of Curtiss A and M and Wright Aeronautical, forming the Curtiss-Wright Corporation, took place on August 29, 1929. Curtiss-Robertson had been fully merged into Curtiss earlier, on June 26, 1929, then Travel Air, initially under Wright Aeronautical, was absorbed into Curtiss-Robertson in 1930.[23] The ultralight CW-A Junior two-seat sportplane, with a design contribution by Walter Beech, followed, with some 270 produced from 1930 to 1932. Beech, already president of Curtiss-Robertson, became president of Curtiss-Wright Airplane Company, when it was renamed, still located in St.

Louis and specializing in light civil aircraft. Ralph Damon and William Robertson were vice presidents, although Robertson stepped aside after completion of the merger.[24] All Travel Air production was consolidated at St. Louis and the Wichita plant was closed. The St. Louis company soon introduced the larger Challenger to complement the existing product line, but the Model 16 Sport, the last aircraft built carrying the Travel Air nameplate, ended in 1933 due to the Depression. The Curtiss Speedwing, a fast open-cockpit model powered by the Wright Whirlwind and originally designed by Travel Air, survived until 1936.

Another Curtiss subsidiary, the Moth Aircraft Company, had been organized in St. Louis in 1928 to produce the De Havilland Moth trainer under license. Production was rather brief, however, and Moth was soon reorganized into the Curtiss-Wright Airplane Company under the Curtiss-Wright holding company.

Cessna by 1929 had grown to rank with Travel Air, Swallow, and Stearman as one of the Wichita "Big Four" in light aircraft, out of sixteen aircraft producers in the city. A new factory also was opened in 1929. There were rumors that Cessna would follow Travel Air and Stearman in joining a large holding company, a factor of no small concern to Wichita, but Clyde Cessna chose to remain independent. The young firm suffered after the October market crash, however, and Cessna struggled for control. Bankers installed a new president over him, and the company was finally forced by bankers and other creditors to shut down production indefinitely on January 31, 1931. The firm never declared bankruptcy, but its production future was very much in doubt.[25] After being forced out of his company, Cessna immediately started a new C. V. Cessna Aircraft Company with his son Eldon, but more for racing aircraft than mass production, and this venture did not enjoy a long life.

Walter H. Beech, uncomfortable in a large corporation, resigned as a vice president of Curtiss-Wright Corporation and as president of Curtiss-Wright Airplane (Curtiss-Robertson) in March 1932, determined to return to Wichita and establish his own company. With his wife Olive Ann he formed Beech Aircraft Company on April 1, 1932, with a capital of $25,000.[26] Most regarded the venture as foolhardy at the time; 1932 was the poorest year for production and sales since the 1922–25 period. Joining Beech was his Travel Air associate T. A. "Ted" Wells, who undertook design of the Model 17, a large, powerful, and fast executive biplane popularly known as the Staggerwing. Beech began production in 1933 with space leased in the then-inactive Cessna factory, with only a handful of employees. The Staggerwing faced a depressed market, but Beech managed to sell 18 in 1933. Beech then was able to move into the old Travel Air factory in 1934, and sales built gradually.

The engineer Dean B. Hammond purchased the rights to the Parks Aircraft Division of Detroit Aircraft Corporation after its collapse, and Parks

2—Growth from the Lindbergh Boom

Beech Staggerwing, the first modern executive aircraft, 1930s (Wichita State University, Special Collections and University Archives).

formed the basis for his Hammond Aircraft Corporation on May 11, 1932.[27] He also bought the rights to the Ryan Speedster sportplane from Detroit. Major development effort, however, was on the innovative twin-boomed, pusher-engined Model Y, supported by a Bureau of Air Commerce contract. Hammond, a pioneer of tricycle landing gear, later developed the design further.

When Sherman Fairchild severed his ties with the Aviation Corporation in 1931, he moved his headquarters to Hagerstown, Maryland, location of the Kreider-Reisner firm. Production of K-R designs had been suspended in the market collapse of 1930, but Fairchild's Kreider-Reisner Division reinstated production of the F-22 two-seat open-cockpit biplane. The most important new design was the F-24 three-to four-seat cabin monoplane developed in 1932. The F-24 in succeeding versions became a long-term production success for both civil and military markets.[28] In 1934 Sherman Fairchild formed a successor Fairchild Aircraft Corporation to control all manufacturing, and the Kreider-Reisner nameplate disappeared.

Curtiss-Wright reorganized along divisional lines, and the Curtiss-Wright Airplane Division was created as an equal with Curtiss Aircraft at Buffalo and with Wright Aeronautical. It then was renamed the St. Louis Division and focused primarily on commercial aircraft as Robin production declined. Its major effort was the Condor airliner of 1932, of which 44 military and commercial models were produced.[29] While not a major success, the Condor at least kept the St. Louis line open. Curtiss still devoted some effort to personal aircraft development, resulting in its more modern Models 19L and 19W Coupe low-wing all-metal two- and three-seat cabin monoplanes. The CW-19R tandem-seat trainer was a more powerful development.

Ed Porterfield reentered the industry in August 1934 by forming Porterfield Aircraft Corporation, still in Kansas City, Kansas. Famed pilot Roscoe Turner was associated. Porterfield acquired the design and production rights for a light aircraft, the Wyandotte Pup, in exchange for stock in his company, and began producing a line of improved Porterfield trainers, beginning with the Model 35–70 (for the year and engine horsepower). He operated in this capacity until transforming to war production in 1942.[30]

* * *

All aircraft manufacturers suffered greatly during the Depression, but the impact was more severe and more immediate for the personal aviation sector than for the military sector. Military procurement continued until 1932–1933 from earlier appropriations, but the personal aircraft almost disappeared overnight. Remaining firms struggled to develop models that could sell in a limited market, but they rarely achieved profitability.

Growth of that market segment involving small aircraft constructed from plans or component kits, despite potentially lower costs, was severely constrained by certification and safety concerns. Home building alternatives existed, but the government offered little encouragement to the field. Homebuilts faced major difficulties in gaining Approved Type Certificates and, consequently, government registration numbers. Many amateur-built aircraft were soundly designed and constructed, of course, but others were not, heightening safely concerns. Further, the priority of the Department of Commerce at the time was commercial service, and there were fears that publicity over crashes of amateur-built light aircraft would detract from public confidence in commercial air safety.[31] One kit model, the Pietenpohl Air Camper, achieved some success, however. Bernard H. Pietenpohl of Minnesota had begun flying and experimenting with aircraft in the 1920s, and designed and tested his Air Camper in 1928. A small and simple two-seat design with a high parasol wing, and powered by a converted Ford Model T engine, it became the first easily constructed small airplane. The name Air Camper was obscure, as it had no storage capacity and could not be used for camping or other utilitarian purposes. Upgraded with a Ford Model A engine in 1929, the complete kit could be purchased for $750, and gained a steady if small market during the 1930s. Unfortunately, stringent new registration requirements imposed by the new Civil Aeronautics Administration established in 1938 effectively forced Pietenpohl out of business.[32]

Another claimant to the distinction of being the first homebuilt manufacturer was Orland G. Corben. An early experimenter, he believed along with others that flying should not be only a rich man's pursuit. He formed his Ace Aircraft manufacturing Company in Wichita in 1929, and offered his Corben Baby Ace, a simple high-wing, open-cockpit design. Unfortunately, he experienced the same difficulties as others in getting established in the field.

The dream of an affordable, mass-produced airplane for the public remained. Eugene L. Vidal, appointed director of the Aeronautics Branch in 1933, was determined to achieve that goal. He noted that in some 15 years of private flying development there were still fewer than 7,000 registered private airplanes, and felt that flying could become far better established if only small airplanes could be made more affordable.[33] In December 1933 he offered $500,000 in grants for development of a two-seat "poor man's airplane," with a target price of only $700. The craft was to be all metal, as it was felt that metal would enhance public confidence in its safety and durability.[34] The "$700 airplane" concept attracted great interest and publicity, but established producers, aware of the economic realities, generally declined to compete, leaving the field to experimenters. Many firms also opposed the program as detrimental to the sector, in that potential customers might postpone their purchases in expectation of lower prices, further damaging their sales prospects.[35]

The grant was withdrawn and the goal became recognized as unrealistic.[36] The Aeronautics Branch became the Bureau of Air Commerce on July 1, 1934. Successor affordable airplane developments included the appearance in 1936 of the tricycle-geared Arrowplane of Waldo Waterman, a predecessor of the first roadable airplane, plus the advanced Hammond Y-1, a roadable autogiro, and other innovative designs. Vidal left his post in 1937 with his efforts having achieved no permanent results and the average personal airplane still costing in the $2,000 range. Prices could be as low as $1,500, but they ascended to more than $25,000 for the largest twin-engined business models.

Whatever the overall economic conditions, the private aircraft market was still limited by cost, both for purchase and operation. The resulting high turnover in personal aircraft ownership in personal aircraft ownership and availability of good used aircraft also limited the demand for new models. But a major market expansion lay just ahead.

3

Market Expansion and War Production

A more modern aircraft industry structure had emerged by 1935, due both to market development and new legislation and regulation. Technical progress had also been steady despite weak demand, inadequate government support, and shaky industry finances. Within the new structure, aircraft and engine manufacturing operations were largely separated, and those commercial airlines previously owned by holding companies or manufacturers were spun off as independent firms. The aerial service definition had narrowed to such functions as aerial photography, cropdusting, weather reporting, and air taxi work. Business and personal flying gained in prominence and became classified separately from aerial service. In addition, light or personal aircraft production by 1935 had become a largely separate and distinct sector of the industry, and numerous personal aircraft producers sought a niche in the limited market.

Design progress had been significant, as monoplanes increasingly displaced biplanes and enclosed cabins succeeded open-cockpit models. Some producers moved toward all-metal structures, and engines and instrumentation became more efficient and reliable. Larger military and commercial firms such as Curtiss-Wright retained some activity in personal aircraft, but firms specializing in the field dominated the market. Aeronca, Piper, Taylor, and Luscombe, primarily producing two-seaters, emerged as the Big Four of the light aircraft segment by the end of the decade. WACO, Bellanca, and later leaders Cessna and Beech focused on larger personal aircraft models, with lower unit volume. Following are summaries of the more significant developments.

Personal Aircraft Firm Survey

The Piper-controlled Taylor Aircraft Corporation continued to expand with its successful Cub. The company finally attained profitability in 1936, with 515 examples of the J-2 Cub being sold.[1] Increasing friction between William T. Piper and Gilbert Taylor led to a management breakup in that year, however,

3—Market Expansion and War Production

as Piper insisted on keeping prices as low as possible, not the priority of Taylor. Taylor also felt himself increasingly undermined and isolated by Piper. Piper confronted Taylor with an offer to purchase his interest, for $5,000, which Taylor felt obligated to accept. Piper then took over as chairman and president while remaining treasurer. The improved J-3 Cub appeared in 1937.

Gilbert Taylor was determined to remain a factor in the industry and moved to Butler, Pennsylvania, early in 1936, where he established Taylorcraft Aircraft Corporation in a small factory. He felt his Model A, with side-by-side seating, would be superior to the otherwise similar J-3 Cub. Needing more production space, Taylor relocated 100 miles west to Alliance, Ohio, on July 8, 1936, and entered into direct competition with Piper.[2] The Model A was in production by 1937. Gilbert Taylor became concerned about a possible Piper lawsuit over use of the Taylor name, although none materialized.

Finances had been precarious, but the company became better capitalized in April 1937 by the participation of local engineer and businessman W. C. Young. The firm was renamed Taylor-Young Airplane Company, with Young as vice president. A public stock offering followed, strongly supported by the city of Alliance, wishing to retain what was viewed as a potentially strong growth company.[3] Although Young soon ended his association, apparently late in 1937, the name remained unchanged at the time.

The firm appeared to be on a sounder base, but Taylor realized that he needed to offer new models in the increasingly competitive market. First, he brought out the more powerful Model 50. Sales were encouraging, but a fire and explosion at the factory on August 23, 1938, further strained finances. Rescue came on October 19 from Fairchild Aviation Corporation, which provided a $30,000 loan in exchange for 50,000 shares of Taylor stock.[4] Fairchild also installed Richard H. Depew as vice president and general manager, and Gilbert Taylor again lost managerial control of a company bearing his name. (Fairchild Aviation was primarily involved with photography and survey operations, while manufacturing was under the separate Fairchild Engine and Airplane Corporation.) The company was renamed Taylorcraft Aviation Corporation in 1939 and progressed as a market competitor.

Another significant development was the award of a production license to Taylorcraft Aeroplanes, Limited, in Great Britain, established by British investors on November 21, 1939. Taylorcraft thus became one of the earliest American aircraft companies to license production abroad. The British Taylorcraft firm produced military adaptations of Taylorcraft designs during the war for spotter duties.

The original Piper-operated Taylor factory in Bradford was destroyed by fire on March 17, 1937. The high flammability of light aircraft construction materials meant that insurance was very costly, and W. T. Piper was grossly underinsured for the loss. He reallocated funds earmarked for expansion to restart production in a temporary factory. But the disaster led Piper to consider relocation, and he received offers from as far away as Oklahoma. He settled, however, on the town of Lock Haven some distance east of Bradford. Already a man of near-legendary frugality, Piper was not known for high wages or tolerance of unions, but these views did not pose a problem in Lock Haven, and local business interests assisted in the move. Attracting generous local financing and reestablishing production in an old silk mill, the venture progressed rapidly. Overcoming the disruption of the fire and the move, the Cub continued as the most popular aircraft in America, with 687 produced in 1937. Renamed Piper Aircraft Corporation in November 1937, the firm by then employed the three Piper sons. Walter Jamouneau continued as chief engineer.

William T. Piper still was faced with significant financial challenges. Production startup expenses in Lock Haven, in addition to the uninsured loss of $200,000, caused a substantial drain, but he succeeded with a $250,000 public stock offering on March 3, 1938, followed soon by a $750,000 stock sale.[5] A Cub nonstop Newark-Miami round-trip flight during May 17–20, 1938, using crude in-flight refueling and covering 2,420 miles, greatly enhanced public recognition of the reliability of light aircraft, and boosted sales. In 1939 1,806 Cubs were sold, and Piper lowered the price of the basic model to $995, becoming the first mass production aircraft ever priced under $1,000.

Finally on the verge of real prosperity, Piper earned an after-tax profit of $157,823 for the 1940 fiscal year. By the end of 1941, 10,000 Cubs had been built, a record at the time for a basic design, and the Cub name became almost generic for a light aircraft. W. T. Piper was becoming known as the Henry Ford of the aircraft industry. Piper in the meantime had introduced the J-4 Coupe, with side-by-side seating, in 1939, followed by the J-5B Cruiser in 1940, its first three-seat aircraft, which was to serve as the basis for Piper's postwar developments.

Don Luscombe located in Trenton, New Jersey, in 1934 for his new venture, attracting sufficient financial backing and enjoying access to a plentiful labor supply.[6] The Luscombe Airplane Development Corporation began operating in leased space in February 1935, initiating production of the luxurious all-metal Phantom, which had won certification in August 1934. The Phantom possessed many advanced features and was one of the first light aircraft to be built with extensive subcontracting. Its $6,000 price was too high for the market of the day, however, as was the case for the smaller Model 90, limiting sales. Realizing he needed a model that could sell in volume, Luscombe thereupon designed the two-seat, 50 horsepower Model 8 in 1937. Named the Silvaire, it sold for only $2,000 and gained immediate popularity.

The company was required to sell stock for production capital, and went public as Luscombe Airplane Corporation in 1938. The major investor was the millionaire Leopold Klotz, originally from Austria, who soon began to

3—Market Expansion and War Production

A double production milestone: The 10,000th Piper Cub and the 5,000th Lycoming engine for the Cub. W. T. Piper and C. O. Samuelson of Lycoming exchange congratulations, Lock Haven, Pennsylvania, 1941 (National Air and Space Museum, Smithsonian Institution).

intervene in management. Early in 1939 Klotz imposed a new manager on the company, sparking protests from the staff loyal to Don Luscombe.[7] Luscombe thereupon sold his interest to Klotz in April 1939 and resigned as president and director. Although only 44, Luscombe ended his involvement in the industry. The company sold 1,200 Silvaires from 1938 to Pearl Harbor and was a major subcontractor on Pitcairn's autogiro production, but private aircraft production was suspended at the outbreak of war due to metal shortages.

Aeronautical Corporation of America (Aeronca) ended production of the veteran C-3 in 1937 in favor of the more modern Model K Scout, with side-by-side seating. The Model L low-wing two-seater had been introduced in 1935, while the high-wing Scout was joined by the more powerful Chief. The Taft family, after sustaining considerable losses, sold Aeronca for $750,000 to Walter J. Friedlander in 1935. He installed his son Carl as manager and relocated production from Cincinnati to nearby Middletown. Jean Roche left, but Carl Friedlander proved to be an astute manager, and the newer Aeronca models provided the strongest competition to the Piper Cub until the Second World War.

By 1935 Skelly had decided to reenter manufacturing with Spartan. He hired the veteran designer James B. Ford to design a business airplane more

Luscombe 8, a Silvaire production at Trenton, New Jersey, late 1930s (National Air and Space Museum, Smithsonian Institution).

advanced than anything built to that time. The result was the streamlined Model 7X, a powerful five-seat luxury business transport, which first flew on January 1, 1936. The prototype required numerous modifications and resulted in the refined Model 7W, which became the famed Executive. Production began in 1937, and though only 34 were built before the war, it gained wide recognition and was adopted by the wartime military as well. A few examples even saw action in the Spanish Civil War. Spartan also designed the NS-1 military primary trainer, which was ordered by the Navy as the NP-1. Like many others, Spartan suspended aircraft production by 1942 due to the war, but the School of Aeronautics remained active.

Pitcairn Autogiro reorganized as Pitcairn-Larson Autogiro Company, recognizing Agnew Larson's increased role. Larson had desired more active management participation, and Harold Pitcairn was already stretched as a manager. Pitcairn and Larson soon developed major conflicts over costs, however, precipitating Larson's departure.[8] The firm maintained low-volume autogiro production, although principally of its PA-33 and PA-34 models for the Army and Navy rather than for the civil market. The company was again renamed AGA Aviation Corporation (for autogiros, gliders, and airplanes) in 1941, with Pitcairn taking a new partner.[9]

Beech progressed as Model 17 Staggerwing sales totaled 36 in 1935. The firm was rechartered in Delaware as Beech Aircraft Corporation on September 16, 1936, with a stock capitalization of $100,000. The company adopted the marketing name of Beechcraft for its products. Its speed and comfort enabled the Staggerwing to gain a significant share of the business market in the late

3—Market Expansion and War Production

1930s, and 424 had been produced by the beginning of the war. Developments of the Model 17 were employed in numerous military roles. On January 6, 1937, Beech was able to purchase the Travel Air Wichita factory from Curtiss-Wright for $150,000. Beech also developed the high-performance Model 18 "Twin Beech," which first flew on January 15, 1937, and which began to find a market as the top-line business transport. Employment reached 250, and the company issued its first stock offering also in 1937.[10] The "Twin Beech" was to be produced in large numbers in several wartime military versions.

In May 1933 Clyde Cessna's 22-year-old nephew Dwane Wallace, a new engineering graduate of Wichita University, took a position with Beech Aircraft Company. He worked on Staggerwing development under Ted Wells but resigned at the end of the year to help his uncle regain control of his company. Aided by his older brother Dwight, a lawyer, Dwane Wallace prevailed in a proxy fight with the banking interests and gained control of Cessna on January 10, 1934. Clyde Cessna again became president, and the firm moved to restart production after a three-year hiatus. Cessna and Wallace set out to design a plane that could sell in the Depression market, resulting in the C-34 (after the design year), which continued Cessna's successful cantilevered high-wing concept. Powered by a Warner Super Scarab engine and priced in the $5,000

First flight, prototype Beech Model 18, January 15, 1937 (Wichita State University, Special Collections and University Archives).

range, the C-34 led to a series of successful developments. Owing to the firm's shaky finances, Wallace found it necessary to forgo a salary during this period and asked Eldon Cessna to do the same. Eldon, newly married, declined and moved to California for other pursuits.

Clyde Cessna's management role eventually declined in his revived company, and he had been deeply affected by seeing a friend die in a crash. Although only 57, he sold his interest to his Wallace nephews and officially retired on October 8, 1936.[11] While Cessna's retirement was described as voluntary, Eldon Cessna maintained in later years that his father had been pushed aside by his nephews.[12] Dwane Wallace succeeded his uncle as president and was in sole control of the company. After building 42 C-34s, Wallace brought out the model C-37 in 1937, which led to the classic Model C-38 Airmaster. Fifty C-37s were sold in 1937, giving the firm a strong market foothold, and a total of 186 Airmasters of all series was sold through 1941. Wallace then developed the Model T-50 Bobcat twin-engine transport/trainer in 1939. Only 30 civil Model T-50s were sold before the war, but large-scale production followed after Cessna gained major military orders for the T-50.

Cessna Airmaster production, circa 1939. A Model T50 Bobcat is at right (National Air and Space Museum, Smithsonian Institution).

Lloyd Stearman, after an unhappy tenure as president of the revived Lockheed Aircraft Corporation, joined the Bureau of Air Commerce in January 1935. While serving there, he assisted Dean Hammond with development of the Model Y. He resigned late in 1936 to join Hammond in organizing the Stearman-Hammond Aircraft Company in San Francisco. The refined Model Y, designated Y-125, entered production, but the company encountered financial difficulties and ended production at only 15 aircraft.[13] Stearman left later in 1937 for other aviation-related ventures, but Hammond continued as a subcontractor with the company under his name.

Henry A. Berliner, after the sale of his Berliner-Joyce military firm to North American Aviation, incorporated the Engineering and Research Corporation (ERCO) in Maryland in 1930 to produce various types of machinery used in aircraft production. The engineer Fred E. Weick, who had developed the NACA streamlined cowl in 1928, resigned from NACA and joined ERCO in 1936 as chief designer as the firm moved into aircraft.

Weick had designed the small W-1 experimental model in 1934, featuring tricycle landing gear, a pusher engine, and a high parasol-type wing, in response to the Department of Commerce low-cost airplane program. With ERCO, Weick redesigned the W-1 into the low-winged, tricycle-geared, tractor-engined W-1A (originally ERCO 310) which first flew in October 1937 and became the famous Ercoupe.[14] The Ercoupe was also noteworthy for its lack of foot pedals, being flown entirely with the control wheel, and was spinproof. Entering the market in 1940, only 112 Ercoupes had been built when production was interrupted by the war, but the Ercoupe became a classic light aircraft.

The Curtiss-Wright St. Louis Division won a Bureau of Air Commerce contract to develop the advanced CW-25 Coupe, a twin-engined all-metal design which interested the agency as appropriate for advancing private flying. Adapting the wing of the earlier CW-19 Coupe, the CW-25 prototype was delivered to the Department of Commerce in 1940, but the design did not reach the civil market. It was to be the last Curtiss effort in civil aviation, but was produced in substantial numbers as the wartime AT-9 Jeep. Conceptually, it presaged the postwar generation of light twin-engined business aircraft.

The Stinson Division of AVCO continued to produce larger cabin monoplanes, principally the classic Reliant, introduced in 1934 and developed from the original Stinson designs. Initially produced with a straight wing, the Reliant soon adopted the gull wing, by which it became strongly identified. Stinson also developed the Model 10 lightplane, designed by Lewis E. Reisner, a founder of Kreider-Reisner. It first flew on February 13, 1939. The developed Model 10A became the long-produced Voyager. Some 500 were produced before Pearl Harbor, and many were acquired by the Army as the L-9.[15]

In a related development, Vultee Aircraft of California, another division of AVCO and gaining in stature in military aircraft, acquired the small Barkley-

Grow Aircraft Company early in 1940. Barkley-Grow had been founded in 1936 by Archibald S. Barkley, whose career dated back to Wright and Curtiss, and Commander Harold S. Grow, with a staff largely of former Stinson personnel. Barkley-Grow designed the twin-engined T8P-1 executive transport. Although a sound design, it did not find a wide market given the competition, principally the "Twin Beech." Then in August 1940, the Stinson Division was combined as Vultee-Stinson, which absorbed Barkley-Grow the following month.

Bellanca aircraft continued their strong reputation into the 1930s, with many record-breaking flights to their credit. The Pacemaker and Rocket were sound designs but did not find commercial success. Neither did their successor, the larger Aircruiser, aerodynamically a sesquiplane with airfoil-section struts. Bellanca also developed military designs, but did not obtain orders. The firm tended to rely on proven concepts and features that had become outmoded with the rapid progress of the late 1930s, and sales were declining even before war requirements forced a production suspension.[16] Bellanca did, however, build the small three-seat 14–9 Cruisair in 1939, a modern retractable-gear design that would be revived after the war.

Under Clayton J. Brukner, Waco remained a leading private aircraft manufacturer through the 1930s. Chief designer Francis Arcier, an Englishman and design pioneer, joined Waco in 1930 and enjoyed one of the strongest reputations in the industry. The Model F biplane, introduced in 1930, was a popular design, as were the C series and S series. The model CSO tandem two-seat biplane was even adapted as a light fighter in 1931 and ordered by Brazil, although serving only briefly in a combat role. The N series of 1937, four-seat cabin biplanes with tricycle gear evolved from the C series, was unique, and was produced in small numbers. The last prewar taildragger model was the E series, produced until 1940. The firm belatedly realized that its biplane designs were becoming rapidly outdated by the end of the decade, and with the coming of war converted to military production.

Grumman, located on Long Island, New York, and primarily a naval contractor, embarked on limited diversification into private aviation. The G-21 Goose twin-engined amphibian transport, first flew on May 29, 1937,[17] and won acceptance in its narrow market segment. It was joined by the smaller G-44 Widgeon, which first flew on June 28, 1940. Military versions of Grumman amphibians served throughout the Second World War, and the company was to return the civil amphibian field after the war.

Lockheed, growing as a military and commercial airliner manufacturer, also considered a stake in private aviation during 1937. Lockheed president Robert Gross first offered Mac Short, then managing the Boeing Stearman division, the management of a private aircraft subsidiary.[18] Short declined at the time. There were subsequent discussions between Gross and Victor Emanuel, who controlled the Aviation Corporation, about selling his three manufac-

3—Market Expansion and War Production

WACO factory, 1930s (National Air and Space Museum, Smithsonian Institution).

turing units, Vultee, Stinson, and Lycoming, with the expectation that Lockheed would merge Lycoming with its Menasco engine operation into a single company. Stinson would then be moved to the Northrop El Segundo factory, which Gross proposed to acquire from Douglas.[19] This proposal, which would have given Southern California a strong stake in the personal aircraft field, likewise did not achieve fruition.

Lockheed instead established a new private aircraft subsidiary, AiRover Aircraft, located adjacent to its main Burbank factory. It was incorporated on August 17, 1937, and Mac Short then joined Lockheed as manager of AiRover. It developed the innovative Starliner executive aircraft, with twin engines coupled to drive a single propeller, but did not proceed with production given dim market prospects at the time. AiRover was renamed Vega Airplane Company on June 1, 1938, and turned to military work.

Fairchild Engine and Airplane Corporation was formed on November 10, 1936, to control all Fairchild aircraft and engine production. The advanced F-45 low-wing high-performance five-seat business aircraft of 1936, somewhat competitive with the Executive, was another success, although built only in small numbers. While continuing personal aircraft, primarily the F-24, the Aircraft Division became increasingly military-oriented, winning a major primary trainer competition for the Army in 1939.

There were further entrants into light aircraft in the late 1930s, including revivals of older firms. Despite its daunting economics, the field still held a strong attraction for many.

The Lambert Aircraft Corporation of St. Louis, which had developed the two-seat low-wing Monosport, sold rights to the Dart Manufacturing Corporation of Columbus, Ohio, in 1937. The Monosport was developed into the Dart Model G and was produced in small numbers. Then Culver Aircraft Corporation, founded by K. K. Culver in 1939 in Columbus, with Al Mooney as chief designer, took over the rights to the Dart Model G. With a design contribution by Mooney, it became the Culver Cadet and entered production in 1940 after the firm relocated to Wichita. In November 1941 the firm was bought by Walter H. Beech and Charles Yankey, a Beech associate since the Travel Air days. Yankey became the firm's president. Monocoupe Corporation was revived in Robertson, Missouri, in 1937 and resumed production of the Model 90 high-wing two-seat design until the wartime suspension in 1942. It also tested the Monocoach, a four-seat business transport design with twin 90 hp engines. One of the first light twin-engined cabin monoplanes, it did not enter production.

Reuel T. Call, in association with his uncle Ivan Call, his brother Spencer Call, and others, established Call Aircraft Company in Afton, Wyoming, in 1939 to produce his rugged light aircraft design. The first Call Model A flew in 1941, but the outbreak of war meant that access to needed materials was almost impossible, and the civil market was also disrupted. Further, the firm's isolated located precluded its winning any military subcontracts. Call survived on repair work and by building propeller-driven snow cars for mountain winter transportation. Active aircraft production had to await the end of the war.[20] The firm was noteworthy, however, because at over 6,000 feet elevation its factory was the highest in the world, and its products advanced the art of mountain aviation. The location proved to be a distinct advantage in testing aircraft in adverse conditions.[21]

The Bennett Aircraft Corporation of Fort Worth, Texas, was formed in 1939 and designed an experimental twin-engined light transport, but soon moved toward development of light aircraft of bonded plywood construction. With reorganization in 1941 the firm became Globe Aircraft Corporation, still at Fort Worth. The company's first design as Globe, the low-wing two-seat GC-1 Swift, held promise, but production was forced to await the end of the war.

Rearwin Aircraft and Engines, Inc., continued with the Models 6000 and 6000M Speedster which had appeared in 1935, followed by the Model 7000 Sportster. The somewhat larger Model 8135 Cloudster, with side-by-side seating, appeared in 1940, and served as a wartime military trainer. About 124 were built, some for export. The more modern Skyranger also was developed in 1940, and 82 were produced until nonavailability of aluminum forced a shutdown. The firm converted entirely to engine production.

The designer Ben O. "Benny" Howard, who won the Bendix Trophy in

1935 with his Mr. Mulligan high-winged racer, established Howard Aircraft Corporation in Chicago on January 1, 1937, to produce aircraft of his own design. His DGA series of cabin monoplanes, beginning with the DGA-8, extending from the Mr. Mulligan, reached the civil market. The models also saw extensive wartime service as the UC-70 for the Army, and others for the Navy as the DG 1–3 Nightingale.

The Interstate Aircraft and Engineering Corporation was formed in California in April 1937, initially manufacturing components and subassemblies for the aircraft industry. Located in the original Northrop El Segundo hangar, Interstate benefited from its proximity to North American, Douglas, and Lockheed. It produced its new two-seat S-1B Cadet in 1940. The Army acquired 250 cadets as the L-6, and eight civil models were later taken over as the L-8.

Max Harlow, an engineer with experience at Northrop, Douglas, Lockheed, and Hughes, formed the Harlow Engineering Corporation, later Harlow Aircraft Company, in California in 1939 to manufacture a light all-metal executive aircraft, the PJC-2. The PJC-2 was rather similar to the Spartan Executive, although smaller. Quantities of the PJC-2 were taken over by the Army Air Forces for war service as the UC-80, but in 1941 the company transformed entirely to subcontracting.

Swallow Airplane, descended from the original Laird firm of 1920, re-entered aircraft production in 1937. It developed a two-seat trainer in 1940, but little series production was achieved and the Swallow name disappeared.

Meyers Aircraft Company was founded by the 27-year-old engineer Allen H. Meyers in Tecumseh, Michigan, in 1936. Its Model OTW-160 three-seat biplane trainer was widely used in the war by contract flying schools and would continue in production postwar.

The twin brothers Howard and Joe Funk began experimenting with small aircraft in the 1930s, and developed the Model B, a two-seat high-wing model powered by a modified Ford engine and somewhat comparable to the Cub. They had been attracted by the Bureau of Air Commerce competition for an affordable airplane, and formed Akron Aircraft Company in Akron, Ohio, in 1939 in pursuit of that goal. Financial problems led them to relocate to their native Coffeyville, Kansas, in 1941, attracting financial support there from the Jensen brothers. Renamed Funk Aircraft Company, it began production of the Model B, now with a Lycoming engine, but production was halted in 1942 with the war.

After the demise of the Ryan nameplate with the Detroit bankruptcy, the pioneer aviator T. Claude Ryan of *The Spirit of Saint Louis* fame formed a new Ryan School of Aeronautics on June 5, 1931, still in San Diego. Subsequently deciding to reenter manufacturing, he formed Ryan Aeronautical Corporation on May 26, 1934. The flying school became a subsidiary.[22] Ryan concentrated on military trainers, but the two-seat open-cockpit all-metal S-T (for

Sport-Trainer) which first flew on June 8, 1934, also reached the civil market. The three-seat all-metal SCW-145 low-wing cabin model of 1937, with advanced features later seen on postwar aircraft, gained a small market share from 1938 through 1941. Then Ryan, with others, turned entirely to military trainer production and flying school operations.

* * *

While the United States remained the only nation possessing a mass market potential in personal aviation, the numbers of privately owned aircraft and licensed pilots were minuscule compared with those for automobiles. A 1938 survey stated that personal aviation was in no sense a mass market, there being only some 10,000 privately owned airplanes compared with millions of automobiles.[23] The field had nonetheless developed significantly during the economically troubled 1930s (see Table 3-1). The four years before Pearl Harbor brought major growth, and the Civil Aeronautics Board (CAB) estimated the private aircraft fleet at 24,000 in 1941. The pre–Lindbergh total probably was less than 2,000. The Aircraft Owners and Pilots Association (AOPA) was founded in May 1939 and its membership and activities expanded steadily.

Another major development resulted from the new Civil Aeronautics Authority (CAA), established on August 22, 1938. The CAA, which replaced the Bureau of Aeronautics of the Department of Commerce, operated as an autonomous agency. The CAA began a nationwide Civilian Pilot Training Program (CPTP) in 1939. Numerous flying schools across the country received CPTP contracts, and the program began training

Table 3-1
Total Civil Aircraft* 1927–1941

As of December 31	Number
1927	2,740
1928	5,104
1929	9,922
1930	9,818
1931	10,680
1932	10,324
1933	9,284
1934	8,322
1935	9,072
1936	9,299
1937	10,836
1938	11,159
1939	13,772
1940	17,928
1941	26,013

*Includes commercial airliners, since records of the day did not break out personal or business aircraft. Commercial airliners did not number more than a few hundred during this period, however, and it may be concluded that most of the civil fleet consisted of personal or business aircraft.
SOURCE: *Civil Aeronautics Administration, Statistical Handbook of Civil Aviation*, 1950, p. 25.

hundreds of new pilots, increasing both aircraft demand and growth of flight schools (see Table 3-2). Not incidentally, the program also facilitated the approaching wartime aviation buildup.

Design progress, an improving economy, and airways and airfield development combined to strengthen business and personal aviation. Numerous manufacturers, including the light aircraft Big Four, growing firms such as Beech and Cessna, plus Waco, ERCO, and Stinson; and smaller producers such as Culver, Howard, Monocoupe, Rearwin, and Spartan, made the field vibrant. Wichita, however, did not dominate production as it had earlier. Manufacturers were widely dispersed across the country, and Beech and Cessna were low-volume producers. Wichita aircraft industry employment was only some 2,000 in 1939. Consumers had enjoyed a broad choice, but the outbreak of war precluded further design progress, and all civil production was suspended for the duration. Most manufacturers became subcontractors to major military firms or converted to other war-related production.

Table 3-2
Number of Certified Planes of Five Seats and Under

As of January 1, 1939	Number
Aeronca	853
Beech	163
Cessna	114
Curtiss-Wright	741
Fairchild	567
Fleet	191
Luscombe	61
Monocoupe	293
Piper	1,658
Rearwin	170
Stinson (Vultee)	779
Taylorcraft	623
Waco	1,050
Total	7,412

SOURCE: John H. Geisse, *Report to W.A.M. Burden on Postwar Outlook for Private Flying*, GPO, Washington, 1944, p. 80.

General Aviation Manufacturers in Wartime

As the Air Corps was reorganized into the Army Air Forces (AAF) on its journey toward equal status with the Army and Navy as a military service, organic army aviation was reborn on June 6, 1942. The roles of military observation and artillery spotting, previously performed by large, heavy observation aircraft with O-designations, were gradually supplanted by light aircraft originally developed and intended for the civil market. The Civil Air Patrol (CAP), a military adjunct using light aircraft, was founded in 1941. It operated throughout the war patrolling the coast.

William T. Piper wrote Secretary of War Henry Stimson on February 18, 1941, proposing light aircraft for such military roles.[24] After some resistance, the Army began ordering light aircraft such as the Cub. John E. P. Morgan, a Piper director, lobbied for the proposal on behalf of Aeronca and Taylorcraft as well as Piper, and became an unsalaried liaison between the manufacturers and the War Department.[25] Tests of the Cub during large-scale army maneuvers in Louisiana in the spring of 1941 were promising, and gained the strong support of the Third Army Chief of Staff, Colonel Dwight D. Eisenhower. With civil aircraft production suspended, orders for L-series (for liaison) military aircraft enabled the industry to sustain light aircraft production. The O-designation was abolished. Piper, Aeronca, Taylor, Stinson, Beech, Cessna and smaller firms filled large orders for liaison and training aircraft of their design.

The primarily private aircraft firms contributed to wartime aircraft production effort in other ways as well. In addition to military adaptations of their civil models, they produced military designs under license and engaged in subcontracting and component production for larger military manufacturers. Some were active in all.

The Stinson Division of the merged (from 1943) Consolidated Vultee Aircraft Corporation produced more than 12,000 light aircraft during the war, including over 3,000 L-5 (originally O-62) Sentinels, developed from the Voyager, plus several hundred AT-19 Reliants for U.S. forces and for the Royal Navy under Lend-Lease. The L-1 Vigilant, originally O-49, was built in the new Vultee factory in Nashville, Tennessee, which opened in 1940 and offered a lower-cost labor force. Inspired by the German Fieseler Storch, the Vigilant still was not regarded as a success and was soon succeeded by the L-5 Sentinel.[26] The Wayne, Michigan, factory remained active with production of the veteran Reliant and large numbers of the Voyager and L-5.

Beech, which had become a major business aircraft firm before the war, transformed into a significant military aircraft producer. Walter Beech missed extensive work time due to health problems in 1940, and Olive Ann Beech became increasingly active in management. At a time when Walter was hospitalized after a stroke, and Olive Ann was also hospitalized giving birth to a daughter, certain Beech directors attempted to take over management. Olive Ann Beech immediately foiled the attempt and remained in control. She negotiated a $50 million loan from a consortium of banks, followed by a Reconstruction Finance Corporation (RFC) loan of $13.5 million later in 1940, to finance a major expansion.[27]

Beech undertook a major subassembly operation from 1943 in supplying wing sets for the advanced A-26 attack aircraft to the Douglas factory in Tulsa, Oklahoma, where the A-26 was assembled and not far from Wichita. Unlike most personal aircraft firms, however, Beech designed

3—Market Expansion and War Production 49

and tested a combat aircraft, the advanced XA-38 Grizzly. The XA-38 was a sound design worthy of production, but the powerful R-3350 engines with which it was powered were urgently needed for the B-29 strategic bomber program and could not be diverted for the new design.[28] Beech produced 5,257 of the Model 18 "Twin Beech" under such designations as C-45, AT-7, and AT-11 for the AAF, plus Navy and allied variants for war service. It also developed and produced 1,771 of the AT-10 Wichita, a smaller twin trainer built largely of wood due to the then-anticipated shortage of strategic metals.

Cessna achieved a major success in 1939 with an order for its Model T-50 light transport for the Royal Canadian Air Force, where it served as a trainer named the Crane. Dwane Wallace negotiated a $500,000 line of credit from a Wichita bank to finance the start of production. Canada became the center of British Empire flying training, and the T-50 played a key role in that undertaking. Although not to the scale of its neighbor Beech, Cessna explained rapidly with war contracts and opened a new factory in nearby Hutchinson, Kansas, in 1942. Sales reached $13.6 million and profits $1.6 million for 1941. T-50 production, including prewar civil models and Canadian orders, totaled 5,402 through the war, most under the AT-8, AT-17, and UC-78 designations. Both Cessna and Beech unionized in 1940, following unionization by most large aircraft firms. Cessna built Waco CG-4A gliders under license, and also developed the C-106 Loadmaster twin-engined cargo transport in 1943. While promising, the C-106 simply lost out in the battle for material priorities. Like Beech, Cessna subcontracted on the Douglas A-26 produced in Tulsa, Oklahoma, and was an important subcontractor to Boeing as well.[29]

From 1941 through 1944 Taylorcraft produced its L-2 Grasshopper, or liaison aircraft, a tandem-seater developed from the civil Model D. The company also built a number of small military glider trainers derived from the L-2. Upon completion of production contracts, Taylorcraft engaged in subcontracting for the duration of the war.[30] Gilbert Taylor was effective removed from management in 1942, as Fairchild's influence increased. Fairchild then sold its interest in the spring of 1943 to outside investors, as the troubled ownership and financial history of the firm continued.

The Piper J-3 Cub, by far the most numerous light aircraft, received the first large military order, for 1,500, on February 10, 1942. The most successful of the light liaison models, it was produced through the war as the L-4 Grasshopper (all light liaison aircraft were named Grasshopper) as well as in a Marine Corps and Navy ambulance version, a total of 6,028 being delivered. Piper also unionized in 1941, a development that displaced William Piper.

After Luscombe ended civil aircraft production and switched to subcon-

Walter and Olive Ann Beech inspecting SNB production line during Second World War (Wichita State University, Special Collections and University Archives).

tracting in 1942, the FBI removed Leopold Klotz from his position in the firm due to his foreign nationality. But Klotz gained U.S. citizenship in 1944 and regained control on June 6, 1944, D-Day.[31] He immediately began planning a move from New Jersey to Texas for postwar production.

Bellanca suspended civil aircraft production in 1941 and undertook military subcontracting. It also completed 21 Fairchild AT-21 Gunner combat trainers under license. Globe's wartime activity included production of 600 Beech AT-10 trainers as well as subcontract work. The Swift, for the expected postwar market boom, first flew in January 1945.

Waco devoted its efforts to war production from August 1941, but its civil models were not selected in large numbers by the military. Its most important contribution was in design and manufacture of troop-carrying gliders. Waco built more than 1,600 of its glider designs, beginning with the CG-3. The widely used CG-4A was also manufactured in large numbers under license by several firms. William Robertson, whose Robertson Aircraft Corporation was a glider subcontractor, died along with several prom-

Beech AT-10 production line, Second World War (Wichita State University, Special Collections and University Archives).

inent citizens in a glider crash on August 1, 1943. His company exited at the end of the war.

Aeronautical Corporation of America changed its name to Aeronca Aircraft Corporation in 1941. The two-seat civil Model 65 Super Chief, developed from the earlier Model 40 Chief, was modified into the military L-3 (originally O-58) Grasshopper, and more than 1,400 were produced. Aeronca produced Fairchild PT-19 and PT-23 primary trainers under license as well.

In 1942 Rae Rearwin, at age 64 and after a 15-year struggle, finally decided to exit aviation. After difficult negotiations, he sold his company to a group of New York investors, led by munitions manufacturer Frank Cohen, in August 1942. The company was then renamed Commonwealth Aircraft, Inc., effective January 7, 1943, and headquarters remained in Kansas City. Rearwin retired to Southern California. Commonwealth gained war contracts for engines and flight training, and also produced more than 1,500 Waco gliders.[32] The Oklahoma oilman J. Paul Getty gained ownership of Spartan in 1942, and the flight school was very successful in training wartime pilots. Howard Aircraft Corporation's DGA-15 cabin monoplane was ordered by the military, and also produced the Fairchild PT-23 under license, but all government contracts were cancelled in 1944 and the company exited. In 1945 Harlow, another wartime subcontractor, purchased rights to the neighboring Interstate firm's designs and production equipment after the latter had exited aircraft production. Culver was noteworthy for its series of radio-controlled target drones used in simulating enemy air attacks, becoming one of the more successful producers of drones.

* * *

Light aircraft manufacturers contributed greatly to the war production effort, and their cooperation with the major military aircraft manufacturers would serve them well for the future. But their focus and aspirations remained on private flying. Those companies reentering civil aircraft production either offered updated prewar designs or developed completely new models reflecting aeronautical advances as they eagerly anticipated a postwar private flying boom.

4

The Postwar Era, 1946–1954

The War Production Board lifted the suspension of civil aircraft production on May 17, 1945, and personal aircraft firms eagerly resumed civil activity. Established prewar firms were joined by new entrants seeking to participate in the widely anticipated private flying boom. Yet stability was to remain elusive. Several firms were quickly forced from what became an overcrowded market, and others sought or were forced into merger for survival. Even the successful Beech and Cessna firms, Wichita neighbors, conducted serious merger negotiations in June 1945, although both had prospered during the war and were optimistic about the future. Walter Beech and Dwane Wallace could find few points of agreement, however, and talks ended.[1] Years later, neither company would publicly comment about the negotiations.[2]

Larger military aircraft firms, which had experienced massive contract cancellations with the end of the war, feared they faced diminished futures in their fields as well. With the general recognition that there simply were too many companies for anticipated business, some explored merger, with the support of or even pressure from the government. But many sought to diversify into personal aircraft, confident in the coming boom. Such a development posed a potential competitive threat to the oft-beleaguered personal aircraft industry sector. The following account traces the complexities of the light aircraft sector, as well as its technical progress.

The General Aviation Industry Upheaval

While the military sector reached a low point early in 1946, production and employment rose sharply in personal aircraft. Similar to the automobile market, there was a virtual flood of light aircraft production to meet pent-up demand.

Despite widespread parts shortages, a total of 35,000 civil aircraft was produced in 1946 (see Tables 4-1 and 4-2), of which 31,594 were small personal models led by such firms as Aeronca, Cessna, Piper, and Taylorcraft.[3] Beech had not placed its new design in production, and its output trailed temporarily. In the same year, only 1,059 military aircraft were delivered.[4]

General aviation as it now exists, broadly defined as all aviation outside the military and scheduled commercial passenger and freight sectors, was born in the immediate postwar period. But forecasting the future of private aviation at the time was in some ways as complex as for the military market. Private aviation, given Depression and war, was recognized as having been a volatile business over the previous two decades.[5] But AOPA membership exceeded 40,000 in 1947, and the number of licensed private pilots approached 250,000. The Aircraft Industries Association, successor to the Aeronautical Chamber of Commerce, established both a Private Aircraft Council (PAC) and a Helicopter Council to address those sectors. The Civil Aeronautics Administration, heretofore strongly oriented toward scheduled commercial service, began to be more supportive of nonscheduled and personal flying. John H. Geisse promoted personal flying for the CAA.

Postwar optimism was such that there were many forecasts that a true mass market would arrive. A figure of 500,000 personal aircraft by 1950 was bandied about.[6] One market survey reported over 78,000 sales prospects for light aircraft, and that 119,000 individuals were interested in personal helicopters. Even the U.S. Department of Commerce developed a forecast of 200,000 personal aircraft a year.[7] In addition to the many veterans who had been trained to fly in the war, civilian flight training was covered by the G. I. Bill, enabling thousands more to gain private licenses. Factors potentially limiting demand, however, included safety concerns, costs, regulations, and airfield availability.[8]

Table 4-1
General Aviation Unit Sales, 1946*

Piper	7,780
Aeronca	7,555
Cessna	3,959
Taylorcraft	2,483
Ercoupe	2,503
Luscombe	2,483
Stinson	1,436
Globe (Swift)	1,054
Temco	563
Beech	299
Bellanca	288
Republic	196
Funk	194
Navion (NAA)	146
Total	30,939

*Other sources also report some 400 Culver Model V sales.

Table 4-2 Civil Aircraft

Total Registered Civil	Summary by Number	Aircraft, Selected Years	Engines, November 1, 1947
December 31, 1927	2,740	Single engine	80,537
December 31, 1929	9,922	Two engine	3,447
December 31, 1932	10,324	Three engine	48
December 31, 1934	8,322	Four engine	484
December 31, 1936	9,229	Unspecified	7,441
December 31, 1938	11,159	Gliders	673
July 15, 1941	22,354	Lighter-than-air	41
December 31, 1945	37,789		
December 31, 1946	81,002		
November 1, 1947	92,644	Total	92,644

Civil Aircraft Registration by Major Manufacturers as of November 1, 1947

Piper	19,007
Aeronca	12,456
Taylorcraft	8,075
Cessna	7,242
Fairchild	5,796
Consolidated Vultee*	5,094
E. & R. Corp. (ERCO)	4,217
Boeing**	3,899
Luscombe	3,945
North American	1,915
Douglas***	1,613
Waco	1,622
Beech	1,484
Globe	1,078
Curtiss-Wright	827
Lockheed***	394
All others	13,980
Total	92,644

*Includes Stinson
**Includes Stearman
***Principally commercial airliners
SOURCE: *World Aviation Annual*, 1948, p. 279.

Light aircraft use by the military had become firmly established during the war, and demand continued in the postwar years as large numbers of the Super Cub, Champion, Navion, and others were ordered. The military also supported the sector by ordering specialized liaison and trainer designs, which general aviation firms might supply more efficiently than large military firms, with their high cost structures. Further, small helicopters originally designed for military use were easily adaptable for civil uses, supporting development of a civil market. The influential Finletter Commission report of 1948, while primarily concerned with the military and national security aspects of air power, recognized the role of the personal aircraft industry, and recommended its preservation and support. NACA, while still focused on military research, held a conference in the summer of 1946 to disseminate wartime research applicable to the design of personal aircraft.[9] Thus the light aircraft sector (see Table 4–3), while lacking the political influence of larger industries, still gained significant support from the military, NACA, CAA, Commerce, and other agencies.

Personal aircraft remained only a small percentage of total aircraft production by value, but most large military aircraft firms considered entering the field, regarding it as a possible offset to the postwar decline of military production.[10] Military firms also felt that their greater resources, including their engineering and production expertise, could be applied to advantage in a booming market. While a large-scale entry into the sector by military firms would have seriously threatened established light aircraft manufacturers, it developed that of the numerous personal aircraft design studies and prototypes undertaken by the larger firms, few entered production.

Table 4-3 Nine Major Personal/Light Commercial Airframe Companies, 1947*

Aeronca Aircraft Corp.
Beech Aircraft Corp.
Bellanca Aircraft Corp.
Cessna Aircraft Corp.
Engineering & Research Corp.
Luscombe Airplane Corp.
Piper Aircraft Corp.
Taylorcraft, Inc.**
Texas Engineering & Manufacturing Corp.

SOURCE: Survival in the Air Age: A Report to the President's Air Policy Commission (popularly known as the Finletter Commission), GPO, Washington, D.C., 1948, p. 51.
*The Stinson Division of Consolidated Vultee was not included.
**Bankrupt end of 1946.

Kaiser Industries briefly considered producing an all-metal four-seat design at its Fleetwings operation in Bristol, Pennsylvania, but declining market prospects ended the idea. Goodyear, the rubber producer, but also a major wartime aircraft manufacturer, tested the small GA-2 amphibian but decided against production. Even Rohr, a major military subcontractor, developed a personal airplane, a small V-tailed tricycle-geared model, but likewise did not proceed with production.[11]

Douglas, reviving the name of its original airplane, tested the innovative Cloudster in 1946. The Cloudster was of advanced configuration, with twin rear-mounted engines geared to a single pusher propeller, but it remained experimental. Lockheed developed the small Little Dipper and Big Dipper personal aircraft, maintaining its practice of astronomical names, but decided both were unpromising and ended development. The single-seat Little Dipper, functionally a flying motorcycle, also was proposed to the Army but attracted no interest. Lockheed's 14-seat Saturn commuter airliner was tested in 1946, but at a projected price of some $100,000, it fell victim to the availability of surplus military variants of the Douglas DC-3 at around $25,000 each.

Consolidated Vultee (Convair) developed several new personal aircraft models, seeking to continue a strong market presence with more modern successors to the Voyager. The Model 106 Skycoach, an all-metal, pusher-engined, four-seat design of the Stinson Division, flew in April 1946. The twin-engined Model 116 followed in July 1946. The Model 111 Air-Car, designed by the engineer T. P. Hall, explored the roadable airplane or flying automobile concept, and was followed by the more powerful Model 118 ConVAirCar, which first flew on November 15, 1947. With rising costs, efforts soon ended for all new models, however, and Convair's only general aviation entry remained the Voyager. Hall pursued the renamed Air-Car independently after Convair ended development, but eventually ended efforts as well.

Grumman's entry into the personal aircraft market, planned before the end of the war, was to offer nothing for its future. Grumman had developed and tested both the small G-63 Kitten I landplane and the G-65 Tadpole amphibian in 1944. Then in 1946 came the G-72 Kitten II, with tricycle gear and somewhat similar to the Ercoupe. Assessing the overall market and concerned about a cost structure somewhat higher than the competition, Grumman wisely decided not to enter the civil market at the time. The prewar Widgeon and the new, larger Mallard twin-engined amphibians also were produced, but their prospects were limited by the availability of cheap surplus military amphibians. Only 59 Mallards and 76 Widgeons were built, but their development at least kept Grumman in the amphibian field.[12] Grumman was to reenter the personal aircraft field later.

Fairchild chief executive J. Carlton Ward determined that the company, in addition to military work, should maintain a major presence in the personal aviation field. He pushed for production of the new F-47 low-wing four-seat business aircraft and established the Fairchild Personal Planes Division in Wichita late in 1945, developments opposed by major stockholder Sherman Fairchild. When Fairchild regained control of his company in 1948, precipitating Ward's departure, the division was disbanded. The Glenn L. Martin Company, also concerned over future military business, conducted a series of design studies for personal aircraft, but none reached the prototype stage.

The only personal aircraft developed by military firms to enter production were the North American Navion and the Republic Seabee. The four-seat low-wing NA-143 Navion (a rough acronym of North American Aviation) first flew on January 16, 1946. The Navion drew on the design of the P-51 Mustang fighter and had considerable customer appeal in the luxury segment of the personal aircraft market, and North American pursued production whereas Lockheed, Douglas, and Convair had not. The Navion also won Army orders as the L-17 liaison aircraft. While North American had regarded the civil market as a necessary diversification move, initially strong demand for the Navion disappeared when the overall market for light aircraft suddenly dried up in 1947. The company thereupon stopped Navion production on April 15, 1947, at 1,108 aircraft, selling all rights to the smaller Ryan Aeronautical Corporation on June 25. North American had sustained a loss of $8 million on the program.[13] Ryan, which had not continued its prewar designs, felt that with the Navion it could compete in the reduced postwar market.

After purchasing the rights, Ryan produced the Navion until 1951, including further L-17 models for the Air Force. But after building some 1,200 Navions for both civil and military customers, Ryan ended the program due to the press of Korean War military requirements and concentrated on subcontracting.[14] The Navion, however, became regarded as a personal aviation classic and would enjoy a long development and production life, including twin-engined conversions, with other firms.

Republic's RC-1 four-seat pusher-engined light amphibian first flew in November 1944. The developed RC-3 Seabee entered production for the civil market, but postwar inflation pushed costs to the point that it was no longer the economy model first envisaged. Underpriced originally at $3,995, the price soon rose to over $6,000, but losses still increased. Although selling well initially, Seabee production ended with the general market contraction of 1947. A further complication was Republic's purchase in December 1945 of Aircooled Motors, maker of the Seabee's engine. Although intended to enhance Republic's cost control, the purchase instead increased pressure on

4—The Postwar Era, 1946-1954

its already strained finances.[15] After the Seabee ended production, Aircooled was resold to the ill-fated Tucker Corporation in March 1948, but the Seabee episode was a factor in a Republic management shakeup.

Whatever the potential advantages of military firms in light aircraft, the early postwar experience served to validate the existence of a personal aircraft manufacturing sector. That distinct sector in fact continued, although many firms would later become controlled by larger corporations, both of the aircraft and other industries.

In the heady immediate postwar period, established private aircraft manufacturers felt that they could price small models for as little as $2,000, and larger four-seat models could sell for $4,000, but rising costs and market uncertainties made these figures unattainable.[16] The major demand in the short term was for proven prewar designs, such as the Champion, Cub, Taylorcraft, Silvaire, Voyager, Swift, and Fairchild F-24, but certain manufacturers, especially Beech and Cessna, readied completely new designs.

It soon became apparent that, among other problems, the industry had seriously overproduced in 1946. Flying schools became saturated. Then the general collapse in new aircraft demand and the industry's inability to provide new aircraft at low prices sealed the fate of all but a few companies and models (see Table 4-4). Personal aircraft deliveries declined to only 7,037 in 1948.[17] New designs generally cost in the $5,000-$9,000 range, too expensive for major market growth. Disposals of war surplus light aircraft by the RFC were another constraint on new aircraft demand. Yet even as numerous firms exited the market, new competitors appeared, and another major development of the 1949-1953 period was the appearance of light twin-engined business aircraft. They would become a major growth segment.

A new investor, Nash Russ of Detroit, bought control of Taylorcraft on May 13, 1945. The company still experienced financial difficulties, however, exacerbated by overexpansion and the expense of developing a four-seat model, and creditors forced a shutdown on November 8, 1946. Taylorcraft declared bankruptcy the following month, and its assets were placed up for sale.[18] Gilbert Taylor along with Ben J. Mauro, a former distributor, reentered the industry by forming Taylorcraft, Inc., on April 25, 1947, purchasing the rights and leasing part of the Alliance, Ohio, factory for limited production. With new financing, the firm relocated in 1949 to the Beaver County Airport in Pennsylvania for development of new production as well as for subcontracting work.[19] The four-seat Model 15 Tourist entered production in 1950, followed by the Model 19 Sportsman, developed from the 1939 Model B. The firm was managed by Mauro on behalf of Taylor. With the benefit of addition financing secured in 1951, Taylorcraft would attain modest success during the decade.

Waco had initially hoped to continue in the military glider field postwar, but the abolition of this category ended that prospect. Having fallen behind the leaders in light aircraft, Waco made a final attempt at a competitive model for the postwar business market with its unusual pusher-engined Aristocraft, which first flew in December 1946. The firm decided market prospects did not look promising, and production was not undertaken. Waco then withdrew from the aircraft field on June 2, 1947, but continued production of aircraft parts, small machinery, and with subcontracting.

Aeronca enjoyed initially strong postwar sales of the Model 7 Champion, developed from its prewar models, and of the L-16 army version. It introduced the side-by-side Model 11 Chief and refined Super Chief, also extending from its prewar designs, and the four-seat Model 15 Sedan in 1947. It then developed the experimental low-wing Arrow. Over 10,000 Champions had been built when all production was suspended in 1951 in the face of weak demand. Design rights were sold to a new Champion Aircraft of Wisconsin, which later resumed production. Aeronca remained a significant component producer and subcontractor.

The renamed Monocoupe Engine and Airplane Corporation was acquired by new investors and relocated to Melbourne, Florida. It resumed production of the prewar Model 90 during 1947, but ended production in 1949. Harlow exited in 1946, but Max Harlow, with partners, reentered the field in 1947 as Atlas Aircraft Company. The modern H-10 four-seat design was tested but did not enter production.

Two new investors bought Culver from Charles Yankey on November 14, 1945. Culver entered the postwar market with its Model V (for Victory), developed from the prewar Model G, but suffered bankruptcy in 1946. It simply fell behind the competition, particularly from Cessna's new Models 120 and 140. Cunningham-Hall, out of the airframe business since before the war, was dissolved in 1948, happily with no loss the stockholders.[20] Spartan tested a modernized Executive with tricycle gear in 1946. Development had been delayed but the design showed much promise. J. Paul Getty decided the market outlook was not favorable, however, and cancelled the program, marking the exit of Spartan from aircraft production. The tricycle-geared Ercoupe was produced in some numbers until 1950, when production ended in the generally weak market.

Commonwealth Aircraft, successor to Rearwin, acquired Columbia Aircraft Corporation of Valley Stream, Long Island, a wartime contractor, early in 1946. Commonwealth then closed its Kansas plant and consolidated operations at Valley Stream, but Columbia retained its separate identity. Designer Gilbert Trimmer sold his small twin-engined amphibian design, the Trimmer C-170, to Commonwealth. The C-170 was tested but not produced. While the cross-country move was not well-managed, Commonwealth still produced

4—The Postwar Era, 1946–1954

276 of the Skyranger 185, developed from a prewar design, before a disastrous strike closed the plant in November 1946.[21] The company exited aircraft.

Among smaller producers, Meyers attempted to compete with the modern MAC 125, a low-wing design but still with taildragger gear. It was followed by the more powerful tricycle-geared MAC 145 and by the MAC 145T, with retractable gear, produced in small numbers from 1949 to 1956 when production was suspended. Call produced the small CallAir A-2 and A-3 strut-braced low-wing models in limited numbers. The rugged Call models enjoyed a reputation in the western states but still encountered difficulty competing against the industry giants. Funk resumed production of its Model B in 1946, and the type won some adherents, but production was ended in 1948 after some 400 had been built.

Bellanca, despite respected designs in the four-seat Cruisair and the larger Cruisemaster, introduced in April 1949, simply lost out in competition to such firms as Piper, Cessna, and Beech, and suspended production in 1952. All patents, rights, and production equipment for the Cruisemaster were sold to Northern Aircraft, Inc., of Alexandria, Minnesota, in 1955.

Luscombe moved to Garland, Texas, in 1945 to continue production of the updated Silvaire and the four-seat Sedan. The company considered for a time a twin-boom pusher-engined personal aircraft developed from the prewar Stearman-Hammond design, but it did not proceed. The Silvaire then

Ercoupe production, Riverdale, Maryland, late 1940s (National Air and Space Museum, Smithsonian Institution).

faded in competition with the new Cessna 120 and 140 models. Ironically, Cessna had been inspired by the Silvaire in developing its postwar all-metal designs. By 1949 Luscombe could not meet its payroll, and efforts to secure an RFC loan were unsuccessful.[22] The firm declared bankruptcy, and Leopold Klotz withdrew from the company and returned to New York. A successor Luscombe Holding Company emerged, which held 85 percent of Luscombe Airplane.

J. B. Baumann, a founder of Mercury Aircraft and later with Lockheed, founded Baumann Aircraft Corporation in 1945 to develop his B-250 Brigadier twin-pusher-engined executive aircraft. The Brigadier first flew in June 1947, and during 1949 Piper, interested in the business market, considered but then rejected acquiring Baumann and its production rights. The more powerful B-290 was tested in 1951, but with no financing, the Brigadier unfortunately never attained production.

The engineers Ben Anderson and Marvin Greenwood had started a small company in 1941 for personal aircraft development. Both joined Boeing in Wichita for the duration of the war, but revived the firm afterward in Houston, Texas. Anderson, Greenwood and Co. produced five of the unusual AG-14 light twin-boom pusher design, the first flying on October 1, 1947, but soon moved into subcontracting. A sidelight to the anticipated postwar private flying boom was the recurring dream of a truly practical roadable airplane. While the concept was not new—Harold Pitcairn had considered a roadable autogiro–M. B. "Molt" Taylor, a former naval aviator, pursued the concept more extensively than had anyone previously. An important feature of his design was that the flying surfaces could be towed behind the automobile section, thereby conferring greater flexibility in operation. Taylor formed Aerocar, Inc., in February 1948, and the Aerocar first flew in October 1949. Taylor refined his Aerocar for years, but a market for such a craft never developed. Other roadable designs, the prewar Waterman Arrowbile and the postwar Fulton Airphibian and ConVAirCar, were short-lived.

Even with the major market reverse of 1947, a general aviation Big Three of Beech, Cessna, and Piper emerged. Their status was enhanced and protected somewhat by the nonentry and quick exits from the private aircraft field by larger military producers, but long-term survival was more attributable to design quality and competitiveness.

Cessna moved quickly to establish postwar design leadership. It led the industry in promoting the "family car of the air" concept.[23] With others, Cessna was severely strained by the severe market contraction of 1947, even diversifying briefly into metal office furniture and industrial products. The Hutchinson factory, closed at the end of the war, transformed into industrial products manufacture. More significantly, however, was Cessna's rapid conversion to all-metal aircraft, ending all production of fabric-covered airplanes in 1949. Cessna also retained the high-wing configuration, although strut-braced rather than fully cantilevered. The two-seat Model 120 and refined Model 140, designed early in 1945, achieved instant success and were followed in 1948 by the four-place Model 170. The Model 170, sat a base price of $4,995, was more expensive than the Piper Pacer or Aeronca Sedan, but its all-metal construction and greater power conveyed strong advantages.

The larger radial-engined Models 190 and 195, similar in configuration to the prewar Airmaster, were produced from 1947 to 1954. The more modern Model 180, with the same wing as the 170 but with a larger fuselage and more powerful engine, appeared in 1953. The Models 170 and 180 and further refinements became market leaders, and Dwane Wallace became recognized for his marketing acumen. Dwight Wallace, however, left in a dispute with his brother, never publicly discussed, and joined Beech.

Cessna successfully entered the light twin-engined business market with the Model 310, which first flew on January 3, 1953. Cessna also became a significant military aircraft contractor, and with expanding business operated three plants in the Wichita area from 1951. The L-19 Bird Dog army liaison aircraft, developed from the Model 170, won a spirited contract competition in June 1950 for a successor to wartime liaison models. The L-19 was widely used in Korea and after, with production totaling 2,460 by 1959. Later, Cessna won the Air Force design competition for a jet-powered basic trainer. The prototype Cessna XT-37 first flew on October 12, 1954, and entered large-scale production. Cessna also participated in the Korean War expansion by manufacturing major components for the Boeing B-47, also produced in Wichita, thus continuing its wartime subcontracting relationship.

Beech, which built a strong military production record during the war, returned immediately to the civil market. The refined G-17S postwar model of the Staggerwing ended production in 1948 after 90 were delivered. Total production since 1932 was 781. Critical for the future was the new Model 35 Bonanza, with its distinctive V-tail, which first flew on December 22, 1945. In 1947, its first full year of production, 1,229 Bonanzas were sold, a strong counter to the overall weak demand of that year. The Bonanza, in one sense a successor to the Staggerwing, gained a commanding position in the high-powered, luxury four-place segment, despite being the most expensive with a base price of $7,975. Benefiting from continuous improvement, the Bonanza was to be produced for decades. During March 6–9, 1949, a Bonanza fitted with wingtip fuel tanks and piloted by William P. Odom made a solo nonstop flight of 5,273 statute miles from Hawaii to Teterboro, New Jersey, a record for a private aircraft design. The flight took 36 hours. Odom, tragically, died in a racing crash later that year.

Beech also tested the innovative Model 34 "Twin Quad" commuter air-

Cessna factory, early 1950s (Wichita State University, Special Collections and University Archives).

liner in 1947. Although a promising design, which paired four 375 hp Lycoming engines buried in the wings to drive twin propellers, and with the V-tail of the Bonanza, Beech decided market prospects were not encouraging and ended development. While moving ahead with new designs, Beech also diversified into nonaviation machinery and equipment, completing a contract for agricultural harvesters in the late 1940s. Production of the Model 18 "Twin Beech" continued uninterrupted. The improved E18S "Super 18" model first flew on December 10, 1953, sustaining its leadership at the high end of the business transport sector. The Model 50 Twin Bonanza, a modern twin with tricycle landing gear and a conventional tail, made its first flight on November 15, 1949. The first of the postwar light business twins to reach the market, it first served as the L-23 Army liaison aircraft during the Korean War, but then succeeded in the business market after military needs had been filled.

Walter Beech continued to lead a stable management team. The veterans Yankey, Gaty, and Wells continued on the board and were joined by Dwight Wallace, who also became the firm's general counsel. Olive Ann

Clyde Cessna and Dwane Wallace standing beside a Cessna 180, 1953 (National Air and Space Museum, Smithsonian Institution).

Beech, holding the titles of secretary and treasurer, remained influential in management. When Walter Beech died unexpectedly of a heart attack on November 29, 1950, at age 59, she became president and chief executive officer and managed the company with conspicuous success. Her nephew Frank Hedrick, who had joined the company in 1940, became her second in command. Of great significance for the company was winning a major military contract with its T-34 Mentor primary trainer. Basically a Bonanza with a tandem glass cockpit and a conventional tail, the T-34 prototype first flew on December 2, 1948. The T-34 first lost to the Fairchild T-31 in a 1949 flyoff competition, but T-31 production was delayed due to funding shortfalls. Walter Beech then persuaded the Air Force to conduct a second competition, which the T-34 won. Delayed by Korean War priorities, the T-34 finally entered production in March 1953, was later adopted by the Navy, and widely exported.

Another military contract, for the T-36A twin-engined crew trainer, resulted in a crisis. The largest aircraft ever designed by Beech, the T-36 was cancelled on June 10, 1953, just as the prototype was ready to fly and a new factory had been completed. Overnight, half the Beech order backlog was lost and the employment level of 13,000 was reduced by half.[24] But the company eventually made up the loss with increased subcontracting business. Beech also became active in pilotless vehicles, or target drones, and would continue to have the largest proportion of military sales of the general aviation firms.

While no personal aircraft producer was unaffected by the sudden drop in demand in 1947, Piper was the most severely affected of the established firms. Piper had produced 7,773 new aircraft during 1946 and was so optimistic that it opened a branch plant in Ponca City, Oklahoma. Piper suffered a setback when flooding caused extensive damage at its Lock Haven factory on May 28, 1946, but recovered quickly. Then the sudden disappearance of the market simply caught the firm by surprise. William Piper had expected a market slowdown, but not to the extent it actually occurred.

There was new product development with the powerful four-place low-wing PA-6 Skysedan and the small PA-8 Skycycle, both appearing in 1946. (Piper switched to the PA prefix for aircraft designations for the postwar market.) The Skycycle, with a fuselage adapted from a military drop tank, proved somewhat unstable and faced a dubious market, but the Skysedan, designed by Jamouneau, showed promise, and Piper committed a major error by not moving ahead with production. Other experimental types included the light twin-boomed pusher-engined Skycoupe and the PA-10 light amphibian. By 1947 Piper production consisted of the PA-11 Cub Special, successor to the veteran J-3 and carrying a base price of $2,195, and the three-seat PA-12 Super Cruiser and four-seat PA-14 Family Cruiser that extended from the prewar J-5B. Its product line, therefore, was concentrated at the "low end" of the market, most vulnerable to competition from cheap surplus aircraft, and still reflected prewar design technology. Clearly the company had stuck with the Cub design too long, but established a production record of 14,125 of the civil models.

After years of strong profitability, Piper lost over $500,000 for the 1947 fiscal year. Dividends were suspended, debts mounted, and major production cutbacks and layoffs followed. An alarmed board of directors, under pressure from Manufacturers Trust of New York and other major creditors, brought in the troubleshooter William C. Shriver, formerly with Chrysler Corpora-

4—The Postwar Era, 1946–1954

tion, as general manager. Shriver was given total authority to reverse the decline and manage the company out of debt, and the move became a textbook case of the rescue of a failing company. Arriving in June 1947, Shriver moved quickly, completely shutting down manufacturing and closing the Ponca City branch plant. Employment, 2,607 in February, had already been reduced to under 1,000 by June, but Shriver pared it to only 157 by the end of the year. Remaining employees were forced to take pay cuts. Shriver moved into the office of William T. Piper, Sr., forcing him completely out of any involvement in day-to-day operations, and removed W. T. Piper, Jr., as assistant treasurer, reassigning him to sales.[25]

Shriver discovered that the conservative senior Piper had developed little in the way of modern business practices, such as cost accounting and market analysis. In addition, he was continuing an outdated product line. Piper's sobriquet as the Henry Ford of personal aviation proved to be accurate in less flattering ways as well. Some felt, however, that Shriver had made the younger Piper a scapegoat for the financial problems in order to preserve the reputation of his father. Although removing most officers, Shriver was impressed with Walter Jamouneau and retained him as an executive and member of the board of directors. He then pushed development of the PA-15 Vagabond, with side-by-side seating, as the best short-term prospect for sales in the diminished market.

The next task was to reassure creditors. The engine supplier Continental Motors had threatened to force the firm into involuntary bankruptcy, but Shriver persuaded Continental and others to hold off action. He also cultivated the necessary political contacts to secure a $390,000 RFC loan, enabling Piper to resume production and to use up its considerable inventory of materials.[26] Restarting production in January 1948, Shriver began expanding the workforce and succeeded in containing losses and repaying creditors. The Vagabond, while an austere and uncomfortable design, did manage to sell well enough during 1948 to generate needed cash for developing new models.

Shriver, who had announced that he intended to stay only 18 months, in one of his final acts acquired the money-losing Stinson Division from Consolidated Vultee on December 1, 1948, for 100,000 shares of new Piper stock. All Stinson assets, rights, and unsold inventory of some 200 airplanes were included. William Piper, Sr., opposed the Stinson deal, but Shriver felt that the acquisition would give the company broader market coverage, and the Voyager was the lowest-priced of the four-seat models on the market. Piper completed a small number of new Voyagers from assemblies, but turned down the idea of new production.[27]

With the Voyager added to Piper's PA-15 and new PA-17 Vagabond trainer, and with a new four-seat development nearing production, market coverage was indeed enhanced and recovery was underway by the end of

1948. The last Voyager was delivered in 1950, marking the end of the Stinson nameplate after 24 years and 12,320 aircraft, of which more than 5,000 were Voyagers. Shriver left at the end of 1948, having earned a reputation as an ogre, but clearly having stabilized operations. Later, the senior Piper grudgingly credited him with having saved the company.

Product changes continued as the veteran Cub Special ended production, succeeded in 1949 by the improved PA-18 Super Cub, which would enjoy a long production life. Korean War orders for the Super Cub as the L-18 and L-21 helped the company significantly, and an agricultural spraying version also found a market. Joining the Super Cub in 1949 was the four-seat PA-16 Clipper, developed from the Vagabond. Running afoul of Pan Am's airliner trademark, the Clipper was redesignated the PA-20 Pacer and was produced in quantity from 1950 to 1954. The tricycle gear version, the PA-22 Tri-Pacer, was introduced in 1951 and became one of the most popular of all postwar light aircraft.

After Shriver's departure, William Piper still did not control the board, and his New York financiers imposed a new executive vice president and general manager, August Esenwein. More friction between the Piper family and

W. T. Piper, Sr, circa 1953 (National Air and Space Museum, Smithsonian Institution).

its bankers ensued. Among other things, Esenwein removed Jamouneau as chief engineer. He also pressed for an entry into the twin-engined market, where Piper's lack of engineering expertise in that segment had led to consideration of the Baumann Brigadier. In the meantime, the senior Piper had acquired more stock in the open market, and by the board meeting of January 10, 1950, regained control and reinstated Jamouneau. Esenwein resigned.[28] Piper, although nearing 70, had no thought of retirement, but did install his second son Thomas "Tony" as administrative vice president and *de facto* chief executive on April 1, 1950. Tony Piper proved to be as conservative and frugal as his father. The elder Piper went on to gain his twin-engined pilot rating in 1953 at age 73.

Piper entered the twin-engined business segment with a new design, probably the riskiest product decision yet undertaken by the company. Originally called the Twin-Stinson, possibly in tribute to an earlier Stinson design study, the prototype, with twin tails, first flew on March 2, 1952. The developed PA-23 Apache soon entered production after Piper undertook the first market survey in its history.[29] The Apache became an immediate success and led to further twin-engine developments. While at $23,000 the most expensive aircraft ever designed by Piper, the Apache was still priced well under the larger but competitive Twin Bonanza and new Cessna 310. Max Conrad's publicized transatlantic solo flights in the Apache were a major boost to general aviation and to Piper, which once again became a strong competitor.

The General Aviation Helicopter

The helicopter had entered military service toward the end of the war, and with peace many saw an enormous civil market potential. The strong overlap in development and performance between military and civil models aided the civil market. Manufacturers progressed with both simple, light designs and larger passenger- and cargo-carrying models. Low-priced helicopters were forecast as the answer to the dream of the "family flivver," taking off and landing in front yards and eventually displacing fixed-wing light aircraft. Other civil uses for the helicopter included business travel, medical emergency evacuation and transportation, law enforcement, and agricultural spraying. But the dream of a light helicopter for the general public would prove to be unattainable, as had been the case earlier with the autogiro. Development efforts were highly active, however, as the following survey recounts.

The first helicopter certificated for civil operation in the world was the Bell Model 47, on March 8, 1946. While primarily a military firm, Bell Aircraft Corporation had begun helicopter development in 1942 under the pioneering engineer Arthur Young. It placed the Model 47B in civil operation in 1948 at an initial price of $21,500. A total of 78 of the Model 47B was built, including crop spraying and cropduster versions. The New York Police Department was among the early customers. Production was moved from Buffalo to Fort Worth in 1951. The Model 47 also was widely exported, further strengthening Bell's market position. The improved Model 47G, appearing in 1953, was also licensed to the Italian firm Agusta. The larger five-seat Model 42 was also planned for the civil market, but only three test models were built as development stopped.

Sikorsky, the leading helicopter manufacturer, did not initially target the civil market, but limited numbers of its S-51 and larger S-55 series were ordered for industrial use in the early 1950s.

The young helicopter pioneer Stanley Hiller formed Hiller Aircraft Company in California in 1942 as a division of his father's Hiller Industries. In partnership with Kaiser Industries, he tested his first XH-44 model in August 1944 with a view toward its military potential. Renamed United Helicopters, Inc., in 1945 for the postwar market, Hiller tested the experimental UH-4 Commuter, which featured coaxial rotors, and the J5 model, with jet deflector vanes at the tail for control. Production success came with the two-seat Model 360, with a conventional main rotor plus tail rotor, which first flew in 1947. In 1948 it became the third helicopter to gain civil certification, after those of Bell and Sikorsky. The UH-12 military variant became the standard training helicopter for both the Army and Navy during the Korean War era, giving

The Bell Model 47 in use by the San Francisco Police Department, late 1940s (Bell Helicopter Textron).

Hiller a sound production base. Then the UH-12N developed civil variant gained certification in 1951, but production had to wait until military needs had been met. The company was renamed Hiller Helicopters in 1950, and by then primarily military, continued civil development and production. The challenge remained that the civil helicopter cost some $30,000, double the price of a Beech Bonanza.[30] The small Hiller HJ-1 Hornet, powered by rotor tip ramjet engines, was tested during 1951–52 and was publicized as a potential mass-market personal helicopter, but it never saw production. Hiller continued to stress affordability and ease of operation, and the later Model 12C found a share of the small civil market of the mid-1950s.

Siebel Helicopters was formed in 1948 Charles M. Siebel, a Wichita native and former Bell engineer, specifically to pursue a small helicopter for the general aviation market. His two-seat Model S-3 showed promise, and Cessna took over the firm on March 1, 1952, in order to diversify into the market, the first established general aviation firm to do so. Charles Siebel was retained by Cessna to further develop the basic design, redesignated CH-1, which first flew in July 1954.

Newby O. Brantly founded a firm for helicopter development in Pennsylvania in 1943, and built and tested a small coaxial rotor model in 1946. The single-rotor production Model B-1 was the lowest-priced helicopter in the United States, leading efforts to make the helicopter more affordable. After moving production to Oklahoma, Brantly developed the Model B-2, which first flew on February 21, 1953, and which led to further progress toward the elusive goal of the small, affordable helicopter. But the company struggled to attain quantity production.

The Market Stabilizes

Despite recurring upheavals, the general aviation manufacturing sector reflected one consistent characteristic, that of entrepreneurship. The light aircraft field, however cyclical and risky, was the only manufacturing sector of the industry that provided entrepreneurial opportunities. Regardless of prevailing market conditions, and in the face of numerous exits by older firms, new ventures appeared. Whatever their educational backgrounds or financial backing, those forming new aircraft production ventures tended to be mechanical tinkerers and innovators, always believing that they could build and sell a better airplane. Yet despite numerous and innovative light aircraft designs, few enjoyed sustained production. Most longer-term market successes were aircraft of conventional configuration. In fact, manufacturers were to be criticized in later years for design conservatism. The following account traces the more significant new entrants.

Colonial Aircraft of Maine was organized in 1946 by David B. Thurston, a former Grumman engineer with extensive amphibian design experience, and other associates.

The firm produced the C-1 Skimmer pusher-engined light amphibian, developed from the Grumman Tadpole with which Thurston had been involved at Grumman.[31] The Skimmer first flew on July 17, 1948, but did not enter production for several years.

Fletcher Aviation Corporation of California, starting in 1941 as a war subcontractor, developed light aircraft designs, although primarily for military rather than civil market. Its first design, the wartime FBT-2 light trainer, of extremely simple configuration and of plastic-plywood composite construction, did not attain orders or production. Postwar, the company designed the FL-23 liaison aircraft, followed by the FD-25 Defender light ground attack aircraft in 1952, both intended for the Army. The FL-23 lost out to the Cessna L-19 for orders, but the developed FD-25B was licensed to Toyo in Japan. Fletcher then turned to civil market developments.

Mooney was incorporated on June 18, 1948, in Wichita, by former Culver executives Al Mooney and Charles G. Yankey, with Yankey providing the financial backing and serving as president. Art Mooney was also associated. Its first design, reminiscent of the wartime Culver drones, was the diminutive M-18 Mite. Despite an initial price of $2,000, sales of the Mite were disappointing. Facing limited space for expansion in Wichita, Mooney move to Kerrville, Texas, in February 1953 and reestablished operations. Mite production was phased out, but the new four-seat M-20 made its first flight on August 10, 1953. The M-20, while offering modern features and high performance, was simpler, with extensive use of plywood in its structure, and less expensive, at around $12,000, than competitive models. It would make Mooney a significant factor in the four-seat low-wing market.

An innovative entry was the Koppen-Bollinger Aircraft Corporation, organized in Massachusetts in 1948 by Professors Lynn L. Bollinger of the Harvard Business School and Otto Koppen of MIT, to develop a practical short-takeoff-and-landing (STOL) utility aircraft, Both had extensive experience in aviation. Soon changing the name to Helio Aircraft Corporation, they developed a small STOL prototype based on the Piper Vagabond. Named the Helioplane, it first flew on April 8, 1949. An early proposal for Aeronca to produce the Helio design was not carried out, and it remained experimental. But a new, fully developed STOL design, the Helio Courier, was manufactured from 1954 under contract by the Mid-States Manufacturing Corporation of Pittsburg, Kansas. The owners had an eye to the military liaison market as well as the civil market, and they attained limited success in both.

4—The Postwar Era, 1946–1954

With the end of the war in 1945, the Defense Plant Corporation began to dispose of unneeded plants built for war production, including those in Dallas and Fort Worth. The Fort Worth DPC plant remained with Consolidated Vultee, but the Dallas "A" and "B" plants used by North American were up for disposal. The engineers Robert McCulloch and H. L. Howard, who had run the North American Dallas operations during the war, saw an opportunity to enter the light aircraft market and take advantage of the Dallas facilities. Attracting outside investors, they established the Texas Engineering and Manufacturing Company, Limited, on November 17, 1945, using the Dallas "A" plant. Aeronautical terminology was deliberately left out of the name for later diversification purposes.

The company began production with the Fairchild F-24 and the Globe Swift, having acquired rights for both designs. In late 1946 the firm was incorporated as TEMCO, Inc. Globe Aircraft Corporation had been optimistic about the postwar market but soon encountered financial difficulties. The Globe bankruptcy was an early crisis for TEMCO, but it acquired Globe's assets and inventory on June 23, 1947, and continued production of the Swift, a classic design, from 1947 to 1950.

TEMCO went on to acquire the assets of the bankrupt Luscombe Airplane Corporation of nearby Garland, Texas, in 1949. The reorganized Luscombe Holding Company became a wholly owned on January 12, 1950. TEMCO resumed Silvaire production in March 1950, producing 50 before suspending it for military work. Soon after, all light aircraft manufacturing was suspended in October as capacity was needed for Korean War subcontracting, and personal aircraft lines were officially discontinued, effective December 31, 1950.[32]

TEMCO soon began development of original designs, including the T-35 Buckaroo trainer developed from the Swift, and again was reorganized as Temco Aircraft Corporation in 1952. Luscombe was fully merged into Temco on April 2, 1953. Additional factory space was leased at Greenville, Texas. Success did not follow, however, as Temco lost out to the Beech T-34, and only 20 were ordered. But Temco did achieve success with adaptations. The original twin-engined conversion of the Navion was completed by Dauby Equipment Company in Los Angeles in April 1952. Entrepreneur Jack Riley bought the conversion, further refined the concept, naming it the Twin Navion. Riley went into production, but sold only 19 before selling the operation to Temco in 1953. Temco further developed the conversion as the Riley Twin, and produced substantial numbers from that year. A separate line of Navion conversions was undertaken from 1953 by Cameron Iron Works of Galveston, Texas, as the Camair 480, with more powerful engines than the Temco model. The company established the Camair Division for the operation.

Table 4-4
Annual Production and Sales,
General Aviation Aircraft

Year	Units	Factory Sales ($ millions)
1946	35,000*	$110.0
1947	15,594	57.9
1948	7,037	32.4
1949	3,405	17.7
1950	3,386	19.1
1951	2,302	16.8
1952	3,058	26.8
1953	3,788	34.4
1954	3,071	43.4

*Estimated.
NOTE: Figures account for fixed-wing aircraft only.
SOURCE: GAMA, *General Aviation Statistical Databook* (1990–1991 edition), p.4.

In the fall of 1944, while the country was still at war, the veteran Douglas engineer Theodore Raymond "Ted" Smith, a major contributor to the design of the A-20 Havoc attack bomber, already was thinking of the postwar civil aviation market. With a small number of Douglas associates, Smith organized the Aero Design and Manufacturing Company in Culver City, California, on December 21, 1944. His objective was to develop a completely new twin-engined light executive transport, to be named the Commander, that would be an advance over other business twins. Smith and several of his colleagues resigned from Douglas on August 15, 1945, with the end of the war, to pursue the venture full-time. The company soon experienced problems raising financing, and initial capital was only $175,000. Consequently, the first prototype, designated L3805 (for Lycoming, 380 horsepower, five-place) did not fly until April 23, 1948. Unusual in its high-wing configuration, the Aero Commander showed much promise and several orders were received, but production was held back due to funding shortfalls.

The company survived by attracting investment from the Pew oil interests of Philadelphia and the Amis brothers construction interests of Oklahoma City. With civic support, the company was reorganized in September 1950 and relocated to a new factory in Oklahoma City.[33] Ted Smith held the position of vice president, research and development. The Aero Commander

520, the developed production version, first flew on August 25, 1951. The first customer deliveries came on February 5, 1952, and 46 were delivered by the end of the year, the beginning of a more than 30-year production life for the Commander series.

* * *

During 1949 there was significant price cutting by most manufacturers in the small industry, to maintain demand and output. By 1950 it could be said the industry had stabilized, although at a lower level of production than even the most pessimistic forecasts of 1945. Such respected firms as Aeronca, Erco, Luscombe, Stinson, and Waco had exited. In 1951 only 2,302 personal airplanes were produced, and no more than five significant manufacturers, Beech, Cessna, Piper, and the new Mooney and Aero Design firms, would survive through the decade.

Private flying no longer gripped the public imagination by the 1950s as it had between the wars, and private aircraft ownership simply was not a widely held aspiration.[34] Yet the Civil Aeronautics Administration still estimated that the active civil aircraft fleet had grown to some 54,000 by 1953, of which only about 1,500 were commercial airliners.[35] CAA administrator Theodore P. Wright undertook special efforts to promote private flying from 1952. But the CAA, also responsible for the certification process for new aircraft, lacked the resources to perform all tests during the late 1940s and delegated much testing to the manufacturers themselves. The CAA then relied on the test results, but that practice would later engender safety controversies.

The Aircraft Industries Association introduced the utility category and formed the Utility Airplane Council in 1952, in succession to the Private Aircraft Council. Dwane Wallace served as the first chairperson. The AIA formally identified six utility roles: business flying, industrial (including pipeline patrol, aerial mapping and survey, forestry, etc.), agricultural, instructional, charter, and pleasure or sport. Noteworthy was that the last category, once the only general aviation role, had become the smallest. The AIA ended use of the term "personal planes," in part to change the public's perception of private flying as the province of the country club set or of wealthy playboys, but also in recognition of the dominance of business flying.

The business market segment began to grow rapidly, and new light twin-engined executive aircraft such as the Aero Commander 520, Twin Bonanza, Piper Apache, and Cessna 310 helped expand the market. In addition, the export market for utility aircraft became a significant factor for the first time. Beech established an export division as early as 1946. Light aircraft were exported to numerous countries, and the export component of total sales rose rapidly. The American general aviation industry remained the *de facto* world general aviation industry. The British industry, for example, very active in personal aircraft during the 1930s, did almost nothing in the field postwar.

The cost of general aviation aircraft would continue to rise, although limited by market pressure. There was little doubt that price was very much the decisive factor in personal and business aircraft purchases. For larger commercial aircraft, delivery dates, operating economics, and financing arrangements could be more influential, but for the general aviation customer, price remained paramount.[36]

5

General Aviation Matures, 1954–1967

The year 1955 was a boom year for all civil aviation. Business flying increasingly became regarded as the future of general aviation, and major marketing efforts focused on business applications (see Table 5–1). The Corporate Aircraft Owners Association, founded in 1947, became the National Business Aircraft Association (NBAA) in 1953 and advanced the field. Twin-engined aircraft became more prominent as larger, luxurious types became increasingly preferred for business use, especially transportation of senior executives. While smaller single-engined aircraft still dominated numerically, sales of light twin-engined models rose from 354 in 1954 to 870 in 1958.[1]

Light aircraft design advanced, but almost entirely by industry-funded research. Major NCAA effort and focus during the 1950s was on high-speed research, irrelevant to general aviation until the advent of business jets. Yet general aviation still reflected basic technology developed by NACA from the 1920s. However limited, most general aviation research was undertaken by the NACA Langley center in Virginia.

Beech, the largest general aviation firm, reported sales of $76 million in 1955, followed by Cessna with $50 million and Piper with $17 million. Such smaller military firms as Republic, Martin, and Grumman each reported sales in the $300 million range for that year, highlighting the still-small size of the general aviation sector.

Light aircraft production expanded steadily in the prosperous economy of the 1950s and 1960s. The term *general aviation*, referring to all civil aviation outside the scheduled commercial transportation sector, came into popular use around 1957–1958. To that point the term *utility* had been preferred both for the field and as an aircraft category. Such terms as private aircraft, personal aircraft, and especially business aircraft were still widely used, however. The public began to recognize the practical value and economic benefits of general aviation. Increasing use of both fixed-wing aircraft and helicopters for agricultural dusting and spraying would lead to development of specialized agricultural designs during the decade. Development of more effective spraying equipment and chemicals underpinned that growth.

The change coincided with the redefinition and expansion of the aircraft industry into an overall aerospace industry, as missile development and space programs became more significant. Smaller commuter aircraft and commuter airline operations also began to be included in the general aviation sector. But a point of possible confusion remained in that helicopters were regarded as a distinct sector of the aerospace industry, although general aviation roles for helicopters were increasing steadily. General aviation helicopters continued to be treated separately from fixed-wing aircraft in industry statistics.

Table 5-1
Annual Production and Sales, General Aviation Aircraft

Year	Units	Factory Sales ($ millions)
1955	4,434	$68.2
1956	6,738	103.7
1957	6,118	99.6
1958	6,414	101.9
1959	7,689	129.8
1960	7,558	151.2
1961	6,788	124.2
1962	6,697	136.8
1963	7,569	153.4
1964	9,336	198.8
1965	11,852	318.2
1966	15,768	444.9
1967	13,577	359.6

NOTE: Figures account for fixed-winged aircraft only.
SOURCE: GAMA, *General Aviation Statistical Databook* (1990–1991 edition), p. 4.

General aviation manufacturers continued to be strengthened by military demand for training and utility aircraft. Those aircraft often overlapped strongly with general aviation designs and could be purchased "off-the-shelf" by the military with considerable savings in research and development expense. Thus general aviation firms could easily develop and advantageously fill military needs and potentially reap an added benefit from a countercyclical effect. Military demand made general aviation firms particularly vulnerable to budgetary constraints, however, as training and utility aircraft generally held a lower priority than combat and other larger aircraft. The Beech T-36 cancellation was a case in point.

Sport and recreational flying remained too expensive for development of a mass market. All active producers struggled to gain and hold market share, but competition was so intense that many small firms with less complete product lines could not survive against the major producers. As a result, general aviation manufacturers declined steadily in number, some by failure and others through merger. But newer competitors persevered, feeling that a new or innovative design could gain a profitable market niche.

The Homebuilt Segment Emerges

One response by sport or recreational pilots to the expense of private flying and to the decline of sport or recreational flying was that of constructing, and in some cases designing, small airplanes for their personal use. Although not new, the business of supplying component kits or plans for completion by amateur builders began to gain some momentum in the 1950s. Development of that market niche was aided somewhat by the lack of interest in the field by the established factory aircraft producers.

Government regulatory authority had been largely negative on the matter of homebuilt or amateur-built aircraft, even for personal flying. The Bureau of Air Commerce and later the CAA had simply made no provision for certification of homebuilts, which consequently could not be granted registration numbers. An experimental or "X" registration number, primarily intended for established manufacturers to test a new type, was valid for only 30 days.

The CAA gradually began to become more supportive of amateur aircraft after the Second World War and also encouraged personal flying. A leading amateur aircraft designer and builder, George Bogardus of Oregon, lobbied the CAA during 1946 and 1947 for rule changes that would facilitate and encourage homebuilts. With the change in the regulatory environment since the 1930s, Bogardus was successful; the CAA established a permanent category for homebuilts in 1949 with the Experimental-Amateur Built (E-AB) license. The ruling permitted X registrations for six months' operation of airplanes that had not been certified by the CAA, and the certificate was renewable. The certification applied to aircraft that were not used for commercial purposes and to those that were at least 51 percent built by the owner-operator. In addition, they could not be built for resale. The CAA regarded such aircraft as falling within the experimental category, and that provided a major incentive for development of a kitplane or homebuilt segment. After being tested according to specified standards, a homebuilt aircraft could be awarded a type certificate by the CAA Aviation Safety Agent in the field.

More specific Civil Air Regulations (CARs) regarding homebuilts became effective January 15, 1951. Then a manual with procedures for issuance of airworthiness certificates was officially adopted on September 19, 1952. The legal basis for development of amateur-built or homebuilt aircraft was complete.[2] The change was also consistent with overall CAA efforts to promote private flying, and was especially important given the cost of recreational flying. The change spurred more widespread amateur experimentation in aircraft, including original designs.

Sport or recreational flying with aircraft of amateur construction remained the smallest segment of general aviation, but regulatory progress and the more supportive attitude of the CAA encouraged the field. A sufficient core of enthusiasts had developed that the Experimental Aircraft Association (EAA) was founded on January 26, 1953, in Milwaukee, Wisconsin, by Paul H. Poberezny, a combat veteran pilot and leading light aircraft experimenter. Under Poberezny's leadership, the EAA became the umbrella organization for the field and grew steadily, expanding internationally and eventually claiming more than 160,000 members worldwide. The term *experimental*, while perhaps misleading, was defined by the CAA generally to include aircraft of original design and construction for personal use rather than for business use or commercial sale. But experimental aircraft had entered the general aviation vocabulary.

The year 1953, as the founding year of the EAA, also could be regarded as the modern founding year of the homebuilt sector of general aviation. Always characterized by individual experimentation and entrepreneurship, the sector had seen numerous efforts toward development of a distinct homebuilt or kit airplane business during the period from the end of the Second World War to that year. Legal and market barriers to entry into the field were low, and required investment also was comparatively low. Further, those firms involved with factory-built general aviation aircraft continued to ignore the kit or homebuilt field.

Among the pioneers in small homebuilt aircraft was Ray Stits, who began experimenting in 1948. He founded Stits Aircraft in Riverside, California, and developed his Playboy and Flut-R-Bug models. He sold both plans and component kits. Stits also claimed the distinction of designing and building the "world's smallest airplane," his biplane SkyBaby with a 7'2" wingspan. The low-wing Playboy entered the market in 1953 but experienced weak demand, a situation faced by all single-seat sport models regardless of merit. Mooney had had a similar experience with its factory-built Mite. The larger mid-wing Flut-R-Bug recorded sales, less engine/propeller assemblies, of 27 kits by 1956.

Another pioneer was Curtis Pitts, a Georgia native who specialized in aerobatic airplanes. He designed his single-seat S-1 Special during 1943–44 and first flew it in September 1944. Pitts built a series of the design over the years, and they were highly regarded performers. Plans were available for home construction, but the Special did not become available in kit form until the 1980s.

A third notable pioneer was Sylvester "Steve" Wittman. A Wisconsin native, Wittman had been an early air racer and experimental aircraft builder. He was also instrumental in founding the EAA. His W-8 and W-10 Tailwind, light two-seat high-wing cabin monoplanes, were developed during 1952–53. Their extremely simple design and conventional configuration helped them earn a strong reputation, and several were successfully assembled from kits.

A fourth early entrant, the Ace Aircraft Company of West Bend, Wisconsin, was the successor to the pioneer firm of O. G. Corben. The company offered a modernized version of the original 1931 Baby Ace, a single-seat model with a high parasol wooden wing, adaptable for home construction. Company assets were acquired by Paul Poberezny in 1954, and his redesigned Baby Ace, using some Cub components, first flew on November 15, 1956. Over 350 kits were sold and completed. In 1961 Poberezny sold the Ace firm to Edwin T. Jacob, who continued marketing the design. In 1955 the EAA also marketed a kitplane of its own design. EAA efforts in the field continued into the 1970s.

Another popular early design for amateur construction was that of Robert Nesmith of Houston, Texas. The Nesmith Cougar, a conventional high-wing taildragger design, first flew in March 1957 and several thousand sets of plans were sold.

Throughout the 1950s other amateur builders constructed numerous small aircraft, some from original designs, but most as experimental models rather than as a basis for sale as plans or kits. The biplane configuration remained popular for single-seat sport models. A popular alternative, which has continued, was to copy designs of classic light aircraft of the 1920s, 1930s, and 1940s, or to develop smaller replicas of wartime fighters such as the P-51 Mustang.

Despite continuous activity and new entrepreneurial efforts, the homebuilt or kit segment progressed very slowly through the 1950s and 1960s. The major incentive for the segment was that private aircraft ownership and operations remained too expensive for most pilots, with kit aircraft or home construction offering major cost savings over new factory-built aircraft, even of such small models as the Super Cub. Also, many amateur builders took particular pride in constructing their own airplanes. Power by modified Volkswagen air-cooled engines was popular in homebuilt aircraft.

Many obstacles and disincentives remained. Home constructors could encounter delays and technical difficulties. The completion rate from kits was low, and the completion rate from plans even lower. Aviation periodicals frequently ran advertisements offering partially completed kit aircraft for sale by those who had abandoned the effort. In addition to construction problems, the economics of the field remained somewhat unfavorable in that good used factory-built aircraft still could be cheaper than home construction when all expenses were factored in. That alternative proved a major deterrent to homebuilt market growth. In addition, there was a general lack of an aftermarket for homebuilts, whatever their quality. And despite the apparent appeal of a single-seat sportplane, a significant commercial market still had not developed.

Technical factors and safety issues presented further problems to growth. The certification process for homebuilts remained a major hurdle. Homebuilts, being small and light, were very sensitive in the weight-and-balance area, with little margin for error. Further the accident rate was quite high during the initial test period; afterward, the safety record improved markedly. Many accidents were attributed to construction shortcuts or to unapproved modifications, but there was a troubling incidence of structural failure. These factors combined to limit the development and growth of the homebuilt field until the 1980s.

The economic impact of the homebuilt or kit construction segment during the 1950s and 1960s was difficult to measure. No organization or agency compiled or maintained complete statistics on the field; national sales figures for plans, kits, or for the value of completed aircraft were unobtainable. Yet there was little doubt that the importance of the segment, however obscure and however gradual, was increasing. Illustrating later growth, *Kitplanes* magazine reported that 25,401 kits from manufacturers were sold in the United States from the years 1963 through 1989.[3]

Industry Survey

With business aviation expanding and aircraft demand growing in a generally prosperous economy, established firms as well as newer competitors benefited. Production rose steadily and new models appeared.

Mooney, with a promising four-seat retractable-gear design in the Mark 20, faced the problem of financing its production. President Charles Yankey, an aviation veteran, died on December 29, 1953, at age 74, and Piper, seeking a more modern four-seat design to complete its product line, considered purchasing the rights to the Mark 20, but negotiations faltered. Al Mooney later expressed regret at not coming to an agreement with Piper when he had the opportunity.[4] Al W. and Art B. Mooney were then forced to sell all stock to outside investors in order to save the design. Under new ownership, Hal F. Rachal became president on July 1, 1954, and the Mooney brothers joined Lockheed as engineers in 1955.

The restructured firm restored the Mite to production for a time, and the Mark 20 was certified in August 1955. The Mark 20 gained popularity and was joined by the Master, a fixed-gear version, and then by the advanced Mark 22 Mustang, with retractable gear and pressurization. The Mark 22 was a market failure however; only 22 were sold before production was suspended. But Mooney steadily built a niche in the low-wing, four-place market, with the simpler, lower-priced Mark 21 joining the product line in 1961. Mooney enjoyed a record production year in 1965, and in 1966 began distributing the Mitsubishi MU-2, a new high-winged twin-engined utility and executive transport which had first flown on September 14, 1963. Mitsubishi had established a production subsidiary in San Angelo, Texas, not far from Kerrville, for the U.S. market. The MU-2 attracted steady orders.

Aero Design produced 150 of the initial Model 520 by 1954 before switching over to the improved Models 560 and 560A. The factory suffered a disastrous fire in August 1957, but with community support resumed production in four months.[5] More advanced developments followed with regularity, including the 680 Super and the pressurized Model 720 Alti-Cruiser of 1958, although only 13 Alti-Cruisers were built. With higher performance and increased size, the advanced models grew further away from the original concept, and Aero Design accordingly developed the smaller Aero Commander 500 and 500A models, named Shrike Commander, for the "low end" of the twin-engined business segment. A liaison model, the YL-26A, was supplied to the Army, while the Air Force acquired 15 L-26Bs as VIP transports. President Eisenhower's publicized use of an Air Force Aero Commander, alleviating lingering safety concerns, was a further boost to business flying.

Aero Design was sold to Rockwell-Standard Corporation of Pittsburgh, principally in auto parts and other machinery, in June 1958, as it decided on aircraft manufacturing as part of its diversification strategy.[6] The subsidiary name was changed to Aero Commander, Inc., in October 1960, as sales success of the twin-engined business segment continued. Current models were refined and new developments proceeded. The lengthened Grand Commander 680F/L, which first flew on December 29, 1962, marked a major advance into the luxury executive market. A further development was the Turbo Commander, powered by two Garrett AiResearch TPE 331 turboprops, which first flew on December 31, 1964.

A strong trend of reviving older light aircraft designs for further development and production continued. Such revivals often were under new corporate auspices where the original firms had entered bankruptcy or other-

Aero Commander 500 production line, Bethany, Oklahoma, 1950s (National Air and Space Museum, Smithsonian Institution).

wise exited the field. Rights to older designs also were sold to new or existing producers. CallAir, for example, produced the Super Cadet, developed from the prewar Interstate S-1A Cadet, while continuing limited production of its A-2 and A-3. CallAir began agricultural aircraft development in 1953, one of the earliest firms to offer a specialized design for this growing segment. The more powerful Model A-4 first flew on December 14, 1954. The Models A-5 and A-6 were agricultural adaptations of the A-4 and achieved some success from 1957 in that role. Some examples of the A-2 were also converted for crop spraying. Agricultural aircraft to that point had been conversions of such older types as the 1930s Stearman trainer.

On January 1, 1959, the company was incorporated as CallAir, Inc., with capital of $1 million. The Call family then sold the corporation to John Mangum, a former distributor, on November 11, 1959. Unfortunately, the new arrangement did not endure as business, always low-volume, declined further and dragged the firm into receivership. Two new investors purchased the assets for only $25,000, which they in turn sold to the Intermountain Manufacturing Company (IMCO) at a public sale in February 1962. IMCO then resumed production. IMCO continued to develop the agricultural aircraft series, leading to the CallAir A-9, which enjoyed considerable sales success

5—General Aviation Matures, 1954–1967

during 1963–1965.[7] CallAir rights and assets were acquired from IMCO by Rockwell-Standard in December 1966. To amalgamate its growing general aviation activities, Rockwell-Standard closed the Wyoming plant in September 1967 and transferred remaining production to a new factory in Albany, Georgia.

Northern Aircraft, Inc., of Alexandria, Minnesota, which had purchased design rights for the Model 14–19 Cruisemaster from Bellanca in 1955, entered production with the 14–19–2 in 1957. Northern then merged with American Aviation Corporation of Michigan. The firm changed its name to Downer Aircraft Industries, on January 1, 1959, under Chairman Jay K. Downer, and continued to develop and market the basic Cruisemaster design. The Cruisemaster countered the prevalent all-metal construction of its main competitors, still using wood extensively in its structure. Production was halted on December 1, 1960, but later resumed with the modernized Downer Bellanca Model 260A with tricycle gear and fiberglass structure. Downer reorganized in 1964 as International Aircraft Manufacturing, Inc., known as Inter-Air, and Bellanca design rights were sold to the successor. Inter-Air continued to produce at the same Minnesota location a further refinement of the Model 14–19 as the Miller-Bellanca 260A, Miller being the distributor. Another reorganization in 1966 resulted in Inter-Air becoming the Bellanca Sales Manufacturing subsidiary of Miller Flying Service. Through the changes, sales volume remained low.

In 1956, after the sale of the Model 14–19 rights, Giuseppe M. Bellanca and his son August T. Bellanca formed a Bellanca Aircraft Engineering, Inc, at its old Delaware location. The firm held rights to all designs other than the Model 14–19, and pursued new developments. Giuseppe Bellanca died on December 26, 1960, at age 74, but August Bellanca continued advanced business aircraft development.

Champion Aircraft Corporation, a subsidiary of Flyers Service, Inc., a fixed-base operator, was established in June 1954 in Osceola, Wisconsin. Having acquired rights from Aeronca for the Champion, the company resumed production of the Champion 7 in February 1955, Improved as the Traveller, it was produced in some numbers and was joined by the tricycle-geared Tri-Traveller. Both were produced until 1964, when production switched over to the further modernized Citabria (airbatic spelled backwards). In 1961 Champion had developed a small, two-seat twin-engined model, the Lancer 402, the lowest priced twin on the market, but it was not produced in quantity.

Rights for the Ercoupe, which had ended production in 1950, were sold to Fornaire Aircraft Company of Fort Collins, Colorado, in 1955. Fornaire was an affiliate of Forney Manufacturing Company, a farm machinery maker dating from 1932. Fornaire first tested its improved F-1 Aircoupe on February 18, 1956, and later offered three basic models of the basic design, but volume sales failed to develop. Fornaire rights then were sold to the City of Carlsbad, New Mexico, in August 1960, which leased the rights to the Air Products Company. The first new Aircoupe flew on December 16, 1960, but the venture ended in 1962; Fornaire and Air Products combined sold only some 30 Aircoupes. The City of Carlsbad then sold rights to Alon, Inc., of Kansas, organized on December 31, 1963. Alon was a venture of former Beech engineers John F. Allen, Jr., and Lee O. Higdon, hence the company name, and planned to produce a successor Air Coupe. While considerably modernized, the Air Coupe still could not compete with the new Cessna 150 in the small two-seat segment. The four-seat A-4 development first flew on February 25, 1966, but was not produced.

Culver rights and assets were sold to Superior Aircraft Company, which had been formed in mid–1956 as a division of the Priestley Hunt Aircraft Corporation in Culver City, California, to continue the line. The Culver Model V, dormant for ten years, was developed as the Superior Satellite. Then first Satellite flew on December 20, 1957, but only some 40 were produced.

A new Silvaire Aircraft Company of Fort Collins, Colorado, was formed in January 1955 by Otis T. Massey, a veteran pilot and former Luscombe distributor, with the purchase of Silvaire rights from Temco. His company undertook production of the definitive Model 8F, with a starting price of $4,950, which sold in small numbers from 1956 to 1960. With declining sales the Silvaire company exited in 1962. Don Luscombe, out of the industry for many years, died January 11, 1965, aged 69.

Clayton Brukner sold Waco, inactive in aircraft production since the Second World War, to Allied Aero Industries in 1963. The Troy, Ohio, plant was closed soon after, and the Waco nameplate disappeared. A new Navion Aircraft Company was formed in Galveston, Texas, to produce the modernized five-seat Rangemaster version of the original Navion. The Rangemaster first flew on June 10, 1960, and entered small-scale production. In mid–1965 this venture was succeeded by a new Navion Aircraft Corporation of Seguin, Texas, organized by the American Navion Society, an association of Navion owners. The company produced a more powerful Rangemaster but also encountered market difficulties.

From the mid–1950s the Big Three, Beech, Cessna, and Piper, steadily introduced new, higher-performance designs, spurred by overall market expansion and their own financial strength. Each made significant aeronautical advances, and Cessna and Beech also developed strong military aircraft and subcontracting businesses. The general aviation sector, particularly the Big Three, developed product line proliferation during the period, even instituting annual model changes in the manner of the auto industry. By 1967 Cessna, for example, was producing no fewer than 28 commercial models in addition to military types.[8] Many were of the same basic design but differed

5—General Aviation Matures, 1954–1967

Piper Apache production line at the new assembly building, Lock Haven, Pennsylvania, 1956 (National Air and Space Museum, Smithsonian Institution).

in engine power, appointments, or equipment. The civil aircraft inventory exceeded 100,000 for the first time in 1966, and continued growth prospects and attempts to meet all customer requirements and serve all segments of the market encouraged such developments.

Piper continued production of the Tri-Pacer and Super Cub throughout the 1950s, and the success of the Tri-Pacer led the company to strong profits. Tri-Pacer production totaled 7,668, making it one of the most popular of all light aircraft. Piper remained a distant third behind Beech and Cessna in size, however. Piper produced the PA-22 Colt, similar to the Tri-Pacer, from 1960, and followed its successful Apache with the similar but slightly larger PA-23-250 Aztec in 1959, and with the refined PA-23-235 Aztec in September 1962. The Apache, along with the later Comanche and Cherokee, marked the beginning of the Piper tradition of Indian names for its aircraft, although this led to some confusion with the U.S. Army, which followed the same practice in helicopter names. In 1960 Piper gained a military order for the first time in several years, with 20 Aztecs supplied to the U.S. Navy as the U-11A.

In considering an eventual successor to the Tri-Pacer, Piper decided on a low-wing model. It was the firm's lack of extensive research and development resources that had led to the earlier consideration of the Mooney M-20, but

Piper decided to develop an original design in 1955. Also at that time Piper began to look for an expansion site and favored Florida for its labor supply, weather, and union-free environment, a particular requirement of the elder Piper. The Piper Engineering Center was opened at Vero Beach, Florida in 1957, and production followed. The PA-24 Comanche, with low-wing and retractable gear, first flew on May 24, 1956. Fred E. Weick, designer of the Ercoupe and a pioneer of agricultural aircraft, joined Piper in 1957 and led Piper into that field. He designed the specialized agricultural aircraft, the PA-25 Pawnee, which entered production in 1959 and became a strong competitor in that growth segment.

The first aircraft completely developed at Vero Beach was the PA-28 Cherokee, designed by Fred Weick, Pug Piper, John Thorp, and Karl Bergey. Similar to the Comanche but with fixed gear, it featured the characteristic "Hershey Bar" wing and first flew on January 14, 1960. Intended to compete with the Cessna 172, among others, it succeeded both the Tri-Pacer, which ended production in 1961, and the smaller Colt, produced until 1964. Deliveries began in April 1961, at an initial price of $10,000. It became a strong seller, with some 5,000 produced by 1965.[9]

The PA-30 Twin Comanche followed in 1961, eventually replacing the Apache. By 1964 Piper production was entirely low-wing except for the veteran Super Cub. Production capacity expanded both in Pennsylvania and Florida, and employment reached a record 4,000 during 1966.

Tony Piper decided to step down from the post of chief executive in June 1960, feeling that his conservatism had held back the company.[10] Bill Piper, Jr., regarded as a more people-oriented manager, succeeded him as executive vice president and chief executive, while the senior Piper remained as chairman of the board and president. Tony and Howard "Pug" Piper continued as vice presidents, and Walter Jamouneau as chief engineer. Even as the firm enjoyed growth and prosperity, Bill Piper, Jr., was determined to broaden the product line to meet the challenges of Beech and Cessna.[11] Among new models appearing was the six-seat Cherokee Six, with lengthened fuselage, intended to compete with the Cessna 206. Piper also entered the growing executive market with the pressurized twin-engined PA-31 Navajo. Its largest aircraft to date, with a capacity of six to eight passengers, the Navajo first flew on September 30, 1964.

Cessna continued to broaden and improve its product line during the 1950s. Clyde Cessna, inactive in the industry since 1936, died on November 11, 1954, at age 75. His former associate and fellow aviation entrepreneur Victor H. Roos died in 1956. In 1957 Cessna established separate Commercial Aircraft and Military Aircraft Divisions, reflecting its major activities. Cessna had lagged Beech and Piper by several years in offering tricycle geared single-engined models, but introduced the feature in 1956 when the Model

5—General Aviation Matures, 1954–1967

172 replaced the tailwheel Model 170. The Model 172 was joined by the deluxe Skyhawk version, and a further refinement was the Model 175 Skylark. The tailwheel Model 180 continued, but was joined by the Model 182 with tricycle gear, and then by the deluxe Skylane. The more powerful Model 185 Skywagon utility version, still with taildragger gear, was ordered by the Air Force as the U-17A for delivery to allied nations. The Cessna 172/175 and 180/182 series eventually became the best-selling general aviation aircraft in history, with total production exceeding even that of the J-2/3 Cub.

Cessna's largest business aircraft, the Model 620, configured as a small airliner with a capacity of up to eighteen passengers and powered by four piston engines, first flew on August 11, 1956. The Model 620 did not enter production, however, as surplus twin-engined local service airliners available at lower prices effectively killed market prospects. Coincidentally, North American Aviation in 1953 had considered entering the civil market with a similar small four-engined executive model but did not proceed. In January 1957 Cessna introduced the Model 210 Centurion, a high-wing model with retractable landing gear. Then in September 1957 Cessna reentered the two-seat trainer market with the Model 150, which succeeded the old Models 120/140 and sold in large numbers. Cessna reached the milestone of 50,000 aircraft produced on February 25, 1963.

In the military field, the L-19 (later O-1) was reinstated in production for both the Army and Marine Corps in 1961 and was also produced under license in Japan. Production in the United States totaled 3,381 for all versions by 1963. From the successful T-37 trainer, which entered service in 1957, Cessna developed the YAT-37D armed light attack or counterinsurgency (COIN) version, with more powerful engines, which first flew on October 22, 1963. It later entered production as the A-37. The Air Force acquired 80 L-27A liaison versions of the Model 310. Later redesignated U-3A, total military procurement of the Model 310 reached 196. The two-seat Model 172E became the T-41A primary trainer, initially delivered to the Air Force in 1964 and later reordered in quantity by both the Air Force and Army (as the T-41B) and for export.

In addition to strong general aviation and military production, Cessna expanded internationally by purchasing a 40 percent share in the French firm Avions Max Holste on February 16, 1960. The firms was renamed Reims Aviation on January 30, 1962. The Model 150 and Model 172 were produced under license by Reims. Cessna also held a major position in the metal propeller market with McCauley, which it acquired on August 1, 1960.[12]

Cessna continued to expand its market coverage in the 1960s, as Dwane Wallace determined that the company would offer an airplane to meet every need in general aviation. Model 180 developments included the Model 205A and Model 206 Super Skywagon utility models of 1962, with fixed tricycle gear, and the Super Skylane, extended to carry six passengers. A further development of the Model 310 was the Model 320 Skyknight of 1961, with turbocharged engines.

The innovative Model 336 Skymaster, with push-pull twin engines and a high-wing twin-boom configuration, first flew on February 29, 1961. Initial sales were sluggish, however, and it was succeeded in 1965 by the considerably redesigned Model 337, with retractable gear. While conceptually sound, avoiding the asymmetrical problems of one-engine operation by conventional twins, the Model 337 was relatively noisy and expensive, and sales never reached the levels anticipated.

Cessna developed the Model 188 AgWagon in 1965, a specialized agricultural aircraft which competed with those of Piper, Grumman, and CallAir. Rounding out its product line was the completely new 400 series of larger business twins. The first entry, the Model 411, with six to eight seats, first flew on July 18, 1962, and entered service in 1965. The Models 401, 402, 411-A, and 421 were further developments of the basic design. In 1964, after 28 years as president, Dwane Wallace moved up to chairman of the board while remaining chief executive. Cessna overtook Piper in total unit production on June 1, 1967, 73,900 to 73,250.[13] Piper had built a strong lead earlier with the Cub series, while Cessna did not attain high volume until 1948. Cessna employment exceeded 12,000 for 1967.

Beech, while maintaining a commanding position in the high end of the general aviation market, still sought to broaden its market coverage. But one disappointment in the military sector was the Jet Mentor primary trainer that Beech had developed somewhat secretly with its own funds. Based on the T-34 airframe but converted for power by a small jet engine, the Jet Mentor first flew on December 18, 1955.[14] Beech hoped to gain interest from the Air Force, but an order never materialized. With continuing growth of general aviation, Beech became the object of takeover rumors during 1956 involving the defense contractor General Dynamics, which had acquired Convair in 1953. Both companies denied the rumors, and in fact no merger occurred.

Beech continued production of the successful Bonanza, Twin Bonanza, and veteran E18, and introduced the Model 95 Travel Air (originally Badger), essentially a scaled-down Twin Bonanza with a Bonanza cabin, which first flew on August 6, 1956. It was joined by the Baron, a more powerful version, which first flew on February 29, 1960. Beech also produced the U-8F Seminole for the Army, similar to the Twin Bonanza but with a more capacious fuselage. The civil version of the U-8F, the Model 80 Queen Air, followed on August 28, 1958. The Queen Air was ordered by the Army as the L-23F, retaining the basic designation of the older Twin Bonanza.

The Queen Air led to a Beech bid for permanent leadership in larger twin-engined business aircraft when the company developed the airframe

5—General Aviation Matures, 1954–1967

Ceremony for the completion of the 30,000th Beech aircraft, circa 1969. From left, Frank Hedrick, Olive Ann Beech, and John H. Batten, president, Twin Disc, Inc. (National Air and Space Museum, Smithsonian Institution).

into the lengthened, pressurized Model 90 King Air, powered by PT6A turboprop engines. It first flew on January 20, 1964. Although many had expressed concern about the high cost of turbine power, the King Air gained a market, and further developments enabled the series to dominate the larger executive aircraft segment. Production of the Twin Bonanza was phased out during 1964, but in that same year the ultimate "Twin Beech" development, the H18 Super-Liner, was introduced in both tailwheel and tricycle-gear versions.

For the low end of the market, Beech offered the small four-seat Musketeer, which first flew on October 23, 1961. The Musketeer III, introduced in 1965, succeeded the initial models. The light Travel Air and Baron twins continued, and an Army trainer version of the Baron was the T-42A. The Model 99 executive transport, a long-fuselage Queen Air derivative with twin turbine power, first flew in July 1966 and would lead to a long series of developments. Commercial sales for the company tripled in eight years, from $32 million in 1958 to $100 million in 1966.[15]

Olive Ann Beech began sharing more management duties with her nephew Frank Hedrick, who was promoted to executive vice president in 1960. Mrs. Beech held the office of president and retained decision authority, while Hedrick assumed a more public role. Veteran executive John P. Gaty retired for health reasons in 1960, then died in 1963. Beech operated branch plants in Liberal and Salina, Kansas, and Boulder, Colorado, to handle both its commercial and military subcontracting businesses. As defense business gained in importance, Beech began development of supersonic target drones in 1955.

Grumman, out of civil aviation for almost a decade, decided to reenter in the mid–1950s, feeling an urgent need to diversify away from its heavy dependency on the U.S. Navy as well as sensing growth opportunities. Its successful entry into the agricultural market was the G-164 Ag-Cat, a biplane design of dated appearance but incorporating the latest agricultural aircraft technology. First flying on May 27, 1957, it was certificated two years later. Given its high overhead as a military contractor, however, Grumman licensed production to Schweizer Aircraft, to that point exclusively a sailplane producer.[16] Schweizer produced 400 of the initial version, and further developments followed.

The Colonial C-1 Skimmer amphibian, delayed for several years, finally entered production in 1955, enjoying an effective monopoly in its narrow segment. Colonial suffered bankruptcy in 1959, however, and rights were sold to a new Lake Aircraft Corporation in October 1959, organized by David Thurston's partner Herbert P. Lindblad. Lake produced a developed version, but shaky finances resulted in its takeover by Consolidated Aeronautics of Indiana in 1962. Production remained in Maine. David B. Thurston remained active as a designer and consulting engineer.

Helio acquired its Kansas contractor in July 1956 and produced the more powerful Super Courier from 1958, which was ordered as the U-10A for the Air Force and Army. The U-10A served successfully in Vietnam, where its STOL capabilities were especially valuable. The Helio U-5A, a small twin-engined development, was also built in small numbers. Military orders kept the company alive as it struggled to develop civil demand for its specialized models. The Courier II, a lighter higher-performance development of the Courier I, entered service in 1965. The most advanced development, appearing in 1964, was the larger Helio Stallion, which was turboprop powered and could carry up to ten passengers.

Taylorcraft developed a new Zephyr 400, with a molded fiberglass fuselage and wing coverings, in 1955, but despite its advantages it was not successful in the market. Fiberglass floatplanes and agricultural models were also developed. The team of B. J. Mauro as president, C. G. Taylor as vice president, and Jack Gilberti as chief engineer continued to manage the firm, but

5—General Aviation Matures, 1954–1967

declining business forced a production shutdown in 1959, followed by bankruptcy. Remaining Taylorcraft assets were sold in 1963. Gilbert Taylor moved to California as chief engineer for the small Saturn Aircraft venture, which was developing the former Monocoupe Meteor high-speed business twin as the Saturn Meteor II. The project was abandoned in 1961, however.

Meyers Aircraft Company, still in Tecumseh, Michigan, attempted to compete in the growing field. It developed the more advanced four-seat low-wing Model 200 to succeed the MAC 145. The Model 200 first flew on September 8, 1953, and Meyers hoped that it could compete with the Beech Bonanza. It did not enter production until 1959, and fewer than 40 were sold. Meyers models were respected for their quality and durability, but still could not find success in the market. Meyers also resumed production of the earlier MAC 145T tricycle-geared model in 1961. After the demise of Taylorcraft, Jack Gilberti launched a new venture, Volaircraft, Inc., in Aliquippa, Pennsylvania, to build a new lightweight all-metal design, the Model 10. The developed four-seat Volaire Model 1050 entered production in 1963 and gained market share.

Volaircraft, simultaneously with Meyers, became another acquisition of Rockwell-Standard, through Aero Commander, on July 12, 1965. Rockwell-Standard continued its aggressive strategy of heavy involvement in the general aviation field. Volaircraft and Meyers were purchased for approximately $1 million cash each. The Volaire Model 1050 filled the gap at the lower end of the Aero Commander range. Under the Rockwell-Standard Aero Commander Division, the Meyers Models 200/200A evolved into the improved Model 200B, renamed the Aero Commander 200. The Volaire 1050 became the Aero Commander 100, and in 1968 the Darter Commander.

Aero Commander headquarters remained in Pittsburgh, but organizational changes ensued with Rockwell-Standard's entry into the light single-engined market. Operating divisions remained at Bethany, Tecumseh, and Aliquippa, but all production eventually consolidated at Bethany and at the new Albany, Georgia, facility.[17] By the end of 1966 the Rockwell-Standard portfolio included Aero Commander, Meyers, CallAir, and Volaircraft, plus the small but growing Snow Aeronautical of Olney, Texas. Leland Snow, a veteran agricultural pilot, began development of original aircraft in 1955 and incorporated in 1961. His first design, the S-2B, gained certification in 1958. With sales of more than 200 agricultural aircraft by 1964, Snow had attained a strong position in the segment by the time of the merger. Earlier, Rockwell-Standard had made unsuccessful merger overtures to Beech, Cessna, Mooney, and Piper.[18]

Fletcher Aviation Corporation, in addition to production of aircraft components and jettisonable fuel tanks, and subcontracting on military missiles, continued to develop small aircraft. After the FD-25 Defender, the firm developed the FU-24 Utility in July 1954, which was produced under license in New Zealand from 1957 as an agricultural aircraft. The firm reorganized in 1960 as the Flair (from Fletcher Aircraft) Aviation Corporation, still managed by Wendell Fletcher. Then Flair was acquired by American Jet Industries, founded in 1951 for aircraft modification and repair, and renamed the Sargent-Fletcher Company in 1964, with the participation of E. J. Sargent. The company continued in other lines, but the FU-24 was its final aircraft development, and all rights were sold to New Zealand in 1964.

One smaller venture that was to endure was that of Ohio native Belford D. Maule. An early experimenter who had built his first airplane in 1931, and later worked for Lycoming, Maule began an aircraft parts business in Jackson, Michigan, in 1940. As the B. D. Maule Company, he designed a small four-seat high-wing model named the Bee Dee M-4. Based somewhat on the old Piper Cub, it first flew in 1957. The developed M-4 prototype first flew on September 8, 1960, and formation of the Maule Aircraft Corporation followed in 1961. The M-4 Rocket, a rugged utility model with STOL characteristics, went into production in 1962. An improved model with all-metal wings followed in 1963, and sales gradually grew.

A minor venture, although interesting, was a light twin-engined, retractable-gear model designed by John Thorp in 1958, which he designated T-17. The businessman George Wing adapted the design as the Wing Derringer, and formed Wing Aircraft Company in Torrance, California, to build the aircraft. Although with only two seats, the Derringer was intended as a business aircraft. It stressed high performance and possessed innovative construction features. The prototype flew on May 1, 1962, but numerous delays and disputes killed the program. George Wing made another attempt in 1978, but experienced financial problems and production ended with only a dozen completed.

Ted Smith departed Aero Commander in 1963 and founded Ted Smith Aircraft Company, Inc., in California, to develop a new design. His Aerostar Model 600 twin-engined executive transport first flew in November 1966. With an innovative mid-wing configuration, unusual in general aviation aircraft, the Aerostar 600 led to a long series of developments. The Aerostar matched the performance of other modern twin-engined business models, but was designed with simpler features and fewer parts for ease of construction and maintenance. Smith added the Model 601 with turbocharged engines, but would encounter persistent problems in establishing the Aerostar in production.

The engineer Edward J. Swearingen, who earlier had worked for Lear, established Swearingen Aircraft in San Antonio, Texas, in 1959 to develop and market modifications of existing light twin aircraft for business and commuter purposes. By 1964 Swearingen had developed the piston-engined

SA-26 Merlin I, which used components from the Beech Twin Bonanza and Queen Air but was essentially a new design. Then the turbine-powered SA-26T Merlin II, first flying on April 13, 1965, marked the completion of the transition of Swearingen from modification to manufacturing. With rising business, Swearingen undertook major factory expansion for production of both models, which led to a long series of developments.

Lockheed again explored the general aviation sector with a single-engined light utility aircraft for use in developing and remote areas of the world. Designed by the Mooney brothers, the LASA-60 (LASA for Lockheed Azcarate S. A.) was built at the Lockheed-Georgia factory and first flew on September 15, 1959. Lockheed did not plan to produce the LASA-60 domestically, but to license production to the Lockheed-Azcarate affiliate formed in Mexico and to other Lockheed affiliates in Italy and Argentina. The program was less than a resounding success, however, as only 44 Mexican models were built, 18 for the Mexican Air Force, and the Lockheed-Kaiser venture in Argentina was abandoned. Macchi of Italy retained exclusive rights and developed the design, but produced only 100, ending in 1965.

Fairchild, with declining military production, entered the utility aircraft segment with licensed production of the Swiss Pilatus Porter, a STOL design powered by a small turboprop engine. Initially named the Heli-Porter, it was renamed Turbo Porter. Some 88 were produced from 1966 at the Hiller Aircraft Division in Germantown, Pennsylvania, after Fairchild acquired Hiller.

Among developmental firms, M. B. Taylor developed the Aerocar Model II Aero-Plane, a non-roadable version of the Aerocar. Taylor also refined the basic Aerocar, which won CAA certification in 1956. A market still did not develop, however, and only six were sold. Willard R. Custer developed aircraft using his channel wing concept, in which pusher propellers would pull air over the channeled wing sections. Custer claimed that much greater lift would be developed than with a conventional airfoil, giving the aircraft capabilities approaching those of helicopters, including near-hovering capability. After years of experiments, Custer first tested his CCW-5 business aircraft prototype, built by Baumann in California and modified from the Brigadier, on July 13, 1953. The Custer Channel Wing Corporation then was formed in Hagerstown, Maryland, in 1956 to produce the CCW-5 and to pursue further developments. Custer rented hangar space earlier owned by Kreider-Reisner and Fairchild.

As was all too common with new aircraft ventures, production encountered numerous delays and financing problems. Plans were announced variously for production at sites in Texas and Canada, but never materialized. Further, widespread skepticism remained that the channel wing would attain the capabilities claimed for it. What was announced as the first production CCW-5 finally flew on June 19, 1964, at Hagerstown, but a long dispute with

Custer Channel Wing prototype, 1964. W. R. Custer at right, with his wife and other family members (National Air and Space Museum, Smithsonian Institution).

the Securities and Exchange Commission over public stock sales and failure to gain FAA certification effectively killed prospects.

Light Helicopter Development

Development of general aviation helicopters progressed steadily during the 1954–67 period. While distinctly subordinate to the military market, the civil helicopter market gradually expanded after the Korean War, with applications in agricultural spraying, law enforcement, geological and forestry survey, medical transportation, and firefighting. But the helicopter as an executive transport had yet to become established.

A new civil design came from R. E. "Rudy" Enstrom, of Menominee, Wisconsin, a mining engineer who aspired to enter the helicopter field. In partnership with Jack Christensen, a local businessman, they formed R. J. Enstrom Corporation in 1959 with Christensen as president. Enstrom first flew his Model F-28 ultralight two-seat design, essentially a homebuilt, on December 12, 1960. After attracting local investors, the company's three-seat development first flew on May 26, 1962, attained certification in 1965, and entered production in 1966. The Brantly B-2, also in development for years, finally entered production in 1959 and more than 200 were produced. It was succeeded by the developed Model B-2A, and a larger five-seat Model B-305 appeared in 1965.[19] From the late 1950s Cessna produced small numbers of the original Siebel helicopter for the Army as well as a few of the CH-1 civil version, but poor sales led to the discontinuation of the line in 1962.

The most successful general aviation helicopter continued to be the Bell Model 47, which underwent continuous improvement. The Model 47H, an updated enclosed-cabin version, appeared in 1954 but did not win a wide market. Then the Model 47J-2A Ranger, a deluxe four-seat development with a streamlined monocoque fuselage, was introduced in 1956 and gained popularity both in civil and military roles. Bell Aerospace, including its Bell Helicopter operating unit, became a wholly owned subsidiary of Textron, Inc., on July 5, 1960.

A development with significant implications for small civil helicopters was the important Army competition in the early 1960s for a light observation helicopter (LOH), to replace the Bell H-13 variants, the Hiller H-23, and the Cessna L-19/O-1. The potential market was for several thousand helicopters. Howard Hughes, among his numerous aviation interests, had entered the light helicopter field by forming Hughes Helicopters as a division of his Hughes Tool Company. The first Hughes-designed helicopter was the two-seat Model

Two Bell Model 47 helicopters involved in logging operations in Canada during the 1950s (Bell Helicopter Textron)

209 of 1955, for both military and civil training roles. Hughes, Bell, and Hiller were finalists for the LOH order, won by the developed Hughes Model 500 as the OH-6A. Hughes hoped to capture a worldwide civil market as well. The Model 269, redesignated Model 200, and the larger Model 500 were produced for that market. Three hundred Model 200s were sold by 1964.

Stanley Hiller negotiated a merger of his company, again renamed Hiller Aircraft Corporation, into Electric Autolite Corporation of Ohio, a longtime business aircraft user, in the summer of 1960. But the autonomous Hiller Helicopters subsidiary continued to lose money. Then Fairchild, in a diversification move sparked by the prospect of the lucrative Army LOH contract, acquired Hiller from the ELTRA Corporation, renamed from Electric Autolite, in May 1964. The company became Fairchild Hiller Corporation in September, with Stanley Hiller becoming an executive vice president of the corporation in addition to heading helicopter operations.[20] Helicopter production remained in California.

While its OH-5A entry into the competition was unsuccessful, the Hiller Aircraft Division carried forward with the turbine-powered FH-1100 civil development. The FH-1100 first flew on January 26, 1963, and entered production in 1966. Stanley Hiller eventually left Fairchild Hiller to return to California and other business interests.

Bell's Model 206A JetRanger light turbine-powered design, also unsuccessful in the LOH competition, first flew as a civil helicopter on January 10, 1966, and entered service in 1967. It led the market in its category and also spurred a general expansion in business use of helicopters.

A sad footnote to an era of rapid rotary-wing progress was the death of Harold Pitcairn on April 23, 1960, at age 62, by his own hand.

* * *

General aviation continued as a growth market through most of the 1950s and 1960s. By 1964, 40 percent of the general aviation fleet was more than 15 years old, extending largely from the short-lived production boom of 1946–47.[21] The requirement for replacement of aging aircraft supported continuing growth. As with military aircraft, piston-engined general aviation aircraft reached a broad performance plateau during this period, but continued to grow in cost and complexity. General aviation had become a key component of the broad aerospace industry, but still remained by far the smallest sector. By 1967, for example, McDonnell Douglas and Boeing were approaching $3 billion in annual sales each, while the largest general aviation firms, Cessna and Beech, posted sales of only $213 million and $174 million respectively.[22] Furthermore, both totals included major military components.

But expectations for continued growth and prosperity were the order of the day. Cessna had forecast annual production of 20,000 general aviation aircraft by 1970, the majority being piston-powered single-engined models.[23] Larger business and executive aircraft continued as a major growth segment, as did specialized agricultural aircraft. The general use of chemical sprays enhanced agricultural aviation growth to the point that there were some 5,000 agricultural aircraft in operation by 1966. Air taxi and commuter services using multi-seat aircraft also grew rapidly during the 1960s.

The United States enjoyed a strong export market in general aviation, as no effective international competition existed in the field. In 1966, for example, 15,700 general aviation aircraft were produce in the United States, of which 20 percent were exported. The British, with their wartime debt burden, had embargoed light aircraft imports from the end of the Second World War until 1960. When the embargo was lifted, American aircraft quickly became a factor.

The Business Jet

Corporate executive aircraft use became generally established during the 1950s, and design advancements facilitated strong growth of the sector. The rapid growth and increasing diversification of large corporations, with geographically dispersed facilities and significant international sales and production facilities, led to corollary growth in corporate air fleets. Business aircraft growth also was spurred by the view that scheduled airlines did not offer the timeliness, flexibility, and comprehensive route structures increasingly required by business, their services being effectively restricted to large metropolitan airports. Manufacturers found that business aircraft could be effectively marketed on their capabilities to visit several sites in one day, impossible on scheduled airlines, consequently enormously beneficial to busy executives and sales teams.

While larger corporate aircraft were widely used, before the 1960s most were conversions of smaller airliners such as the Douglas DC-3 and Convair 340, or of Second World War bombers such as the Douglas B-23, Lockheed Model 18, and Martin B-26. Colonel Robert R. McCormick, owner/publisher of the Chicago Tribune, famously employed a converted B-17 four-engined bomber as his personal transport for years. The inventor, industrialist, and aviation entrepreneur William P. Lear, long attracted to the executive market, formed a division of his Lear, Inc., to develop and market the Learstar, a modernized conversion of the Lockheed Model 18 Lodestar, as a fast and long-range executive transport. Deliveries began in 1955, and Learstars were operated by several major corporations.

With the advent of the large jet-powered airliner, small business jets became regarded as feasible. But in that emerging market the largest general aviation firms, Beech and Cessna, faced a potential threat from large military and airliner manufacturers whose capabilities might be used to great advantage in small business jets. Several military firms in fact designed specialized corporate jet transports to replace the mix of propeller-driven smaller business and converted military and commercial aircraft. Business jet development was to influence significantly the future structure of the general aviation industry.

The Grumman Gulfstream was an early and successful specialized corporate transport. A further manifestation of Grumman's diversification strategy, the G-159 Gulfstream first flew on August 14, 1958, and led to a long series of Grumman corporate aircraft designs. Almost of small airliner size, the Gulfstream was powered by two Rolls-Royce Dart turboprops. The Gulfstream represented a considerable risk for Grumman, with an initial price in the $1 million range, but gained popularity as well as a reputation as the Rolls-Royce of business aircraft. After initial production on Long Island, Grumman opened a new Savannah, Georgia, factory specifically for the Gulfstream on September 29, 1967.

The French were the first to produce a turbojet business or executive aircraft, the small Morane-Saulnier MS.760 Paris of 1954, itself developed from a prototype jet trainer. Beech acquired American rights to the MS.760 in 1955 but decided against marketing or license production.[24] Cessna tested a comparable business jet developed from its T-37 trainer but likewise did not proceed with production. The United States later captured world leadership in business jets, although other nations would gain and maintain significant market shares.

Major spurs to development of business jets were the Air Force UTX and UCX competitions beginning in 1956. The UTX and UCX involved small jet passenger aircraft for military training and utility transport missions, respectively, but which possessed obvious potential for business use. Development of economical and reliable small turbojet engines such as the Pratt & Whitney JT12 and the General Electric CJ610 also facilitated practical business jets. The Lockheed JetStar, the North American Sabreliner, and the McDonnell Model 119 were developed originally for the UTX/UCX competitions. Fairchild did not continue its M185 project after it lost the Air Force competition, however, and McDonnell's Model 220, the business counterpart of the Model 119, also did not proceed.

The Lockheed JetStar, to which the Mooney brothers had contributed, first flew on September 4, 1957, and won the UCX competition as the C-140. The smaller Sabreliner, which first flew on September 16, 1958, won the UTX competition as the T-39. The base of military orders supported development of both models as business jets, the first to attain production. Entering operation in 1962, the JetStar became the top business jet until the arrival of the turbojet Gulfstream II, but orders for the JetStar and Sabreliner business models were comparatively slow in building. Both were still regarded as too expensive for all but the largest corporations. Real growth came with the LearJet.

William P. Lear moved to Switzerland, where he held existing business interests, early in 1962 and established the Swiss American Aviation Corporation (SAAC) to develop what became the LearJet. Lear was confident in the future of the small business jet. Originally designated SAAC-23, his design used the wing and basic structure of the experimental Swiss AFA P-16 strike fighter then being tested. Lear felt at the time that he could better control costs in Switzerland, but numerous problems with suppliers led him to move the project, including production tooling, to the United States later that year. Lear also benefited in designing the LearJet from NACA/NASA-developed design technology, as he lacked resources for basic research.[25] He located his renamed Lear Jet Industries in Wichita, where he won economic incentives as well as access to a large pool of experienced labor. Cessna's T-37 program had created a reservoir of production skills in small jet aircraft, and Wichita issued the first industrial revenue bonds in its history to attract Lear. Lear Jet Industries was, incidentally, the first firm to be formed specifically for the business jet market.

William P. Lear, Jr., aviation entrepreneur and originator of the Learjet series (Learjet, Inc., now Bombardier Business Aircraft).

The LearJet Model 23, configured for six passengers and powered by twin rear-mounted GE CJ610 turbojets, first flew on October 7, 1963. Lear had staked his entire $10 million fortune on the venture but soon ran dangerously low on capital as he pushed to beat the rival Jet Commander to the market. The first customer

The prototype Learjet Model 23 taking off on its first flight, October 7, 1963 (Learjet, Inc., now Bombardier Business Aircraft).

delivery took place on October 13, 1964, and soon thereafter, on November 30, 1964, a successful stock offering provided required capital. At an initial price of $540,000, the LearJet gained instant popularity, with over 100 sold by the end of 1965. The improved and refined Model 24 replaced the Model 23 in production in March 1966 and was joined by the larger Model 25, first flown on August 12, 1966.[26] An around-the-world LearJet flight, completed on May 29, 1966, and taking only 65 hours, garnered much favorable publicity for the design.

In an expansionist period, Lear even briefly contemplated development of a 40-seat feederliner based on the LearJet configuration. Then in May 1966, Lear Jet acquired Brantly Helicopter Corporation, still trying to perfect and market a two-place, simple, affordable helicopter. Newby O. Brantly accompanied the move, but continued losses forced a later sale of the helicopter operation.

Lear, in common with many industry pioneers, was a better designer and engineer than corporate executive, and after initially strong LearJet sales, the firm experienced a sales decline as well as major difficulties with a haphazard distribution network. Over-diversification, operating losses, and increasing competition led to a financial crisis, requiring a rescue by merger. Cessna, planning to develop its own business jet, was uninterested. Beech, favored by several Lear executives as a logical candidate, declined due to longstanding differences between Bill Lear and Frank Hedrick.[27] Then in April 1967, Charles C. Gates, head of Gates Rubber Company in Denver and a veteran pilot, agreed to purchase Lear's 62 percent holding for $21 million. His Gates Aviation Corporation, a sales and service company, initially became a subsidiary of Lear Jet Industries, but the two eventually merged as the Gates Learjet Corporation. The future of the design seemed assured under new ownership.

Rockwell Aero Commander entered the executive jet market with the Jet Commander, chiefly designed by Ted Smith and directly competitive with the LearJet. Also powered by twin rear-mounted GE CJ610s, but with a mid-mounted wing, the Jet Commander actually preceded the LearJet in the air, making its first flight on January 27, 1963. Entering service in 1965, it also attracted initially strong orders.

A Douglas business jet, the PD-808, was designed by the El Segundo Division in cooperation with the Italian firm Piaggio. The first prototype flew on August 29, 1964. Piaggio was licensed to produce the PD-808 for both military and civil uses, but it eventually entered service only with the Italian Air Force. Douglas retained but did not exercise the U.S. manufacturing and marketing rights.

With the LearJet, Jet Commander, Sabreliner, and JetStar already on the market, Grumman followed its turboprop Gulfstream I with the Gulfstream II, an entirely new swept-wing design powered by Rolls-Royce Tay turbojets. Produced at Savannah, it first flew on October 2, 1966, and became an immediate success. The largest in the field, the Gulfstream II was regarded as the ultimate in business jets and led to further developments.

One aspect of corporate jet utilization with significant implications for the future was represented by Executive Jet Corporation of Columbus, Ohio, founded in 1964. The firm was initially founded to charter and manage a fleet of Learjets, but would grow over the next four decades to become a major factor in business jet leasing and fractional ownership.

* * *

Roughly concurrent with the development of executive jets was the development of so-called third-level, or feeder, airlines, which also carried significant implications for general aviation manufacturers. The term *third-level airline* began to be used in the early 1960s to distinguish that category from major trunk carriers and regional or local service carriers, and third-level service steadily expanded throughout the country and the world. This led to a requirement for modern small airliners reminiscent of the Lockheed Saturn and Beech "Twin Quad" designs in 1946 and 1947.

Rule changes by the Federal Aviation Agency (FAA), which had succeeded the CAA on December 31, 1958, facilitated development. Federal Air Regulation (FAR) Part 23, dealing with aircraft under 12,500 pounds gross weight, as less stringent than regulations for larger aircraft, making commuter operation more feasible. Moreover, single-pilot operation, virtually an economic necessity at that level, was restricted by FAR Part 298 to aircraft carrying no more than 19 passengers and weighing no more than 12,500 pounds. But those carrying 20 or more passengers were required to have radar and complete instrumentation, and consequently more regulation, covered by FAA Part 25.

Air taxi operators were exempted from full airline regulation and permitted to operate scheduled services as long as they stayed within the weight limits. This exemption was extended by the FAA indefinitely in 1965. One sidelight to these developments was that the previous distinction between larger general aviation aircraft and commercial aircraft became less distinct. General aviation aircraft had been classified as those with capacities of 19 seats or fewer and under 33,000 pounds gross weight, but such aircraft as the Gulfstream tended to push the definition.

Commuter airline growth was also aided by the trend of trunk airlines away from service to smaller cities, leaving their limited passenger markets to the smaller carriers. Adaptations of business jets were regarded as unfeasible given their cost and the economics of short-range operation, but general aviation firms readied specialized designs for the commuter market, generally with twin-turboprop configuration.

6

The Modern Era, 1967–1979

General aviation had made significant technological advances during the 1950s, but as the industry matured during the 1960s its products became rather similar in design and performance. Light aircraft aeronautical technology continued largely static during the 1970s, and the old dream of an affordable mass-market aircraft had long been abandoned. A particular problem in general aviation design was that requirements were not spelled out precisely by potential customers as was the case with military and commercial aircraft. Accordingly, manufacturers did not develop new designs from customer specifications but simply tried to forecast which would be most likely to sell. In marked contrast to relatively static piston-powered aircraft technology was the intensive development of larger turbine-powered executive models, particularly business jets. Business flying dominated general aviation, with 72 percent of the general aviation fleet devoted to business (see Table 6–1).[1]

Personal and recreational or sport flying remained limited by cost, but business users were more willing to pay for technological advances. One advance from the 1970s was that single-engined business aircraft were increasingly offered with turbocharged engines, enabling them to compete in speed and altitude performance with turbine-powered models. Cessna, Piper, Beech, and Mooney eventually offered single-engined turbocharged models. Another significant benefit was that the National Aeronautics and Space Administration (NASA, successor to NACA) began to devote more research to general aviation, specifically in such design innovations as canard wings, simulation and analytical techniques, laminar flow airfoils, and drag reduction; in such safety-related areas as stall/spin phenomena; and in composite materials and weight reduction.[2]

Even as overall flying safely improved, a conflict between business and commercial flying emerged and posed another threat to general aviation growth. Several widely publicized collisions between smaller business aircraft and airliners in the late 1960s led to allegations that private pilots were less skilled and less cautious than commercial pilots, and that increasing business aircraft traffic threatened commercial scheduled airline safety. Investigation generally concluded that the crashes were due as much to commercial pilot error as to private pilot error, and the controversy gradually eased. One conclusion, however, was that the overburdened and antiquated air traffic control (ATC) system needed major upgrading. Increasing use of business airports in major cities eased the strain on commercial airports, also alleviating safety concerns.

Table 6-1
Annual Production and Sales, General Aviation Aircraft

Year	Units	Factory Sales ($ millions)
1968	13,698	$425.7
1969	12,457	584.5
1970	7,262	337.0
1971	7,466	321.5
1972	9,744	557.6
1973	13,646	828.1
1974	14,166	909.4
1975	14,056	1,032.9
1976	15,451	1,225.5
1977	16,904	1,488.1
1978	17,811	1,781.2
1979	17,048	2,165.0
1980	11,877	2,486.2

SOURCE: GAMA, *General Aviation Statistical Databook* (1990–1991 edition), p. 4.

The Aerospace Industries Association (AIA, renamed in 1959), which had represented general aviation interests through its Utility Airplane Council since the 1950s, saw those interests spun off into an independent organization. The General Aviation Manufacturers Association (GAMA) was formed in January 1970 to advance the cause of general aviation and to enhance the environment for growth. The mature general aviation sector then was represented by NBAA, AOPA, EAA, and GAMA. General aviation aircraft sales exceeded $1 billion for the first time in 1975.[3] Time took its toll on light aircraft pioneers during this period, however, as Rae Rearwin died on November 16, 1969, at age 89, and Lloyd Stearman died on April 4, 1975, age 76. He had returned to Lockheed as an engineer in 1955, where he remained until retirement. Clayton Brukner of Waco died on December 26, 1977, at 81, and Sherman Fairchild on March 28, 1971, age 75. Alfred Verville died in 1970, age 79. He had worked for the Navy Bureau of Aeronautics until retirement, and remained active in aviation until the end of his life.

Industry Survey

Production boomed through most of the 1960s (see Tables 6-2 and 6-3), but suffered a sharp drop during the recession of 1970-1971. Wichita was especially affected, as area unemployment rose sharply. But shipments and dollar value of sales began to rise again in 1972 and increased throughout the remainder of the decade as general aviation growth continued. Prosperity was not spread evenly through the sector, however, as most smaller firms still struggled to compete against the Big Three of Beech, Cessna, and Piper. But Mooney maintained a niche in its segment, as did Rockwell Aero Commander with its line.

The period was also characterized by frequent company reorganizations and ownership changes, and long-term stability remained elusive. There was a trend toward acquisitions of general aviation manufacturers seeking diversification, with both aerospace and nonaerospace firms taking positions in the field.

Product development was especially active in major firms. The new North American Rockwell Corporation (NAR) was formed in November 1967 by merger with the military firm North American. NAR combined its then-extensive general aviation aircraft operations, all from acquisitions, into the Commercial Products Group, which also encompassed most activities of the predecessor Rockwell-Standard Corporation in Pittsburgh. Most general aviation production was controlled by the Aero Commander Division, with plants in Bethany, Oklahoma, Albany, Georgia, and Olney, Texas.

All aircraft in the Aero Commander line were given bird names. The Volaire 1050, first redesignated Aero Commander 100, was renamed the Darter Commander. From the Darter Commander was developed the Lark Commander, a refined, more luxurious version. But sales of the former Volaire line were below expectations. The Aero Commander 200, originally the Meyers Model 200D dating from 1953, also experienced poor sales, and production was ended and rights were sold.

North American Rockwell continued production of the established Aero Commander twin-engined line, including the Shrike Commander, Courser Commander, and Turbo II Commander, later renamed Hawk Commander. Antitrust considerations arising from the North American merger required the divestiture of either the Sabreliner or Jet Commander. Subsequently, all rights to the Jet Commander were sold to Israeli Aircraft Industries in 1968 after 149 had been built. In the extensive agricultural aircraft line, the original CallAir A-9 was renamed Sparrow Commander and was joined by the Quail Commander, with an uprated engine, and then by a further upgraded Snipe Commander. The new Thrush Commander, from the Snow acquisition and the largest agricultural model on the market, completed the line.

North American Rockwell further reorganized on September 30, 1969, with its Commercial Products Group succeeded by an Industrial Products Group. The new Group controlled all general aviation production, marketing, and other services within a new General Aviation Division. Departing from its practice of adapting existing designs, the division developed the new Aero Commander 112, announced in December 1969, which went into production in 1972. The General Aviation Division by that time offered the Lark Commander, the Aero Commander 112, Shrike Commander and Shrike Commander Esquire, the Turbo Commander 681B (again renamed), plus the agricultural line. The Sabreliner was also included in the new division, and NAR thus offered almost comprehensive coverage of the general aviation market. A new piston-engined Aero Commander 685 was developed from the Turbo II Commander. The Model 112, renamed Alpine Commander, was joined by the Model 111 fixed-gear variant and by the deluxe Gran Turismo Commander.

Despite strong development and marketing activity, NAR's general aviation production remained unstable. The company sold rights to the Thrush Commander and Quail Commander models in 1971 to a new Mexican operation in which it held 30 percent ownership. Mexican production was troubled, however, and the venture soon ended. Lark Commander production ended in 1972, and remaining general aviation manufacturing other than the Sabreliner was consolidated at the Bethany plant in 1974.

In 1971 Leland Snow formed a new Air Tractor, Inc., to continue independent development and production of large agricultural aircraft. The company remained in Olney, Texas.

Renamed Rockwell International in 1973 and embarking on a strategy of reducing its aviation interests, the company sold its final Thrush Commander 600 and 800 series to the new Ayres Corporation in November 1977. Ayres operated from the former Rockwell facilities at Albany, Georgia. Of the original Aero Commander twin-engined line, only the refined Turbo Commander 690B, which succeeded the Turbo Commander 681B in 1972, remained in production through 1979. Production of the single-engined Alpine Commander and Gran Turismo Commander models ended in September 1979, but the advanced Aero Commander 840, which first flew on May 17, 1979, succeeded the earlier Turbo Commander. By that time, however, Rockwell faced dim prospects in the overcrowded market and planned to exit general aviation entirely.

Table 6-2 Shipments of General Aviation Aircraft, Selected Manufacturers, 1947–1968

Year	Total	Beech	Cessna	Champion	Lear
1947	15,764	1,288	2,390	—	—
1948	7,037	746	1,631	—	—
1950	3,386	489	1,134	—	—
1952	3,058	414	1,373	—	—
1954	3,071	579	1,200	—	—
1956	6,843	724	3,255	162	—
1958	6,414	694	2,926	296	—
1960	7,588	962	3,720	248	—
1961	6,797	818	2,746	112	—
1962	6,723	830	3,124	91	—
1963	7,603	1,061	3,456	99	—
1964	9,371	1,103	4,188	60	3
1965	11,967	1,192	5,629	271	80
1966	15,747	1,535	7,888	331	51
1967	13,577	1,260	6,233	267	34
1968	13,698	1,347	6,578	255	41

Year	Lockheed	Mooney	Piper	NAR*	Other
1947	—	—	3,634	—	8,452
1948	—	—	1,479	—	3,181
1950	—	51	1,108	—	604
1952	—	49	1,161	39	22
1954	—	14	1,191	67	20
1956	—	154	2,329	164	55
1958	—	160	2,162	97	79
1960	—	172	2,313	155	18
1961	—	286	2,646	139	50
1962	9	387	2,139	121	22
1963	10	502	2,321	114	40
1964	6	650	3,196	109	56
1965	18	775	3,776	110	116
1966	24	917	4,437	354	210
1967	19	642	4,490	386	246
1968	16	579	4,228	471	183

*Includes Sabreliner and original Aero Commander Company.
SOURCE: *Aviation Fact and Figures, 1969*, Aerospace Industries Association, Washington, D.C., 1969, p. 34.

Although completely unrelated, Mooney and Aerostar would become associated by acquisition. Mooney Aircraft, Inc., acquired Alon, Inc., which held the original Ercoupe design, on October 10, 1967. The Alon A-2 Aircoupe was added to the Mooney line, joined by the refined, single-tail M-10 Cadet model. The program was transferred to the Texas factory, but few were produced, ending the long production history of the Ercoupe. Mooney models continued, and the popular Mark 21 was renamed the Ranger. Mooney also progressed from marketing to assembly of the Japanese-designed MU-2 twin-turboprop business aircraft at its San Angelo factory. Mooney then was acquired by American Electronic Laboratories of Pennsylvania on March 26, 1969, and operated as Mooney Aircraft Corporation. This arrangement was short-lived, however, as Butler Aviation International of Texas bought Mooney from A.E.L. on November 21, 1969, operating it as a wholly owned subsidiary.

The Aerostar design of Ted Smith experienced a checkered ownership and production history. Rockwell-Standard, just prior to the North American merger, allowed its purchase option on Ted Smith Aircraft Corporation to expire in April 1967. Ted Smith then moved independently to open a new factory for production of the Aerostar on January 5, 1968, in Van Nuys, California, but persistent financing difficulties slowed deliveries. Smith later sold control to American Cement Corporation. Then Butler Aviation International, already owning Mooney, acquired Aerostar on February 16, 1970. The subsidiary, combining both lines, was renamed Aerostar International Corporation, and production attained some stability. Aircraft were marketed under the Aerostar nameplate, with four original Aerostar series employing the same basic airframe. The subsidiary name was again changed, this time to Aerostar Aircraft Corporation, on July 1, 1970, and Mooney models were marketed under the Aerostar nameplate as well. But market weakness then led Aerostar to suspend all production in 1972.

Ted Smith, having lost his company earlier, saw an opportunity to regain control and formed a new venture, Ted Smith and Associates. Reacquiring Aerostar components from Butler International at a distress price, he restarted production in Santa Maria, California, and planned more advanced developments. The venture became Ted Smith Aerostar Corporation, but Ted Smith died in 1976 at age 70, and the company was acquired by Piper. In the meantime, Republic Steel Corporation of Cleveland (and not to be confused with the old Republic Aviation) announced its acquisition of the Mooney line from Butler on October 14, 1973. The deal became effective in 1974, recreating Mooney Aircraft Corporation in the process. The Mooney line again enjoyed success in the market. The lengthened M-20F Executive led to the improved Model 201 and turbocharged Model 231 of 1976, largely designed by LeRoy LoPresti. The lower-priced Ranger also followed.

Piper enjoyed overall prosperity during the 1960s, but remained the smallest of the Big Three, possessed the smallest military segment, and offered the narrowest product line. The company delivered its 10,000th Cherokee in August 1967. Traditionally, Piper had competed with simplicity and affordability, but was increasingly pressured by Beech, Cessna, and Rockwell. The company suffered a sharp profit drop in the 1967 market downturn, largely due to a lack of broad market coverage. It faced a growing problem in not having a contender in the small commuter airliner market to compete with the Beech 99 and others. Project development remained active, but the six-eight seat PA-31 Navajo did not enter service until April 1967, later than the competitive Cessna 411 and Beech Queen Air. An improved PA-39 Twin Comanche appeared in 1971, but the Twin Comanche line ended in 1974. Single-engined production, down to the veteran Super Cub, remained strong.

The initial commuter airliner entry, and the largest aircraft ever designed by Piper, the 15-seat PA-35 Pocono, first flew on May 13, 1968. Production was planned for a new factory in Lakeland, Florida. William T. Piper, Jr., dubious of turboprop power for smaller aircraft, selected turbocharged piston engines instead. He felt that the price advantage of a piston-powered, unpressurized aircraft would enable it to capture a market from far more expensive turbine-powered, pressurized competitors.[4] The Pocono proved to be seriously underpowered, however, and production was shelved in 1970, leaving Piper still without an entry into the commuter airliner market.

Bill Piper, Jr., finally succeeded his father in the office of president on February 6, 1968, although the senior Piper remained chairman of the board. Younger brothers Tony and Pug Piper continued as executives. By 1969, with the Piper family holding only 31 percent of the company stock, sales approaching $100 million annually, with a strong cash position and strong profits, the firm was an attractive acquisition candidate.[5] On January 23, 1969, Herbert J. Siegel, head of Chris-Craft, Inc., known as a boat manufacturer but actually a highly diversified company, announced the acquisition of a substantial block of Piper stock with the intent to gain control. It tendered for 300,000 shares in the open market. The Pipers resisted the takeover attempt, and a protracted battle ensued.

The Pipers first approached Grumman about acquiring control, but discussions eventually failed. Piper finally found a corporate rescuer in the Bangor Punta Corporation of Greenwich, Connecticut, which acquired more than 500,000 shares held by the Piper family plus others to constitute 51 percent to Chris-Craft's 42 percent.[6] The transaction, at the end of 1969, netted the Pipers more than $30 million, but control passed from the family. Chris-Craft pursued a legal battle against Bangor Punta, but unsuccessfully. After the takeover the senior Piper resigned as chairman of the board and as a director. Tony and Pug Piper and Walter Jamouneau also resigned from the board, but remained officers of the company. William T. Piper, Jr., remained president and a board member.

William T. Piper, Sr., died on January 15, 1970, at the age of 89, after a 40-year career in the industry. In September 1970, Bill Piper, Jr., relinquished the presidency to Joseph T. Mergen, previously vice president and general manager of Avco-Lycoming, and earlier vice president of Curtiss-Wright Corporation.[7] Tony Piper moved to Texas and severed all ties with the company. In addition to the managerial upheaval, the general market decline at the time affected Piper more seriously than others and forced the temporary closure of both the Lock Haven and Vero Beach plants beginning in the summer of 1970.

In a second attempt to enter the commuter market, Piper discussed acquisition of privately held Swearingen Aircraft, makers of the successful Metro, in 1971, but a deal did not reach fruition.[8] Success came in the higher end of the executive market with the first Piper-designed turboprop, the PA-31T Cheyenne II, which first flew on August 20, 1969. Derived from the Navajo, and first converted by Swearingen, the Cheyenne (later Cheyenne II), after some delay, finally went into production in 1973 at the new Lakeland plant. Piper also introduced the smaller PA-34 Seneca (originally Twin Cherokee), eventually to succeed the older Twin Comanche, on September 23, 1971. The PA-31–350 Chieftain, a lengthened Navajo with up to ten seats, was offered from 1972 for the commuter market. Further single-engined developments introduced concurrently in 1970 were the Cherokee Arrow, with retractable gear, and the Pawnee II agricultural model. The larger and more advanced PA-36 Brave joined the Pawnee II in 1974.

Bill Piper, Jr., left the board and Howard "Pug" Piper resigned as an officer in January 1973, formally ending involvement of the Piper family. Mergen succeeded in turning the company around by the end of 1973, with strong sales and profits returning, but then resigned early in 1974 after a series of health problems and frustration with conflicts between the Bangor Punta and Chris-Craft interests.[9] He was eventually succeeded by J. Lynn Helms, formerly of United Aircraft and later chairman of the FAA. Helms pushed ahead with twin-turboprop executive transports, commuter models, and modern twin-engined designs. Piper once again became a strong competitor in other than the business jet segment. The firm reached the production milestone of 100,000 aircraft in April 1976.

Diversification efforts continued. Piper had always lagged Beech and Cessna in military business, and in 1971 it purchased the rights to the Cavalier Mustang II, a modified, turboprop-powered attack version of the famed P-51 Mustang fighter. Trans-Florida Aviation, owned by entrepreneur David B. Lindsay, Jr., developed the Mustang II and proposed it to the military as low-cost battlefield close-support aircraft. Piper moved the program, renamed the PA-48 Enforcer, to its Vero Beach plant. Piper's efforts failed, however, as the Air Force

6—The Modern Era, 1967-1979

maintained it had no requirement. But Piper suspected that the Air Force was more interested in protecting its investment in the more complex and expensive Vought A-7 Corsair II and Fairchild Republic A-10 Thunderbolt II.[10]

While unsuccessful in the military market, Piper expanded its international activities, concluding licensing agreements with Argentina in 1971, Brazil in 1974, and Poland in 1977. Brazil in particular had been a major general aviation export market during the 1971-1974 period, but the market had disappeared rapidly as Brazil, protecting its domestic aircraft industry, imposed a high tariff for aircraft under 15,400 pounds. Brazil was the most active of the international operations, with Embraer (the Portuguese acronym for Brazilian Aircraft Corporation), Piper's licensee, undertaking complete manufacturing rather than assembling aircraft from imported components, although some subassemblies were imported. Piper was thus able to continue serving the market, while Cessna was effectively frozen out. As was frequently encountered in new foreign license production ventures, aircraft built in Brazil cost up to 50 percent more than those made in Vero Beach, but the cost premium later dropped to around 25 percent with efficiency gains.[11] PZL of Poland produced the PA-34 Seneca II under license, while the Argentine and Brazilian operations soon cooperated in production and marketing.

On March 27, 1978, Piper acquired Ted Smith Aerostar Corporation, which it operated initially as the Santa Maria Division. Further developments included the longer, more powerful PA-42 Cheyenne III of 1977 and the PA-38 Tomahawk, a small two-seat trainer intended to challenge the Cessna 150/152, in 1978. The Cheyenne III proved to be a viable competitor to the turbine-powered Cessna Conquest and Beech King Air, and the simplified Cheyenne I, with an attractive base price of $600,000, also sold well.

The basic four-seat low-wing PA-28 line originating with the Cherokee grew to include the Warrior, Archer, Arrow, and Dakota. The larger six-seat PA-32 line included the Cherokee Six, Lance 2, and more powerful Turbo Lance 2, some with fixed and others with retractable gear. The T-tail was adopted for many Piper aircraft during this period. The new PA-32 Saratoga, a roomier, more modern executive model developed from the Cherokee Six, appeared in 1979 and succeeded earlier six-seat models.

With continuing production of such established models as the Super Cub, Aztec F (introduced in 1978), Navajo, Cherokee, Chieftain, and Pawnee, plus the Aerostar line, Piper finally approached the comprehensive market coverage of its major competitors. Its degree of product proliferation approached that of Cessna. Bangor Punta purchased the Chris-Craft shares in 1977, ending the control question, and Piper enjoyed a string and increasing market share. Helms brought in Max M. Bleck, previously with Cessna, as president and chief operating officer in 1978.[12] Sales exceeded $400 million for 1979, exports were strong and growing, and the future appeared favorable.

Table 6-3
Production of General Aviation Aircraft by 14 Manufacturers, 1968*

Manufacturer	Number	Billing Price ($000)
Aero Commander	435	$22,039
American Aviation	33	-291
Beech	1,347	115,737
Bellanca	94	2,128
Cessna	6,578	138,784
Champion	255	2,248
Lake	30	-801
Lear Jet	41	28,650
Lockheed	16	N/A
Maule	25	-332
Mooney	579	24,707
North American Sabreliner	36	N/A
Piper	4,228	85,484
Ted Smith	1	-71
General Aviation Total	13,698	$421,522**

*Excludes military sales, helicopters, and gliders.
**Excludes North American Sabreliner and Lockheed JetStar.
SOURCE: *Aviation Facts and Figures, 1969*, Aerospace Industries Association, Washington, D.C., pp. 31–33.

Frank Hedrick became president of Beech on January 18, 1968, as Olive Ann Beech, then age 65, assumed the office of chairman but remained active in management. Edward C. Burns, a nephew of the late Walter Beech, headed the Boulder Division and became regarded as heir apparent. Thus the family influence continued, although family connections were never discussed openly within the company. Howard "Pug" Piper, after departing from his firm, joined Beech as a full-time consultant on light aircraft in 1973.[13] By that time possibly the strongest general aviation firm, Beech also became regarded as an attractive acquisition candidate, especially by larger aerospace firms. Merger discussions with Grumman, experiencing trouble in its traditional naval business and seeking greater civil diversification, were broken off in October 1973 after Beech determined no mutually beneficial terms were possible.[14]

The Arab oil embargo beginning in October 1973 was a major shock for Beech as well as for the entire general aviation industry. An initial government-imposed 42½ percent reduction in general aviation fuel allocations threatened to devastate the new aircraft market. The General Aviation Manufacturers Association led the effort to ease the restrictions. The reduction was modified to 25 percent and the market improved. In 1975 President Ford reduced general aviation export restrictions, also strengthening the market.[15]

The Musketeer series of smaller fixed-gear models was renamed in December 1971, with variants marketed as the Sundowner, Sport, and Sierra, and production continued of all three. The V-tailed Bonanza and the Debonair, a derivative with a conventional tail, continued in production, and the Debonair was renamed the Model 33 Bonanza in 1967. The larger Model 36 six-seat straight-tail Bonanza appeared in mid-1968. The Duke, a new pressurized, piston-powered twin, sized between the Baron and the Queen Air, first flew on December 29, 1966, and entered production during 1968. Production of the Travel Air ended in 1968, but production and development of the popular Baron continued. Representing a considerable departure for Beech was the new Model 77 Skipper, a low-cost two-seat trainer with a raised cockpit and fixed tricycle gear. Intended for flying schools, the Skipper first flew on February 6, 1975.

At the higher end of the product line, production of the "Twin Beech" series ended in 1969 after 32 years, then a record for a basic design. More than 750 of the definitive Super H18 variant had been built since 1964. Production of the Queen Air series began phasing out, finally ending in 1970. All larger business aircraft then were turbine powered. The initial King Air, effectively replacing the Super H18, was joined by the larger King Air 100, with more powerful PT6A-28 turboprops, in 1969. The lengthened, T-tailed Super King Air 200, flagship of the corporate line, made its first flight on October 27, 1972, and deliveries began in 1973. A new light twin intended for both business and multiengine training use, the Duchess 76, first flew on May 24, 1977, and attained major market share.

The first production Model 99, largest in the Beech line, flew on May 2, 1968, and was developed for both business and commuter use. The more powerful Model 99A appeared in 1969 and was joined by the Model 99 Executive, with a luxury corporate interior. The variants were later designated the B99 Airliner and B99 Executive. Sales of the B99 declined, however, and Beech suspended the line in 1975 with 164 produced, pending a market recovery.

One cloud over Beech, and over the general aviation industry, was that of liability for design-related crashes. The company became a target after four crashes of Beech aircraft were attributed to fuel cutoff during a "slip" turn and bank maneuver, causing power failure. Beech claimed pilot error but was accused of reluctance to face possible design flaws.[16] The company was not harmed at the time and went on to enjoy a prosperous decade in the 1970s, but the episode presaged a growing product liability problem.

While primarily a general aviation firm, Beech maintained its strong military involvement, including supersonic drones. Beech became a major subcontractor to the Bell JetRanger helicopter program in January 1968, producing airframes. Demands of the program on Wichita plant capacity were so great that Beech was forced to shift most general aviation production to the Salina plant. The company also built major subassemblies for the McDonnell Douglas F-4 fighter. The YT-34C turbine-powered model of the veteran trainer first flew on September 21, 1973, and 334 were delivered to the Navy between 1977 and 1984. All four military services ordered versions of the King Air for numerous missions, under various utility and transport designations.

Beech merger discussions in 1977 with General Dynamics, then interested in commercial diversification, were inconclusive.[17] Beech marked the delivery of the 10,000th V-tail Bonanza in February 1977 and in December of that year reached the production milestone of 40,000 aircraft since its founding in 1932.

Cessna retained its position as the largest general aviation manufacturer and offered the broadest product line. Unlike its competitors, it retained the high-wing configuration on all its single-engined models except for the agricultural line. In the military sector, the T-37 trainer was joined by the A-37B attack version in September 1967. The A-37B went into production for the U.S. forces and for export, a total of 577 being completed. Both the T-37 and A-37 remained in production until 1977. The Air Force ordered further T-41A trainers, and the Army ordered the more powerful T-41B. The type was also exported, and orders for military derivatives of the Model 172 totaled 855 by the end of 1978. The push-pull Model 337 was ordered by the Army for Vietnam service as the O-2A, for Forward Air Control (FAC), and as the O-2B for psychological warfare. Deliveries began in 1967 and extended into the mid-1970s.

Cessna reached the milestone of 10,000 Model 150s produced in December 1967, and in May 1972 became the first company to have produced 100,000 aircraft. Production of the Model 401 finally ended in 1972 after 406 were completed, but newer twin-engined executive models, including the Model 402, continued. More than 1,000 of the Model 402 were built, including convertible passenger/freighter versions. Production of the Model 411A, which first appeared in 1968, ended in June 1978 with 303 delivered. The Models 414 and 414A Chancellor, appearing in 1969, represented the upscale, pressurized end of the segment. A further refinement of the executive line was the Model 421 Golden Eagle, which first flew on October 14, 1965. Over 1,500 Golden Eagles were produced.

While continuing the veteran Model 310, Cessna introduced the pressurized Model 340, an advanced development incorporating certain features of the larger 400 series. The Model 340 appeared in December 1971 and effectively replaced the Model 320 Skyknight, which had ended production in 1968.

The Models 172 Skyhawk/175 Skylark and the Models 182/185/Skylane series continued their popularity throughout the 1970s, and further entries appeared in the twin-engined executive line. Departing from numerical designations, Cessna announced the Conquest, pressurized and powered by two TPE331 turboprops, on November 15, 1974, and the larger Titan, a piston-engine version, on July 6, 1975. Cessna's executive models held a competitive advantage in being priced considerably lower than the Beech King Air series. Cessna offered no fewer than 58 civil aircraft models in 1976.[18] The Model 152 two-seat model was announced in 1977 to replace the veteran Model 150 and strong sales continued, but the market for the Model 337 Skymaster declined. In September 1977 Cessna introduced the Model 177 Cardinal luxury four-seat model, which found a strong market. It was joined by the Cardinal RG with retractable gear, unusual in a high-wing design. More than 5,000 Cardinal and Cardinal RG models had been built when production ceased at the end of 1978 because of declining sales. Somewhat ironically, the Cardinal had been intended to replace the Skyhawk/Skylark series, but the older models continued in production.

The Pawnee Division produced single-engined models, while the Wallace Division produced military, twin-engined, and business jet models. The McCauley Division and fluid power activities also remained important. Although generally successful in all market segments, there was little doubt that the most important aspect of Cessna's business and the key to its future was the projected Citation business jet.

Russell W. Meyer, Jr., a lawyer and president of American Aviation Corporation until its acquisition by Grumman in 1973, was recruited by Dwane Wallace in June 1974 to become executive vice president of Cessna. Wallace, a strong believer in retirement at age 65, did so in 1976 after more than 40 years at Cessna. Meyer succeeded him as chairman and chief executive officer. Malcolm S. Harned, an industry veteran, became president.

Among smaller companies, Champion Aircraft Corporation, with a product line descended from the original Aeronca, as acquired by Bellanca Sales Corporation on September 30, 1970, which was in turn the successor to the Inter-Air subsidiary of Miller Flying Service. After the Champion acquisition the firm was renamed Bellanca Aircraft Corporation. In addition to producing the Model 260C and Viking 300, Bellanca further developed the Citabria and also produced the Scout, the Champ, and the Decathlon, another development of the veteran Champion. The Champion operation, while very small, remained active in new model development, but eventually only the Citabria remained in production. Then the four-seat Bellanca Model 260C ended production in 1971, The Viking continued, and its largely wood structure marked a contrast with the dominant all-metal structures of competitors.

In 1976 Anderson, Greenwood and Co. of Texas, inactive in aircraft production since the late 1940s, acquired a 100 percent ownership of Bellanca Aircraft Corporation, still in Minnesota. The unrelated Bellanca Aircraft Engineering, Inc., headed by August Bellanca and descended from the original

Bellanca company of 1927, was reorganized in 1971. Its advanced Skyrocket II five-seat business aircraft, under development for years, was first tested in 1975, but the company could not proceed with production.

A new Taylorcraft Aviation Corporation was formed on April 1, 1968, by members of the Taylor family, which held rights to the original designs. It provided parts and service support to the previous aircraft and from 1973 also built the new F-19 Sportsman, based on older Taylorcraft designs. Production of the F-19 ended in 1980, but the higher-powered F-21 continued in production at a low level.

Willard R. Custer, tireless proponent of the channel wing concept, retired in February 1968. He still pursued certification of the CCW-5 and promoted the aircraft, but his company was essentially dormant. The Aerocar roadable airplane development of M. B. Taylor also largely ended by 1975. The combination of automotive safely, environmental, and fuel economy standards finally doomed market prospects. The model remained available by special order, however.

A new Navion Rangemaster Company was organized in 1972, still in Texas, from the assets of the previous Navion Aircraft Corporation, which had gone bankrupt in 1969. The new company planned to introduce the Rangemaster into production from 1975. This venture also encountered market and financial problems, however, bringing to a close the long history of efforts to continue that classic aircraft design.

Helio was acquired in 1969 by General Aircraft Corporation, also formed by Dr. Lynn L. Bollinger. It was renamed the Helio Aircraft Company. The large 10-seat Helio Stallion failed to sell in the civil market, and Helio was effectively forced out of business in the early 1970s. Production was suspended and the firm was sold in 1976, with the new owners moving to subcontracting.[19] Rights to the Helio designs were again sold, but no new production ensued.

Swearingen progressed with production of both the piston-powered Merlin I and turboprop-powered Merlin II. From these were developed the uprated and refined Merlin III, followed by the further upgraded Merlin IIIB, which flew on December 1, 1968. Even more ambitious was the SA-226A Merlin IV, which involved a major stretch of the fuselage. The plane first flew on August 26, 1969, and was intended for both corporate and commuter use. The commuter version, renamed Metro, was developed in a joint venture with Fairchild Hiller. The Metro first flew on August 29, 1969, and soon captured a share of the 19-seat third-level airliner market segment. After Swearingen experienced financial difficulties, Fairchild acquired 90 percent ownership on November 2, 1971, operating it as the Swearingen Aviation Corporation subsidiary. Still managed by Ed Swearingen, it ceased production of earlier models, but Fairchild marketed the improved Merlin IVA as the Metro II for the third-level segment. Fairchild acquired the remaining 10 percent of the stock in 1979.

6—The Modern Era, 1967–1979

Maule Aircraft Corporation continued with its M-4 Rocket series, which gained a reputation for ruggedness. The model was also produced in Mexico from 1964 as the Cuauhtemoc M-1, although only for the Mexican Air Force. By 1968 some 250 aircraft had been delivered, including those for export, and Belford Maule began considering a new location that would offer lower labor costs, better flying weather, and expansion space. He selected a closed air base at Moultrie, Georgia, and moved operations there in September 1968. Production of the Maule M-4 ended in 1975, but the M-5 Lunar Rocket, which first flew on November 1, 1971, and subsequent developments enjoyed long production lives.

The Lake Aircraft Division of Consolidated Aeronautics continued as the only producer of small amphibians. The basic LA-4 model continued to be refined. The firm was reconstituted in 1981 as Lake Amphibians, Inc., of Laconia, New Hampshire, under control of the French entrepreneur Armand Rivard.

A rare success in a new general aviation venture was the American Aviation Corporation, formed in 1964 in Cleveland, Ohio, with Russell W. Meyer, Jr., as President. American Aviation had acquired the rights to the BD-1 design of James Bede and his Bede Aviation Corporation, which it developed as the AA-1 Yankee. The Yankee gained attention for its low-cost aluminum honeycomb construction, as well as for its STOL performance. By 1972 it had achieved a measure of sales success in the two-seat segment long dominated by the Cessna 150/152.

Grumman, implementing its strategy of reducing its dependence on the U.S. Navy, acquired American Aviation Corporation on January 2, 1973. The subsidiary was renamed Grumman American Aviation Corporation (GAAC), with operations remaining in Cleveland. Russ Meyer was succeeded in May 1973 by the unrelated Corwin (Corky) Meyer, a Grumman vice president with a long background as a test pilot. Grumman's Ag-Cat, still built under license by Schweizer, and Gulfstream II models were brought under GAAC, giving Grumman a broad range of general aviation aircraft. The turboprop Gulfstream I ended production in February 1969 with 200 delivered. More than 2,000 Ag-Cats had been produced by 1979.

With Grumman financial support, GAAC introduced new models from 1974, including the Trainer and the AA-5 Traveler four-seat model, both from the AA-1 Yankee, and the Model Tr 2 combined trainer and sportplane. The Grumman tradition of feline names continued with the AA-5B Tiger, designed by the engineer LeRoy LoPresti. Then the GA-7 Cougar, a completely new light twin, first flew on December 20, 1974. GAAC also seriously studied a 30–40 seat commuter airliner development of the Gulfstream I during 1979–1980, but decided not to proceed. It appeared logical to many for larger general aviation firms to move into 30–50 seat commuter airliners. NASA, in fact, sponsored a Small Transport Aircraft Technology

[STAT] program to advance commuter aircraft technology.[20] No firm produced a new design, however, primarily owing to a poor record of profitability in that segment. The category was left to foreign producers, many with government subsidies.

Grumman's increased investment in general aviation proved to be of short duration, however. In another strategic move it sold its GAAC interests to the aviation entrepreneur Allen Paulson through his American Jet Industries of California. American Jet Industries (AJI) purchased Grumman's 80 percent shareholding on September 1, 1968, and purchased the remaining 20 percent held by others with cash. AJI, which had earlier acquired the original Fletcher company, determined to reenter aircraft production. In 1970 it purchased the new plant built by Lockheed to produce its Cheyenne attack helicopter, which had been cancelled, and centered its activities there. After purchasing the Grumman interests, Paulson combined all operations as Gulfstream American Corporation and headquarters moved to the Savannah factory. Gulfstream, however, soon ended production of the small single-engined designs, then of the Cougar in 1980.

Helicopter Survey

The established general aviation helicopter producers experienced frequent ownership changes during this period. Financial struggles reflected the difficulty of the small civil helicopter market more than any other factor. Helicopter usage expanded for hospitals and police forces, however, where its capabilities could not be matched by fixed-wing aircraft. In addition, business and executive use of helicopters finally began to grow in the late 1970s. Turbine-powered smaller models became more commonplace, and the Allison 250 turboshaft series became an industry standard. A difference between fixed-wing and helicopter marketing was that helicopters sales generally were negotiated directly from the factory; dealerships had never been widely established. A narrower market and fleet orders were the major reasons. Exports became increasingly significant (see Table 6-4). Another growth area was offshore oil platform service. Petroleum Helicopters, Inc., (PHI) was founded in 1951 and expanded to become the largest fleet operator in the world. The first oil drilling platforms had been set up in the Gulf of Mexico in 1946, and the first helicopter flight to an oil platform, by a Bell Model 47, was in 1947. PHI led the development of oil service operations.[21] Other commercial helicopter operators entered the field, which expanded rapidly from the 1960s, with offshore platforms added in the North Sea and elsewhere. The oil service function spurred development of larger and more capable helicopters for the task, with other manufacturers entering the market.

Table 6-4
Exports of Commercial Helicopters by U.S. Manufacturers, 1960–1987

Year	Total Output	Export Number*	Export Value ($000)
1960	266	89	$11,446
1961	755	122	10,483
1962	407	78	11,124
1963	504	60	10,982
1964	579	102	20,080
1965	598	173	25,121
1966	583	161	11,500
1967	455**	223	25,200
1968	522**	242	32,900
1969	534	252	29,100
1970	482	332	26,900
1971	469	298	45,700
1972	575	256	50,300
1973	770	428	83,300
1974	828	395	107,600
1975	864	336	104,700
1976	757	315	113,000
1977	848	321	106,000
1978	904	368	156,000
1979	1,019	459	207,000
1980	1,366	525	249,000
1981	1,072	453	346,000
1982	587	254	206,000
1983	401	216	232,000
1984	376	233	234,000
1985	376	137	210,000
1986	326	210	277,000
1987	358	281	239,000

*Export figures include Bell, Fairchild Hiller, Hughes, Sikorsky, and Vertol.
**Excludes foreign licensees of Bell.
SOURCE: *Aerospace Facts and Figures, 1969*, pp. 31 and 37; *Aerospace Facts and Figures, 1977–1978*, p. 112; *Aerospace Fact and Figures, 1981–1982*, p. 35; *Aerospace Facts and Figures, 1988–1989*, pp. 131–132.

Brantly, previously acquired by Lear and including in the Lear acquisition by Gates, was sold early in 1969 to the new Aeronautical Research and Development Corporation (ARDC), led by the noted defense attorney and helicopter enthusiast F. Lee Bailey. Late in 1970, ARDC was in turn acquired by Brantly Operators, Inc., of Lakeland, Florida, led by Michael K. Hynes. Hynes briefly considered but rejected acquiring the FH-1100 from Fairchild in 1973. The company became Brantly-Hynes helicopters, Inc., in January 1, 1975, reflecting the ownership interest of Hynes, and operations were moved to Frederick, Oklahoma. The Model B-2B and Model 305 remained in production.

Outside investors forced Rudy Enstrom out of his company, but production of the F28 moved ahead, with sales eventually exceeding 1,000, including the more advanced Models 280 and 480. Enstrom was acquired by Purex Corporation in 1968, becoming a subsidiary of its Pacific Airmotive (PacAero) operation. Purex wanted PacAero to take over management, and Jack Christensen resigned. In the event, poor sales led PacAero to shut down production in February 1970. Enstrom then was acquired in January 1971 by an investor group led by F. Lee Bailey, who brought Christensen back. Having just sold Brantly, Bailey undertook development and marketing efforts in his second helicopter venture, and pushed development of the new Model 280 Shark.

A new contender in the small personal helicopter market appearing the 1970s was the Robinson Helicopter Company of Torrance, California. Franklin Robinson, an experienced helicopter engineer, began designing the two-seat R22 in June 1973, and the prototype made its first flight on August 28, 1975. First deliveries were in October 1979, and output expanded gradually. Emphasizing low cost, and powered by a 160 hp Lycoming engine, the R22 soon led the light two-seat helicopter segment.

Fairchild Hiller transferred its remaining helicopter production to Hagerstown in 1966 in order to centralize all light aircraft production. Production of the veteran Model 12 ended in 1967. Although market prospects for the FH-1100 initially appeared favorable, rising prices and increasing insurance costs diminished the market. Competition from the Bell JetRanger was also a factor, and FH-1100 production ended in 1971 with 250 sold. Fairchild Industries, Inc., renamed from Fairchild Hiller Corporation in 1971, disposed of the Hiller helicopter operations in its restructuring of 1973. In the same month a new Hiller Aviation Company was formed by Stanley Hiller in California. It acquired all helicopter rights with the exception of the FH-1100 from Fairchild. Hiller Aviation resumed production of the UH-12E for the civil market.

The light four-seat Bell Model 206 JetRanger, and at the high end, the 11-seat twin-turboshaft Sikorsky S-76, became increasingly popular executive transports. The S-76 first flew on March 13, 1977, and entered service early in 1979. Sikorsky, hitherto almost exclusively military, regarded the S-76 as a means of increasing civil market share. The Bell JetRanger led to a long series of civil de-

A new Bell Model 412 accompanied by a Bell Model 406 flying over Dallas (Bell Helicopter Textron).

velopments. The initial Model 206A was succeeded in 1972 by the Model 206B JetRanger II, with a more powerful Allison 250, followed by the further improved JetRanger III from 1977. The larger Model 206L LongRanger, announced in September 1973, filled the gap between the JetRanger and heavier types. More than 5,000 Model 206s had been built by 1977, including some 2,200 civil models. The Model 47, the original general aviation helicopter, finally ended production in 1976. More than 5,000 had been built, of which about 2,600 were civil.

Bell's large Model 212, based on the military UH-1N and marketed as the Twin Two-Twelve, appeared in 1971. The Model 412, an update of the Model 212, followed in August 1979. Then the new intermediate Model 222, the first commercial twin-turbine helicopter built in the United States, first flew on August 13, 1976, and became popular both for executive use and for servicing offshore oil drilling platforms.

Hughes Helicopters remained a minor presence with its Model 500, competitive with the JetRanger.

Business Jet Progress

The corporate jet segment, represented in the United States by the JetStar, Sabreliner, Gulfstream II, the LearJet series, and until 1968 by the Jet Commander, became increasingly important to general aviation. While initial sales were slow, the market expanded steadily in 1965 and 1966. LearJet sales totaled 305 by the end of 1970, making it by far the most popular of the business jets. Bill Lear departed on March 31, 1969, after his sale to Gates, and the company became the Gates Learjet Corporation in January 1970, with production still in Wichita. Lear pursued further business aviation ventures.

Although hurt by the recession of 1970–1971, the executive jet market soon experienced a strong recovery, led by the LearJet, Gulfstream II, and the French Dassault Falcon. The market in fact became grouped into three distinct segments, the small, represented by the LearJet and the new Cessna Citation, the medium, represented by the Sabreliner, the Falcon 20, the British BAe 125 (originally DH 125), and the large, represented by the Gulfstream II and the later Canadair Challenger. The market also became strongly international, as American designs competed with those from Britain, France, Canada, and Israel. Pan Am established a Business Jets Division to market the Dassault Falcon in North America. Israeli Aircraft Industries (IAI) undertook a long series of developments of the original Jet Commander acquired from North American Rockwell, resulting first in the IAI Westwind and later the Astra Jet. The Canadair Challenger, entering the market in 1982, and the Mitsubishi Diamond also became factors. Mitsubishi, expanding its Texas subsidiary where the MU-2 remained in production, brought the locally developed twin-jet MU-300 Diamond, which first flew on August 29, 1978, to the American market. Cessna's business jet strategy was to offer a smaller model for the lower-cost segment. It announced the straight-wing Fanjet 550, powered by twin CJ610 turbofans, in 1968. Soon renamed the Citation, it first flew on September 15, 1969. But with the business jet field becoming overcrowded and with development costs in the $20 million range, the Citation represented a major financial risk.[22] Furthermore, sales of the Citation were sluggish when it entered the market in 1972. Cessna maintained, however, that its simpler and somewhat slower design would motivate operators of turboprop-powered business aircraft such as the King Air to move up to a business jet. Sales eventually rose, and the Citation series became the most prolific of all business jets. Numerical suffixes began with the larger Citation II, announced in September 1976, and the improved Citation I, which followed in December 1976. The Citation II first flew on January 31, 1977.

Beech, unlike Cessna, Lear Jet, Grumman, and Aero Commander, did not develop a business jet of its own design. Instead, it entered into a marketing and distribution agreement with Hawker Siddeley (later British Aerospace) to form Beechcraft Hawker Corporation in 1970, marketing the originally de Havilland DH-125 in North America as the Beechcraft Hawker BH-125. But Beech ended the Hawker marketing agreement in 1975, the reason being simple economics.[23]

Grumman had planned a Gulfstream III as a refinement of the Gulf-

6—The Modern Era, 1967–1979

stream II, but development was halted in 1977 in favor of a later, even more advanced version incorporating a highly efficient NASA-developed supercritical wing and winglets. Having sold the Gulfstream to Gulfstream American, Grumman resumed development in 1978 under contract to the new owner, and the new Gulfstream III first flew on December 2, 1979. Grumman continued as a production subcontractor to Gulfstream as well. Gulfstream II production ended in 1980 with delivery of 256, succeeded by the Gulfstream III.

Lockheed introduced the developed JetStar II, with advanced Garrett TFE 731-3 turbofans, in the summer of 1976. But after production of 40, the JetStar program ended in 1979. More than 200 had been produced, but the design simply lost out to newer competitors. Rockwell International continued to develop and manufacture the Sabreliner in Los Angeles, although marketing was controlled by a new division in St. Louis. All Sabreliner production and support operations then were transferred to St. Louis in March 1977, by which time some 500 Sabreliners had been delivered. Both the Model 60 and larger Model 75 remained in production.

Gates Learjet announced major model improvements on October 28, 1975, including the advanced, long-range Model 55. It followed with the Models 28/29 Longhorn, improvements of the Model 25 featuring longer wings and winglets. First flight came on August 24, 1977. Further developments included the Models 35A/36A, also similar to the Model 25 but with turbofan power. Airframe production remained in Wichita, but "green" aircraft were transferred to a facility in Tucson, Arizona, for final furnishing and equipment installation.

The business jet market continued its generally strong growth through the 1979s. Production stability was aided by recurring military orders for certain models for training and high-priority transport missions. Governments also ordered business jets for transportation of high-level officials (VIPs). Business jets continued to be marketed on the premise that they would save valuable management time over scheduled commercial air travel, thereby maximizing productivity as well as bringing remote plants and other sites such as oil fields not served directly by commercial airlines within easy reach. The increasing popularity of hub-and-spoke routing by airlines, causing inconveniences for many business travelers, was a further incentive.

The productivity case was supported with statistics showing that corporations owning and operating business jets enjoyed higher profitability than those that did not. The objective was to establish causality between business jet use and profitability, although that remained tenuous. More realistically, given their high cost, the economics of the corporate jet for most companies appeared rather dubious. Further, not all successful firms used business jets. Boeing, for example, never owned or operated corporate jets, relying entirely on commercial airlines for its travel needs. Instead, ownership of corporate jets and entitlement to their use became known as the ultimate corporate perk.[24]

With a rise in sabotage and terrorism affecting commercial airlines, corporate jets increasingly were marketed on security grounds. Then as the market matured, many jets owned by corporations were chartered or leased during periods of inactivity. Manufacturers also offered leasing to their corporate customers as an alternative to the relentless escalation in selling prices, as well as accepting older models in trade toward new models. Specialized business jet leasing firms also appeared.

* * *

Despite economic fluctuations and periodic political disturbances, general aviation manufacturing had enjoyed a strongly expanding market and wide prosperity during the 1970s (see Table 6-5). That strength and prosperity were not to continue, however. By the beginning of the new decade, several factors converged to nearly devastate the industry.

Table 6-5
General Aviation Shipments, 1976–1980

Firm	1976	1977	1978	1979	1980
Ayres	—	—	134	99	44
Beech	1,220	1,203	1,367	1,508	1,394
Bellanca	315	252	370	443	103
Cessna	7,888	8,839	8,770	8,400	6,393
Gates Learjet	84	105	102	107	120
Gulfstream	762	866	933	400	167
Lake	88	99	98	96	79
Lockheed JetStar	3	16	9	7	4
Maule	96	108	88	67	59
Mooney	227	362	379	439	332
Piper	4,042	4,499	5,272	5,255	2,954
Rockwell	595	432	244	164	164
Swearingen	30	28	51	70	86
Ted Smith Aerostar	100	101	—	—	—
Totals	15,450	16,910	17,817	17,055	11,881

SOURCE: *Aerospace Facts and Figures, 1981–1982*, p. 35: and GAMA Reports.

7

The General Aviation Crisis

General aviation manufacturers appeared well-positioned to continue their strong growth into the 1980s. Production volume, dollar sales, and employment peaked in 1979, and optimism for the future was widespread. Cessna led with sales of $939 million for that year, followed by Beech with $602 million and Gates Learjet with $302 million, all including military sales.[1] Total general aviation aircraft sales, $2 billion in 1979, were projected to reach $3 billion by 1981. The sales figures represented fixed-winged aircraft only, as rotary-winged aircraft were statistically separate. But as the American economy enjoyed a strong overall expansion during the decade of the 1980s, the general aviation industry declined sharply, and the decline turned out to be severe and long term, not just cyclical. The reasons were many, but the most damaging factor was the rash of product liability lawsuits against manufacturers stemming from aircraft accidents.

Aircraft prices had already escalated substantially in the 1970s. Liability insurance costs forced manufacturers to raise prices even more, sharply reducing new aircraft demand. The market decline was felt earliest and was most pronounced in the single-engined segment, as growth continued until 1981 in twin-engined propeller-driven models and business jets. A record 389 business jets and 918 turboprop-powered models were delivered in 1981, but overall executive aircraft production declined sharply thereafter. Exports of general aviation aircraft (see Table 7–1) which generally had ranged from 20 percent to 35 percent of total output, accounted for more than 40 percent by 1990 due to the domestic market collapse.[2] Concurrently, imports of general aviation aircraft into the American market increased markedly, reaching 35 percent by value in 1985, although concentrated in the high-value business jet and turboprop-powered commuter segments rather than in small single-engined types.[3]

Table 7-1 General Aviation Exports, 1959–1995

Year	Total Units	Helicopter Exports	GA Exports
1959	1,033	(not reported until 1969)	
1960	1,528		
1961	1,646		
1962	1,458		
1963	1,583		
1964	1,834		
1965	2,457		
1966	2,985		
1967	3,125		
1968	2,879		
1969	2,713	252	2,461
1970	2,369	332	2,037
1971	1,864	298	1,566
1972	2,328	256	2,072
1973	3,591	428	3,163
1974	4,658	395	4,263
1975	3,604	336	3,268
1976	3,533	315	3,218
1977	3,790	321	3,469
1978	4,839	368	4,471
1979	4,337	459	3,878
1980	3,703	525	3,178
1981	3,070	453	2,617
1982	1,194	254	940
1983	735	216	519
1984	658	233	425
1985	621	137	484
1986	674	210	464
1987	729	242	487
1988	923	280	643
1989	1,604	294	1,310
1990	1,158	349	809
1991	852	318	534
1992	570	212	358
1993	508	175	333
1994	539	154	385
1995	573	210	363

SOURCE: *Aerospace Facts and Figures, 1969*, p. 73; and *Aerospace Facts and Figures, 1996/1997*, p. 30, based on company reports, GAMA, and International Trade Administration, Department of Commerce.

Yet U.S. production still accounted for approximately 70 percent of all turbine-powered general aviation aircraft in operation, and the United States remained by far the largest general aviation market in the world. It was estimated in 1984 that some 36,000 American businesses used aircraft. Product development remained active, particularly at the high end of the market, even with sales declining (see Table 7-2). In the midst of the market decline, general aviation noted the death of E. M. "Matty" Laird, a pioneer of the industry, in Boca Raton, Florida, in December 1982, age 87.

Table 7-2 Annual Production and Sales, General Aviation Aircraft

Year	Units	Factory Sales ($ millions)
1981	9,457	2,919.9
1982	4,226	1,999.5
1983	2,691	1,469.5
1984	2,431	1,680.7
1985	2,029	1,430.6
1986	1,495	1,261.9
1987	1,085	1,363.5
1988	1,143	1,918.4
1989	1,535	1,803.9
1990	1,144	2,007.5
1991	1,021	1,968.3
1992	899	1,839.6
1993	964	2,143.8
1994	928	2,357.1
1995	1,077	2,841.9
1996	1,132	3,141.0

SOURCE: *General Aviation Statistical Databook* (1996 edition), p. 4. Washington, D.C.: GAMA.

Industry Survey

Piper's cumulative production reached 125,000 on May 4, 1982, but by that time output was falling rapidly in the overall decline. After J. Lynn Helms departed for the FAA in 1981, Max M. Bleck, already chief executive officer, succeeded him as chairman as well. Piper then came under a new corporate parent when Lear Siegler Corporation acquired Bangor Punta Corporation on March 1, 1984, for $282 million.

Continuing its attempts to broaden market coverage, Piper formed an Airline Division on June 4, 1981, to support third-level operators of the Chieftain and to produce new versions for that market. The piston-engined T-1020 and the turbine-powered T-1040, both roomier versions of the Chieftain, were offered. The Airline Division became inactive in 1986, however, after only 23 T-1020 and 23 T-1040 models had been produced.

Aerostar operations, under Piper ownership, were transferred to Vero Beach in October 1981. Several variants of the basic Aerostar, differing in pressurization, power, and equipment, were offered. But production of the Aerostar 601P was suspended in 1982 due to weak market conditions, followed by suspension of the Model 600A. Total Aerostar production of Models 600, 601B, and 601P by all corporate owners totaled 875. Then the remaining 602P and 700P models were suspended in 1984, bringing the production history of that design to an end.

Production of the PA-38 Tomahawk, PA-23-250 Aztec F, and PA-44 Seminole light twin, which had entered service only in 1978, was suspended in 1982. Rights for the veteran Super Cub and the PA-26 Brave were sold to WTA, Inc., of Lubbock, Texas, in 1983, but both models were still manufactured by Piper on behalf of WTA. Then the Super Cub operation ceased in 1987. Navaho production also ended, but product development continued with the entirely new PA-46 Malibu, a large single-engined business aircraft with a roomy cabin offering twin-engined comfort. Announced on November 20, 1982, the Malibu supplemented the slow-selling Saratoga, and was regarded as Piper's future in the declining market. Walter Jamouneau died on September 13, 1988, at age 76, after a 50-year career with Piper.

Beech finally gave up its independence on October 1, 1979, with its acquisition by Raytheon Corporation of Lexington, Massachusetts. The culmination of years of merger considerations, Beech agreed to the friendly takeover after being assured that it would retain its distinct identity, a concern that had weighed against any agreement with Grumman or General Dynamics in earlier talks. The acquisition also promised synergy; there were no overlapping product lines. Raytheon would gain commercial diversification, and Beech would benefit from Raytheon's technical capabilities, especially in defense contracts.[4] It was anticipated at the time that Beech would become the largest profit contributor to Raytheon. Another concern was that of aging management: Mrs. Beech was 76 at the time of the merger and Frank Hedrick was 69.

The merger was approved by stockholders on February 6, 1980, and became effective on February 8.[5] Payment was by an exchange of stock, with the transaction valued at some $800 million, an advantageous price to Beech, but one that later brought Raytheon intense criticism, coming as it did just before the market decline.[6] Olive Ann Beech and Frank Hedrick became directors of Raytheon. A series of management changes followed as Beech nephew Edward C. Burns became president on January 10, 1981, with Frank Hedrick moving to vice chairman. Burns was forced to make significant layoffs during 1982, when Beech, along with others, was adversely affected by the market collapse. Burns then retired on June 15, 1982, followed by Hedrick on July 1. Olive Ann Beech retired as chairman of the board in September 1982, assuming the title of chairman emeritus, and D. Brainerd Holmes, chairman of Raytheon, also became chairman of Beech. The aviation entrepreneur Linden S. Blue, formerly with Learjet and LearFan, Inc., succeeded Burns as President and CEO but served only 26 months before departing. With his brother he took control of General Atomics from Chevron in 1986. He was followed in those positions at Beech by James C. Walsh in 1984. Then Max M. Bleck, formerly CEO of Piper and later with Learjet, became president and CEO of Beech in 1987.

Beech entered business jet production in December 1982 by purchasing rights to the Mitsubishi Diamond 2, which had first flown on January 28, 1985. Mitsubishi, which had ended its cooperative agreement with Mooney, had also decided not to continue Diamond 2 production in San Angelo after having built only 11 before the sale to Beech. More than 500 MU-2 models also had been produced, but Mitsubishi ended all its general aviation activities on March 31, 1986, and exited the market. Beech took over production of the renamed Beechjet, still using Mitsubishi components, and completed transfer of total manufacturing to Wichita in June 1989. Demand developed slowly, chiefly due to competition from the established Citation and Learjet, but the improved Beechjet 400A, manufactured entirely in Wichita, boosted sales.

A revised Beech Model 99, a 15-passenger model for third-level service improved from earlier versions, was announced on May 7, 1979, and first flew on June 20, 1980. It was placed in production at a new factory in Selma, Alabama, on the site of the closed Craig Air Force Base. Then the successor to the Model 99 series, the completely new Beech 1900C, first flew on September 3, 1982, and entered production in 1983. Possessing 40 percent design and component commonality with the Super King Air 200, the 1900C accommodated 19 passengers.

Beech continued to rationalize its product line even as it developed new and improved models. Production of the Duke, the King Air 100, and the Duchess 76 ended in 1984. The E55 Baron ceased production after 1,201 had been completed, but the improved E58 Baron continued. Beech also suspended production of the single-engined Sierra and Sundowner in 1984. The Model 35 Bonanza, finally bowing to diminished demand and increasing questions over the safely of its trademark V-tail, ended its 38-year production life early in 1985, with a final production total of 10,390. Beech had consistently denied recurring accusations that it covered up safely problems with the design. Straight-tail Bonanza production continued, as did the twin-turboprop line. The Super King Air 300 was succeeded late in 1989 by the much-improved Super King Air 350. The King Air C90A and Super King Air 200 continued concurrently with the more advanced model, and military versions continued to receive orders.

Criticized at times for its design conservatism, Beech replied by announcing the radical Starship 2000 in 1982. Featuring an innovative canard configuration, twin pusher turboprop power, and a structure of advanced composite materials, the Starship was intended to be competitive with business jets. Projected as the eventual replacement of the King Air series, but with a development cost of some $550 million, the Starship represented a major risk for Raytheon. A proof-of-concept test model at 85 percent scale, built by Burt Rutan's Scaled Composites development firm in California, was first flown on August 29, 1983. Then the full-scale prototype was first flown on February 15, 1986. Scaled Composites, Inc., founded in 1982, was acquired by Beech in June 1985, but was then resold to Burt Rutan in November 1988, reportedly after some differences between Rutan and Beech management.

Cessna, successful with smaller business jets, moved up the scale with the large Citation III. Designed with a supercritical swept wing, the Citation III first flew on May 30, 1979, and went into production in 1980. Cessna delivered the 1000th Citation early in 1982. The Citation S/II, with a supercritical wing, appeared in 1984, succeeding the earlier straight-winged models. The lower-cost Citation VI and more powerful Citation VII were developments of the Citation III, but another development, the Citation IV, was cancelled in 1990.

Another major product development was the Caravan, a capacious single-turboprop utility design which first flew on December 9, 1982. A logical step up for Cessna from its Skywagon and Stationair utility models, as well as a potential replacement for the veteran De Havilland Canada Beaver and Otter bush aircraft, the Caravan could also be equipped with floats. The Caravan captured a substantial worldwide market, and in addition was ordered by the Air Force as the U-27A for supply to foreign air arms under the Foreign Military Sales (FMS) program.

Cessna's cumulative production total reached 172,000 in 1982, but production of its smaller models was declining rapidly. The push-pull Model 337 ended in April 1980, and the veteran Models 180 and 310 ended their long production lives in 1981. More than 5,000 of the 310 series had been built. A new T303 Crusader light twin, initially powered by 160 hp piston engines, first flew on February 14, 1978. The T303 entered production in 1981 with 250 hp engines, but then was suspended in 1985 in the continuing retrenchment by Cessna. In any event, the T303, while more spacious, became regarded as somewhat inferior to the 310 series. The three Cessna production plants were consolidated into a single aircraft division in 1984, reflecting the drop in demand, a move that also involved major layoffs.

The last major independent general aviation firm, Cessna agreed to become a subsidiary of General Dynamics Corporation on March 3, 1985, for $660 million cash. General Dynamics chairman David S. Lewis already served on the Cessna board. The merger became effective on September 13, 1985. Dwane Wallace, possibly the most consistently successful executive in the history of general aviation, died in 1989, age 77. He reportedly had become disenchanted with his successor Russ Meyer, and left the board and sold most of his Cessna stock in 1983.

Remaining smaller general aviation firms sustained production, but at sharply reduced levels. Republic Steel, owner of Mooney, was acquired by the conglomerate LTV Corporation in 1984. Continuing its ownership odyssey, Mooney thereupon was sold to a private investor group which formed the Mooney Holding Company. The subsidiary Mooney Aircraft Corporation was under the management of LeRoy P. LoPresti, previously with Grumman American. Then French Investors, led by the entrepreneur Alexandre Couvelaire, acquired 70 percent of Mooney in the spring of 1985. The remaining 30 percent was acquired by Armand Rivard, another French entrepreneur who also controlled Lake Amphibians. A restructuring in February 1986 was followed by Rivaud's sale of his interest in September. Couvelaire served as chairman of Mooney and controlled strategy.[7] Robert Cromer was brought in as general manager, and Jacques Esculier later became CEO under Couvelaire. Annual production fell from more than 400 in 1979 to 90 in 1985, but development continued of the basic four-seat low-wing retractable gear M-20 design. Al Mooney, long retired from Lockheed, died in 1985 at age 79.

Production of the Lake LA-4 Buccaneer continued steadily in New Hampshire, with the 1,000 model of the series delivered in 1980. The Buccaneer was phased out of production in 1984, being succeeded by the refined Renegade, which could seat up to six. The factory relocated to Kissimmee, Florida, in 1987, although headquarters remained in Laconia. The Renegade, while rather expensive for the time at some $250,000, remained the only piston-powered amphibian in the world. The market for the model was, in fact, primarily international. The Renegade was joined by the Turbo 270 Renegade and by the SeaFury model for saltwater operation.

Bellanca production consisted of the Viking and the new Aries T-250, an Anderson, Greenwood design. But with increasing financial problems due to declining business, Anderson, Greenwood, and Co., liquidated the Bellanca Division in 1981. Then Viking Aviation, organized by most of the former managers and officers of Bellanca, purchased the rights and organized a new Bellanca, Inc., on May 7, 1982. Production of the Viking was eventually reinstated in 1984, at low volume. The firm filled an order from the Turkish Army for 30 Citabria trainers during 1982–1983, the only military order for the type. The Champion line was sold by Bellanca, Inc., in August 1982 to a new Champion Aircraft Company in Houston, Texas, but that venture failed in 1985.

Ayres maintained low-volume production of its Thrush Commander line of agricultural aircraft. But as was the case with other market segments, demand for agricultural aircraft declined, Maule Aircraft Corporation entered Chapter 11 bankruptcy late in 1984, largely as a defense against product liability suits, but the successor Maule Air, Inc., resumed production of the upgraded MX-7 series from its veteran basic design. Taylorcraft, with a low level of activity, was purchased by a group of former Piper executives, including William T. Piper, Jr., on July 9, 1985. Production was moved to the recently closed Piper factory in Lock Haven, but the company soon became financially shaky again and entered Chapter 11 proceedings late in 1986.

Fairchild's Swearingen subsidiary, exclusively in the 19-seat commuter segment, was renamed Fairchild Aircraft Corporation in September 1982 but remained operationally autonomous from the parent Fairchild Industries. Ed Swearingen departed Fairchild Aircraft afterward and established a new Swearingen Aircraft Corporation at the end of the year to pursue new business aircraft developments.

Spurred in part by its difficulties in the military and commercial sectors at the time, Fairchild Industries sold Fairchild Aircraft Corporation and rights to the Metro to GMF Investments of California, a venture capital firm. The transaction took place in December 1987, after negotiations with Aeritalia of Italy fell through. The sale appeared to end the uncertainly over the Metro, and the improved Metro III, with longer wingspan and four-blade propellers, appeared in 1988. But under its new owner, the company soon became embroiled in a lawsuit with British Aerospace Corporation in which BAe alleged that Fairchild had acted to undermine prospects in North America for its competitive Jetstream. Fairchild first sued BAe late in 1988, but BAe responded with a $225 million countersuit. After Sanwa, its major Japanese financier, withheld credit, Fairchild Aircraft declared Chapter 11 bankruptcy on February 1, 1990, to defend itself against the contingent liability created by the lawsuit. GMF ousted the Fairchild management but continued production at low volume.[8] There were subsequent discussions with Mooney's French owners of a Fairchild-Mooney combination, but in September 1990 the firm was acquired by Carl Albert, formerly a regional airline executive, backed by $35 million in new Japanese financing. Metro production continued, including the C-26 version for the Army.[9]

Gulfstream American continued to expand in general aviation, and its success with the Gulfstream made it a major firm along with Beech, Cessna,

Piper, and Learjet. Rockwell International had reluctantly decided that the single-engined and business aircraft market was not viable for a primarily military firm, and planned to exit. Gulfstream purchased the Rockwell International General Aviation Division on February 3, 1981, effectively ending Rockwell's involvement but enhancing Gulfstream's stature in general aviation. Its status as a comprehensive general aviation manufacturer would also prove of short duration, however, as its Commander division soon ended production of the Shrike Commander. Production continued of the pressurized Aero Commander models 840, 900, 980, and 1000. The models 840 and 980 originally were intended to replace the Turbo Commander 690B, but production of those models also ceased late in 1983. Only 21 Aero Commander models were delivered in 1984, reflecting to a high degree the seriously overcrowded twin-engined business aircraft segment.

The market decline then led to the phaseout of all original Aero Commander models, with production permanently discontinued in January 1985. The Bethany, Oklahoma production facility was closed.[10] The event marked the end of more than 35 years of production, extending from the late 1940s and totaling some 3,000 units of the basic Aero Commander design.

Having ended production of the former Grumman American models earlier, Gulfstream American again became an essentially single-product company. It initiated the extensively developed Gulfstream IV in April 1982, with lengthened fuselage, redesigned wings, and more advanced Rolls-Royce Tay engines. The Gulfstream IV first flew on September 19, 1985, and gained immediate market acceptance. Although costing in the $25 million range, the Gulfstream IV held a market advantage in that potential purchasers were less likely to be affected by a recession than those considering smaller jets. Grumman remained a subcontractor, and wings were manufactured by Vought Aircraft in Texas.

Allen Paulson renamed the firm Gulfstream Aerospace Corporation on November 15, 1982. He sold the company to Chrysler Corporation on August 16, 1985, for $637 million, but remained as manager. Chrysler, strongly profitable at the time but the least diversified of the auto companies, viewed aerospace diversification as a priority. In a later auto market downturn, however, Chrysler decided that it could not afford the investment necessary to keep Gulfstream competitive. Paulson then repurchased the company from Chrysler through the investment firm Forstmann Little in February 1989, paying a premium price of $825 million.[11] Forstmann Little became the major stockholder in Gulfstream.

Rockwell International disposed of its last civil aircraft program, the Sabreliner, by selling the Sabreliner Corporation subsidiary to the investment banking firm of Wolsey and Co. in July 1983. The operation remained in St, Louis, but with activity primarily in modification and product support. Sabreliner new production ended in 1981, but the new corporation sustained the significant fleet of more than 800 Sabreliners as well as attracting subcontracting business.

Production of the Learjet Models 28/29 Longhorn was suspended in 1982 due to the slow market. The Model 55 Longhorn, a major redesign and the first of the larger 50-series, first flew on April 19, 1979, and entered production. The Longhorn name was later dropped. By the end of 1984 Learjet production had reached 1,000, but all production was suspended in that year due to market conditions. In addition, the radical Lear Fan 2100 pusher-engined development, undertaken by a separate company with Saudi financial backing, was terminated in June 1985, with FAA certification unattained after some $120 million had been spent.[12]

When Learjet production resumed, the Model 31, combining the fuselage of the Model 35/36 with the new wing of the Model 55, was delivered from 1987. The Air Force ordered 80 Model 35s as the C-21A. Gates Learjet, holding a valuable tax loss carryback, in September 1987 sold a 64.8 percent interest to Integrated Acquisition, Inc., a subsidiary of Integrated Resources, primarily a real estate investment firm. The firm was renamed Learjet Corporation, and production returned to Wichita by January 1988.

The Homebuilt Sector Grows

Development of a viable homebuilt or kitplane segment of general aviation had been largely achieved by the late 1960s. The major impetus for the segment remained that steadily escalating prices of factory-built aircraft enhanced the cost savings of kit construction, a primary consideration of sport and recreational pilots. Pride of construction also remained a factor, but a major obstacle to further growth was that the market for very small single-seat sportplanes, many of which were biplanes, was very narrow. Thus development of a stable and profitable business on that basis alone appeared almost unattainable. Those interested retained their enthusiasm, but there appeared to be little potential for a sustainable industry in that sector. Enthusiasts for such aircraft almost inevitably built them for personal use only.

Another obstacle to development of the homebuilt segment had been that all required certification by the FAA in either the normal or utility categories, which often was a protracted process. But recognition of the experimental category by the CAA, later FAA, had given flyers an alternative to often-restrictive certification procedures. Flight test requirements were far less complex. The experimental category incidentally, included racing, exhibition, and pure research and development aircraft, as well as aerobatic and sport airplanes.

A new or emerging factor that expanded the potential of the kitplane segment was the increasing business use of homebuilt aircraft. Design emphasis expanded from small single-seat aerobatic or sport models toward more capacious models suitable for business use. Aerodynamics became more advanced. Once again, entrepreneurship in general aviation was enhanced, as expanded roles for kitplanes, including business use, attracted new competitors. Further, entry costs for a new kitplane firm remained far lower than for an entry into factory production of complete aircraft.

Prominent among those attracted to the field by its growth and potential for further growth was James Bede. An innovative designer of light aircraft, Bede founded his company in Springfield, Ohio. The two-seat Bede BD-1, which first flew on July 11, 1963, was developed into the successful American Aviation AA-1 Yankee production version previously described. Bede then developed a series of innovative designs under his BD designation prefix for home construction. Over 2,000 sets of plans for the BD-4 two-seat cabin model were sold. He followed with a developed BD-4 and four-seat BD-6, and still later with the BD-8 single-seat light aerobatic model.

But the radical BD-5 Micro engulfed the company in controversy. A very small, swept-wing, mid-engined pusher design, the BD-5 was claimed to be capable of 200 mph even though powered by only a 26 hp engine. It was also claimed to required only 300 hours of assembly time and was promoted as a mass-market small aircraft. The airplane was sold to home builders in a series of sequential subkits, but serious delays in shipments of the engine subassemblies developed, and there were also severe cooling problems with the pusher engine installation. (Pusher engines did not enjoy the natural engine cooling effect by the propwash of tractor installations.) As a result, the Bede company experienced unstable operations throughout the 1970s, and its reputation suffered. It finally declared bankruptcy in 1979, leaving many builders without the necessary subkits to complete their aircraft.[13] While perhaps unique, the Micro episode served to illustrate the numerous pitfalls of the homebuilt or kitplane business.

The homebuilt dichotomy remained that sets of plans were sold for "scratch" construction, and sets of components were sold for amateur assembly. Some firms offered both, and some kit producers also offered ultralight/microlight models. There were, in addition, offerings of kit-built autogiros and helicopters, and of light pusher-engined amphibians. Regardless, all kits or plans were marketed on the claim that they were relatively east to build by those of average skills and that man-hours required were manageable, but the low rate of actual registered aircraft to plan/kit sales belied the claims. Aviation trade periodicals were replete with advertisements of partially completed kit models for sale by their owners.

The EAA had been founded for experimental designers and builders.

But as it grew, the EAA was somewhat surprised to learn that it had effectively inherited a complete segment of the general aviation industry, that of smaller single-engined sport and aerobatic aircraft. That status, however, was largely due to the withdrawal from that category by the factory producers, a reaction to product liability costs and overall economics.

A major spur to growth of the homebuilt segment was the 51 percent rule of the FAA, extending from that established by the CAA. The rule stated that if a homebuilder completed 51 percent of an aircraft, that builder also qualified for a repairman certificate. The practical benefit of the rule was the recognition by the FAA that anyone building 51 percent or more of an airplane also was qualified to service the aircraft and thus could perform 100-hour inspections and other maintenance, realizing major cost savings.

The 51 percent rule also pointed out the trade-off inherent in kit construction, that is, the more complete the kit, with preassembled components, precut holes, and precut parts, the less is required of the homebuilder, but at a much higher cost. A rule of thumb developed that for a given amount of cost for work performed by the kit supplier, the cost to the homebuilder is double that amount. Consequently, the less done by the kit supplier, the more that is required by the homebuilder, subsequently with greater potential for error, but at much lower cost. Decisions thus were required over such matters as predrilled holes and preassembled components by the kit supplier. The Christen Eagle, a popular small aerobatic model, was threatened with violation of the 51 percent rule, and designer Frank Christensen made changes to increase the amount of home construction required, thus winning approval from FAA inspectors.[14]

In practical terms, the 51 percent rule meant that the builder must complete between 51 percent and 100 percent of the aircraft. Thus a supplier simply providing plans and a few components that required the amateur builder to build 90 percent would still comply with the 51 percent rule.

A further advantage of the 51 percent rule was that it circumvented product liability for the manufacturer or supplier. If more than 51 percent of an airplane was built by an amateur, the manufacturers of the kit could not be held liable for any design or construction flaws. The rule further protected the kit producers in that factory producers were effectively prevented from offering nearly complete aircraft for which purchasers could finish details for cost savings. Since the factory built more than 51 percent, product liability still applied. Further, such aircraft still were required to be serviced by a certified mechanic.

The contemporary homebuilt segment dates from the mid–1970s. As before, the purely sport or recreational flying segment simply offered little market potential for factory-built aircraft, but rapidly escalating prices of all factory-built aircraft increased market potential for kit aircraft. The additional growth potential of kit-produced business aircraft led to new and advanced kit designs for that purpose. Some featured aerodynamic advances over factory aircraft. Single-engined design by established producers had not progressed significantly since the 1960s, and production declines during the product liability crisis did not aid aeronautical advances. Further, such popular designs as the high-winged Cessna models dated from the 1940s, leaving a potential design gap for kit designers to exploit. A structural advance was the increased use of composites in kitplanes, but composites also possessed drawbacks for small aircraft over traditional materials such as wood or aluminum. Composites had no "give" and tended to shatter on impact, which created a new safety concern.

The homebuilt/kitplane industry segment finally attained major importance in general aviation in the 1980s, appearing to join the mainstream. The major market opportunity for competitors in the field lay with the decline or virtual disappearance of factory-built light aircraft, especially small trainers. Accordingly, whatever market existed for small single-seat sport or aerobatic aircraft was filled, as before, by the kitplane suppliers, as those models had never been a significant factor in factory-built aircraft. The homebuilt sector thus helped preserve the sport/recreational segment and also served as a partial offset to the decline in factory production. Business aircraft use, also price-sensitive, enabled homebuilt business aircraft to grow, and even homebuilt agricultural models appeared. In addition, export potential for kits increased, especially to Europe, where general aviation operations, including fuel, remained substantially more expensive than in North America.

Choice of designs for home construction was widespread and the price range was broad, but one problem remaining for potential amateur builders, and for the growth of the segment, was that the business was unstable; kit manufacturers went out of business regularly. And as a growth industry, most active firms were of recent origin. The average age of kitplane companies was only six years, and designs were traded among firms frequently. Yet maintenance of stable demand or strong market growth required the base of a stable industry. The segment also possessed an international dimension, as European and other foreign designs were licensed to U.S. firms. In addition, the small Rotax engine from Austria, a light two-stroke model in the 50–100 hp class, was a popular powerplant for the smaller homebuilts.

The 1995–1996 Edition of *Jane's All the World's Aircraft* listed no fewer than 36 suppliers of plans or kits (or both) in the United States, although even more existed. Level of activity varied, of course. The following survey describes the more important firms during that time, including some that also built complete aircraft in addition to kits and plans. Interestingly, many firms were located in the Pacific Northwest states of Washington, Oregon, and Idaho.

Stoddard-Hamilton Aircraft, Inc., of Arlington, Washington, was founded in 1979 by Tom Hamilton, assisted by partner Ted Setzer. Stoddard-Hamilton offered the Glasair line, originally designed by Tom Hamilton, with a structure of molded composites and advanced electronics. Hamilton was regarded as a pioneer of composite construction for small aircraft. The original Glasair flew in 1979, and the Glasair II-S and III, with retractable gear and higher performance, succeeded the earlier model. Representing the high end of the homebuilt field in performance, the new Glasair Super II offered 250 mph speed and was available in retractable, fixed tricycle, and taildragger landing gear configurations. Broadening its coverage, the company introduced in 1996 the GlasStar, an entry-level small model, with a kit priced at $19,000. GlasAir models emphasized expedited construction, and were joined by the Sportsman 2+2, with Lycoming power. The original company was sold to employees in 1987, and Hamilton formed a new Glasair Corporation in that year. Glasair was later acquired by the Chinese Jilin Hanxing Group, and operated as Glasair USA, LLC.

Europa Aviation, Inc., of Lakeland, Florida, offered the Europa line. The Europa, a simple low-wing taildragger-gear design powered by an 80 hp Rotax, was designed and developed in the United Kingdom. The U.S. subsidiary marketed the line for the American market.

Neico Aviation of Santa Paula, California, originally manufactured parts for the industry and provided aircraft modification services. It soon expanded into kit production with the Lancair line, named after the designer and founder Lance Neibauer. Neibauer, originally from Michigan, had experience with Meyers Aircraft before starting his own firm. He then founded Lancair in 1981 to develop small high-performance kit designs with advanced aerodynamics. With a relocation to Redmond, Oregon, the firm was renamed Lancair International, and the first Lancair flew in June 1984. The two-seat models 200 and 235 featured a Kevlar composite structure. The later four-seat Lancair IV was claimed to be the fastest kitplane, and its promise led the company toward full factory production. Other models included the 360, ES, and Super ES, which was developed as the LC40, a fixed-gear four-seat model.

Volmer Aircraft of Glendale, California, offered the VJ-22 Sportsman amphibian. Volmer Jensen, a noted sailplane designer, broadened his activities to include amphibians. Possibly the most promising firm was Cirrus Design Corporation, founded in Baraboo, Wisconsin in 1984. Cirrus was established originally for kit production but relocated to Duluth, Minnesota, with plans to move toward full factory production of its designs. President Alan Klapmeier became a leading figure in the field. The first Cirrus Design model to receive FAA certification was the ST-50, developed in collaboration with Israviation of Israel. The ST-50, a five-seat high-performance pusher turboprop for business use, went into production in Israel. The domestic Cirrus Design VK30 advanced pusher-engined 4–5 seat model first flew on February 11, 1988. The initial kit price was $42,500, including engine, propeller, and electronics, but the VK30 program suffered a setback when a test pilot was killed in a crash on March 22, 1996.

7—The General Aviation Crisis

An entirely new Cirrus Design model, the SR-20, was developed beginning in 1990. A modern, economical, low-wing four-seat all-composite model for factory construction, the SR-20 was initially projected to sell for $130,000. Major components were built at a new factory in Grand Forks, North Dakota. The state had enacted laws to head off aircraft product liability suits, which attracted Cirrus.

Scaled Composites, Ltd., founded by Burt Rutan in 1982, continued to be a factor in the homebuilt field, although its activities were much broader. Scaled Composites was a separate venture from the original Rutan Aircraft Company formed in the 1960s. The Rutan-designed VariEze was begun in 1974 and first flew on May 21, 1975. The larger, more powerful LongEZ first flew on June 12, 1979. It became a popular homebuilt model for cutting-edge pilots. Both were then-radical composite designs with canard configurations. Rutan had worked for Bede earlier, and much Bede influence was evident in his emphasis on composites and advanced electronics. Rutan continued as a leader in advanced concepts, especially with the VariEze. Although powered by an aft-mounted pusher engine, it avoided the cooling problems experienced by the BD-5. The design provided stability as well as high performance. Rutan operated Scaled Composites independently after reacquiring it from Beech in November 1988.

Another growing firm was Aviat Aircraft, Inc., of Afton, Wyoming. Frank Christensen, a California native and Stanford University graduate, had founded his original Christen firm in the early 1970s. He designed the Christen Eagle, mentioned earlier, a small fully aerobatic biplane which competed with the designs of Ray Stits. While superficially similar to the Stits models, it was in fact considerably different. Christensen earlier had attempted to purchase rights from Stits, who declined to sell. The Eagle kit was originally priced in the $25,000 range. Curtiss Pitts had operated in Afton, and Christen instead acquired Pitts Aerobatics rights in November 1983, but later ceased marketing plans or kits. The Christen Eagle II, a high-performance model with a 200 hp Lycoming and intended for kit construction, made its first flight in February 1977. The Eagle II led to the formation of Christen Industries in 1984. Activities of Christen and Pitts eventually were consolidated at Afton. Curtiss Pitts remained active in experimental aircraft.

Christen then was acquired in April 1991 by Aviat, a subsidiary of a British company, and took the name Aviat Aircraft, Inc. Malcolm White became the new owner and Frank Christensen retired. Aviat operated in the old CallAir facilities, which it expanded over time. The Aviat A-1 Husky, a factory-built two-seat light utility aircraft reminiscent of the Super Cub, was designed by Herb Anderson and Christensen in 1987 and enjoyed steadily increasing sales. In fact, the Husky bid to replace the Super Cub in utility roles. Aviat also offered factory-built Pitts models S-1T, S-2B, and S-2S to order.

The Aviat Husky, a successful light utility aircraft (Aviat Aircraft, Inc.).

The Eagle II remained on the market, but kit production was a minority of total Aviat business. While remaining popular, the Eagle II kit rose in price to $55, 000, less engine and propeller. Then a new investor, Stuart Horn, purchased Aviat in December 1995 and further expanded operations. Aviat later acquired the type certificate to the old Globe Swift from Piper, intending to restart production in the future.[15]

SkyStar of Nampa, Idaho, took over the popular KitFox design, which first flew on May 7, 1984, from Denney Aerocraft Co., its original developer. *Fortune* reported in 1983 that the KitFox, a simple-side-by-side, high-winged STOL model, was the best-selling kit model, with 2,000 sold from 1984 to 1993. Denney thereafter was reported to have purchased the Pulsar line from Aero Designs of San Antonio, Texas. The basic Pulsar, a low-wing two-seat modern design with Rotax power, carried a kit base price of $21,500, rising to $27,500 for the more powerful Pulsar XP.

Sequoia Aircraft Corp., of Richmond, Virginia, was founded in 1975. Sequoia developed its original models 300 and 302 for kit construction, but a more significant move was the acquisition of rights to the Italian Falco (Falcon) F-8L. The Falco was a progression from an original design by the noted Italian engineer Stelio Frati which had first flown in 1955. A modern two-seat retractable-gear low-wing model, the Falco was offered by Sequoia for home construction at a basic kit cost of $60,000.

The Pitts S-2B aerobatic airplane, as built to order by Aviat Aircraft (Aviat Aircraft, Inc.).

James Bede, determined to remain in the industry, established a successor in St. Louis, Missouri. He pursued advanced developments of the BD-12 and BD-14 pusher-engined models that continued the basic concept of the ill-fated BD-5. Both were powered by an 80 hp Rotax. BD-12 kit prices ranged from $21,500 to $40,000 at 1995 levels, less engine, propeller, and instrumentation. A further marketing innovation was that Bede announced plans to market kits through upscale automobile and boat dealerships. Bede also designed the BD-10 civil two-seat supersonic personal craft, production rights for which were sold to Peregrine Flight International of Nevada. Peregrine planned full factory production but also planned to offer the BD-10 in kit form. Completed cost at the time was expected to be approximately $1.4 million, but the BD-10 never flew.

Further strong market contenders included Rans, Inc., of Hays, Kansas, and Zenith of Mexico, Missouri. The name Rans came from its owner and designer, Randy J. Schlitter, and the firm had designed and marketed a series of small homebuilt designs. The S-7 Courier, a Rotax-powered two-seat STOL model, appeared to be a strong contender. Zenith was established in Missouri in 1993 after acquiring rights to originally Canadian designs, and offered the

Zenair CH series of light monoplanes for the U.S. market. A third contender was Van's Aircraft, Inc., of North Plains, Oregon, with a name derived from its founder and engineer, Richard VanGrunsven. Beginning in 1973 with his first original design, the RV-3, Van's went on to success with production of a series of kitplanes.

Among older names, Taylor Aerocar, Inc., after deciding that regulations and economics had effectively blocked a flying automobile market, attempted an entry into kit construction for its roadable airplane, without success. David B. Thurston, still active in amphibians, designed and marketed the TA-16 Trojan four-seat pusher amphibian for kit assembly, but sales were limited.

A more recent factor in the homebuilt sector, gaining in significance, was the increasing crossover between traditional factory builders and kitplane or plans suppliers. Aviat, Cirrus Design, and Bede were prominent examples. But there was no evidence of the reverse, of factory builders interested in offering kits of their models.

Numbers of amateur-built aircraft on the civil registry grew fairly steadily. Registration totaled 2,865 in 1971, growing to 7,496 by the end of 1981. By 1985 the number exceeded 10,000 and grew to 19,104 registered by July 1, 1997.[16] In addition, there were several hundred racing aircraft on the registry. Attendance at annual EAA Fly-Ins grew to more than 800,000 people. While the actual number of homebuilt aircraft remained difficult to track, it was determined that by 1990, the number of kits supplied to homebuilders exceeded shipments of factory-built small aircraft by at least two to one.[17] A key role of the EAA was assisting aspiring homebuilders in their task. The homebuilt pioneer Bernard Pietenpohl died on January 14, 1984, at age 83. He had lived long enough to gain wide recognition for his efforts of 50 years earlier.

It remained difficult to compile annual values of aircraft built from kits due to the range of value added by homebuilder and to high noncompletion rates. One recent estimate was that the completion rate from kits was 63 percent, while that from plans was less than 5 percent. But there was no question that the impact of the experimental and homebuilt segment had effectively replaced the traditional factory-built small trainer segment.

Helicopter Survey

The civil helicopter market suffered a serious decline from 1980, even as helicopter capabilities advanced and functions and roles broadened. Among other factors, the helicopter had acquired increasing importance in traditional bush flying and in logging. Canada, in fact, was the second-largest civil helicopter market in the world. Still, most competitors struggled. Reasons for the market decline were many, but strongly reflected the slump in offshore oil activity at the time, previously a strong growth area; sharply rising product liability costs; expense and availability of operator's insurance; a large fleet of good used helicopters; noise and safety concerns; and continuing high operating costs.[18] A further limitation in demand for new helicopters appearing from the late 1980s was the increased release of surplus smaller military helicopters to the civil market.

Military downsizing meant, among other things, an excess helicopter inventory, and many were similar to civil models and readily adaptable. Police forces in particular were beneficiaries. Yet development continued to be active, and competitors determined to enter or remain in the market, as the following survey recounts.

Brantly-Hynes, in another name change, became Hynes Helicopter, Inc., in 1984, but with declining business the firm closed and all assets were placed up for sale in 1987. New interests purchased all rights for the B-2B and Model 305 from Hynes Aviation Industries in March 1989. A new Brantly Helicopter Industries was incorporated on May 8, 1989, in Texas, with plans to restart production, but that venture faded also.

F. Lee Bailey, facing heavy development expenses, sold Enstrom to a private investment group, Bravo Investment, B.V., of the Netherlands in January 1980. Bailey left the helicopter field. Then in September 1984, Bravo resold Enstrom to a new American investor group, including the inventor Dean Kamen. The developed TH-28 competed for the Army New Training Helicopter (NTH) contract, but lost to Bell. Civil production continued, including turbine-powered models, but Enstrom still suffered in being underpriced by the Robinson line. Rudy Enstrom reentered the helicopter field in 1979 as chief engineer for Douglas Hillman, who was developing a new light helicopter in Phoenix. Hillman, however, died in a crash, and the project ended as well.

Robinson continued to lead the light piston-powered helicopter segment. The company delivered its 1,000th helicopter on March 30, 1989. In the recession year of 1990, a conspicuous success was the delivery of 402 R22 models, and total production reached 2,260 on November 30, 1992. Robinson announced the four-seat R44 in 1989, still relatively inexpensive, which won 50 orders by 1992. Robinson emphasized the export market for the R44 to avoid the product liability situation in the domestic market.

Hiller Aviation finally acquired rights to the Fairchild FH-1100 in April 1980. The company could not finance a resumption of series production, however, and suffered bankruptcy on January 23, 1984, leading to its sale to Rogerson Aircraft Corporation in April 1984. Hiller Helicopters then operated as a wholly owned subsidiary of the renamed Rogerson-Hiller Corporation. The firm relocated to Port Angeles, Washington, where it won some subcontracting orders from Boeing, but helicopter production remained suspended.

The sailplane manufacturer Schweizer, having purchased all Ag-Cat rights from Grumman in January 1981, and continuing production of an advanced version, also acquired rights to the Hughes 300 civil helicopter on July 13, 1983. Schweizer thus became more heavily committed to powered aircraft. Hughes sold its smaller civil line after demand had declined, and Schweizer produced the Model 300 primarily for the training market. The developed business Model 330, with a base price of $517,000, also entered production. The Model 330 also lost the competition for the Army NTH order.

Bell Helicopter Textron was incorporated as a wholly owned subsidiary of Textron, Inc., on January 3, 1982. BHT then established a wholly owned Bell Helicopter Canada (BHC) subsidiary in Montreal in October 1983 to specialize in civil market production, which allowed the parent to concentrate on military production in Texas. The investment was spurred by incentives provided by the Canadian government.

Production of the JetRanger line began to be transferred to the new location during 1985. The larger Models 212 and 412 were transferred to Canada in mid–1988 and 1989, respectively, and the Model 206LT Light Twin was added to the 206 series in 1992. The Model 412 also was produced under license by Agusta in Italy, The 412 was intended as the successor to the 212, but the 212 remained in production in response to steady demand. But initially strong demand for the Model 222 intermediate twin, still produced in Texas, faded in the general market decline, and production ended in 1988 with 182 built. The improved successor Model 230, first flying on August 12, 1991, also sold slowly in the sluggish market, and production ended in 1995 at 38 machines.

Helicopter development was undertaken both at Fort Worth and Montreal, but approximately half of all components for Canadian production were supplied from Fort Worth. All BHC helicopters, with the exception of those for the Canadian market, were sold to the Texas parent for resale. (For purposes of this study, BHC is covered as a U.S. firm, as is Learjet, owned by Bombardier from 1991.) A major order came in 1991 for 66 JetRangers and 88 LongRangers from Petroleum Helicopters, Inc. (PHI), for its oil service operations.

Another important step for BHC was the Army NTH competition, won by the TH-67 Creek, which was derived from the JetRanger III. An initial order for 102 was placed in March 1993. The TH-67 was built in Canada as well.

In March 1982, Sikorsky began deliveries of the improved S-76 Mark II. The largest general aviation helicopter at that time, the S-76's capacity and performance made it favored over smaller models for servicing oil platforms despite its $6-$7 million price. McDonnell Douglas acquired Hughes Helicopters of Mesa, Arizona, from the Hughes estate in January 1984. The operation was renamed McDonnell Douglas Helicopter Company (MDHC) on August 27, 1985, with headquarters remaining at Mesa. While primarily involved with military attack helicopters, MDHC became increasingly oriented toward the civil helicopter market. The Model 500, developed from the LOH military design, won some orders. Then the advanced NOTAR (no tail rotor)

The Sikorsky S-76A first production delivery, February 27, 1979, in oil service configuration (Igor I. Sikorsky Historical Archives © November 2018).

development, with lateral control by deflected air flows, resulted in the MD 520N (NOTAR) of 1989, based on the Model 500 but extensively redesigned. It was funded by a defense contract. The MD520N held promise for civil markets as well as military applications, with the first civil delivery occurring in November 1991.

Product Liability

Product liability lawsuits, in which manufacturers were held financially liable for crashes and resulting injuries and fatalities due to findings of design or production flaws, began to devastate general aviation aircraft production by the early 1980s. Although reflecting in part the overall litigiousness of American society, the trend had a greater impact on general aviation than on other, larger industries. Product liability became defined so broadly in legal proceedings that even an engine failure could be ruled a design or manufacturing defect, although it had always been recognized in aviation that any man-made engine could fail, however rarely. For that reason, no single-engined aircraft were allowed to operate as commercial airliners. Increasing court awards began to inhibit production of single-engined models, always the heart of general aviation and numerically the most prominent. This in turn precipitated a downward spiral in which enrollment in flight schools, always expensive, declined further, leading to a decline in demand for new trainers. Light trainer production in the United States ended entirely.

The crisis developed slowly. By 1971 it was realized that liability costs to manufacturers had increased 15-fold over the decade. Previous amounts were nominal by comparison. Bill Piper, Jr., first raised the product liability concern with GAMA in that year. Product liability suits appeared with increasing frequency during the 1970s but appeared manageable at the time. Beech, for example, after defending itself against several suits, won a major class action suit in federal court in January 1973, in which all pending product liability litigation against the firm was dismissed.[19]

By the early 1980s, however, product liability had mushroomed into a major crisis. Insurers began to base premiums not on the value of the airplane but on the potential magnitude of a court-awarded liability settlement, and liability insurance became so expensive that it threatened the financial viability of general aviation manufacturers. As more lawsuits occurred, the broad societal choice, as represented by juries, was toward the manufacturer as the provider of relief. Attorneys for the manufacturers increasingly advised out-of-court settlements when possible as the more expeditious solution, but that in turn damaged the firms' reputation for quality.[20]

The average manufacturer's liability insurance premium per single-engined plane rose from about $2,000 in 1972 to the $60,000 to $100,000 range by 1998, often doubling the cost of a single aircraft.[21] Actual cash outlays by the industry for court judgments, settlements and defense costs soared tenfold, from $24 million in 1977 to $210 million in 1985.[22] Moreover, there was no time limit; the "liability tail" extended to all aircraft ever produced by a firm, which in some cases covered more than 50 years. A new owner of an established general aviation firm thus faced potential liability for aircraft built decades before by a predecessor company, and resulting insurance costs were reflected in the price of new aircraft. Furthermore, the fact of FAA certification was no defense against claims of design flaws, which ironically served to inhibit product improvements in that they might be interpreted as an admission by the manufacturer that it was correcting a design flaw.[23] Despite the deepening problems, manufacturers won most product liability suits, but the litigation expense and massive awards involved in those suits lost still proved to be nearly devastating. Manufacturers in general pressed for imposition for a Statute of Repose for product liability, advocating a time limit of 10 to 12 years as reasonable, But legislative relief encountered strong opposition, particularly from the Association of Trial Lawyers of America (ATLA). An early bill stalled in the U.S. Senate in 1985. It appeared that the general aviation industry simply lacked the political influence necessary to obtain relief.

John W. R. Taylor, editor of the authoritative *Jane's* aviation reference publication, in his preface to the 1989–1990 Edition, characterized the general aviation problem as "crippling and ludicrous liability litigation waged by unscrupulous lawyers." He went on to praise new Piper owner M. Stuart Millar's attempt to fight such suits in the courts with staff attorneys rather than relying on insurance.[24]

In addition to product liability, unfavorable changes in federal tax laws, including lower allowable depreciation for business aircraft and elimination of the investment tax credit (ITC) in 1986, previously applicable in business aircraft purchases, further diminished aircraft sales. Generally high interest rates through the decade also were an adverse factor, and high interest rates continued from 1979. Costs of replacement models, driven by liability insurance, were sharply higher than earlier models, leading to declining new aircraft demand. Airline deregulation from 1978 also resulted in a long-term deleterious effect on the general aviation market, in that the expansion of third-level airlines opening or resuming service to smaller and more remote communities lessened the need for many business users to own and operate their own aircraft.

The general aviation industry bore some responsibility for its decline, however, in that technology and performance of its models during the decline remained similar to those of the late 1950s and early 1960s. In fact, many aircraft in production in the 1990s were developments of 1960 and earlier designs. While there was continuous product refinement, no technological revolution in general aviation aircraft had occurred, and critics charged that the industry followed a cookie-cutter approach to design and production. Yet design conservatism may have been partially dictated by certification difficulties often attending a radically new design. Certification had delayed the Beech Starship, and certification problems also weighed against the innovative Lear Fan 2100, as had been the case earlier with the Custer channel-wing design. Another complication was that most general aviation aircraft were so durable and reliable that with proper maintenance they could last indefinitely. Owners and operators simply felt no need to trade in aircraft every three to five years as automobiles might be replaced. There was no planned obsolescence in aircraft.

The industry also began to realize that, somewhat reminiscent of the market collapse of 1947, the decline was in part due to overproduction in the 1970s. Production had been in excess of underlying demand. One stimulus was that as prices rose rapidly with inflation, speculative buying became a major factor, as buyers in many instances resold their aircraft later at a profit.[25] The market simply became saturated. A decline in demand, particularly in the single-engined segment, inevitably would have occurred even without the product liability crisis.[26] The general aviation sector also appeared to have insufficient competition; it was definitely oligopolistic, with a four-firm concentration ratio of above 85 percent of total business.[27] A possible explanation was that smaller firms simply could not acquire the financial strength and product line diversity to compete in the product liability environment against the larger, financially stronger firms.

The general aviation industry, despite myriad problems, still had not completely collapsed, nor had it been completely destroyed. One view was that it had instead undergone, albeit at great distress, a fundamental structural and technological transformation.[28] As one manifestation, after factory production of small single-engined trainers had been halted, the kitplane segment took off in direct consequence, effectively replacing the factory-built segment and enabling thousands to continue sport flying. Kit aircraft for amateur construction made flying and ownership more affordable in an unfavorable economic environment. In addition, improved kitplane technology enabled the segment to move more closely to the mainstream of general aviation.[29] Growing political influence of the EAA and increasing FAA support for homebuilts also helped.

The general aviation industry, as did the much larger military aerospace sector, regarded itself as a national resource, worthy of societal and political support, especially in a period of crisis. But real stability and sustained prosperity could come only from market expansion, unlikely given the negative legal and economic environments and the pricing structure of general aviation aircraft. Ironically, the market problems worsened as private flying became safer, with fatalities extremely low in relation to hours flown.

Dramatically illustrating the market decline (see Table 7-3), GAMA reported that shipments by its ten manufacturing members totaled only 2,691 aircraft in 1983, the lowest total since 1951, although the value of those aircraft was almost $1.5 billion.[30] The decline in single-engined aircraft production from more than 14,000 in 1978 to only 613 in 1987 further underscored the crisis.[31] Employment in general aviation manufacturing was down to 21,000 by 1985. Cessna commercial aircraft sales declined to 1,217 in 1983 and to only 978 in 1984, down from 6,393 in 1980, and the company sustained a financial loss for 1983.

By 1990 general aviation production was only a shadow of the boom days of the 1960s and 1970s. GAMA members delivered only 1,021 aircraft in 1991, in an environment of overall recession.[32] The civil helicopter market was also depressed. The decline led manufacturers to distribute their products directly, weakening their well-established dealer network.

Table 7-3 Civil Aircraft Shipments, 1980–1995
(Figures are consistent with totals in Table 7-2)

Year	Total	Helicopters	General Aviation
		Quantity	
1980	13,247	1,366	11,881
1981	10,529	1,072	9,457
1982	4,853	587	4,266
1983	3,094	403	2,691*
1984	2,814	376	2,438
1985	2,413	384	2,029
1986	1,825	330	1,495
1987	1,443	358	1,085
1988	1,526	383	1,143
1989	2,050	515	1,535
1990	1,747	603	1,144
1991	1,592	571	1,021
1992	1,223	324	899
1993	1,222	258	964
1994	1,236	308	928
1995	1,369	292	1,077
Year	Total	Helicopters	General Aviation
		Value ($ millions)	
1980	$3,163	$656	$2,507
1981	3,517	597	2,920
1982	2,364	365	1,999
1983	1,773	303	1,470*
1984	2,028	330	1,698
1985	1,937	506	1,431
1986	1,550	288	1,262
1987	1,641	277	1,364
1988	2,252	334	1,918
1989	2,055	251	1,804
1990	2,262	254	2,008
1991	2,179	211	1,968
1992	1,978	142	1,836
1993	2,257	113	2,144
1994	2,542	185	2,357
1995	3,036	194	2,842

*Includes three off-the-shelf Gulfstream IIIs delivered to the U.S. Air Force as C-20 VIP transports.
SOURCE: *Aerospace Facts and Figures, 1996/1997*, p. 32.

One enduring strength and advantage enjoyed by the American general aviation industry was that it remained effectively the world general aviation industry, since no other country possessed a comprehensive technical and production capability in the field. But exports could not offset the domestic decline. Export demand, while always a significant factor, declined as sharply as domestic demand due to economic problems in other markets comparable to those in the United States. In addition, the U.S. dollar, generally strong in relation to other currencies during the 1980s, did not help exports to remain competitive.[33]

* * *

In the midst of a crisis in the general aviation industry, the last remaining major flight record, an unrefueled nonstop around-the-world flight, was achieved during December 14–23, 1986. The Voyager design of Burt Rutan, essentially a general aviation experimental aircraft powered by push-pull Lycoming engines and piloted by Dick Rutan, Burt's brother, and Jeana Yeager, covered more than 25,000 miles. Rutan lacked major financial support, building and testing the craft with his own resources. The feat captured the pioneer spirit of record-setting flights by adventurous aviators, particularly significant during the product liability crisis.

8

The Path to Recovery

By the end of the 1980s general aviation aircraft production had declined to the point that the industry was practically moribund. The year 1985 saw not only twin-engined Aero Commander production ended and Learjet production suspended, but also production shutdowns of numerous smaller models. Piper closed its Lock Haven plant in August 1984 after completing more than 76,000 aircraft at that location.[1] The Lakeland factory closed in October 1985. Beech closed its Liberal, Kansas, plant in August 1985, and soon thereafter closed its Selma and Boulder facilities. Largely out of light business aircraft by that time, Beech consolidated production at a single factory, as had Cessna earlier. The remaining smaller firms essentially produced to order. Business jet sales experienced a modest recovery at the end of the decade, but it was not to endure.

Yet in the face of seemingly overwhelming negative prospects about the general aviation industry and its future, there was no question of its economic importance. Estimates for 1990, for example, were that general aviation contributed $40 billion to the Gross Domestic Product (GDP), accounted for 540,000 jobs, and served 120 million people in the United States in some manner.[2]

Company Developments

Russ Meyer remained CEO of Cessna after the General Dynamics acquisition. He moved immediately to suspend production of all piston-engined aircraft. The Conquest I and II were the last of Cessna's once-extensive twin-engined line to remain in production, but all aircraft other than the Citation series and the Caravan were suspended indefinitely in May 1986. By that time, however, Cessna had built an extraordinary record, producing 35,772 of the 172/Skyhawk/175/Skylark series, 31,340 of the 150/152 series, and 19,812 of the 180/182/Skylane series. Except for the Models 150/152, the figures included those produced by Reims Aviation. In a further contractionary move, Cessna sold its 49 percent interest in Reims, which it had held for almost three decades, in February 1989.³ Reims had produced more than 6,000 aircraft of Cessna design. Cessna was more vulnerable than Piper to product liability awards because of the resources of its large corporate parent, which hastened the decision to suspend production. Employment fell from more than 14,000 in the late 1970s to 3,600 by 1985, the year of the GD acquisition. Meyer, probably the leading spokesman for the general aviation industry, stated that his company would not resume production of single-engined models until product liability laws were reformed.⁴

Cessna continued its business jet leadership, with the Citation series providing continuing profits for the company before and after suspension of other models. The Caravan utility aircraft also continued strong sales, with over 400 produced by 1990. Federal Express remained the largest customer. The lengthened Model 208B Grand Caravan, with a capacity of 14 passengers and priced in the $1 million range, entered production in September 1990, and also found customers.

Mooney continued with its single-engined four-seat line, adding the advanced MSE in 1989 and the turbocharged M-20R Ovation in 1994. Overall production averaged some 100 per year, and in 1995 Mooney passed the production milestone of 10,000 aircraft in its 47-year history. Mooney entered into an international joint venture with the Socata subsidiary of the French national firm Aerospatiale on June 12, 1987, to develop the TBM 700, a large single-turboprop business aircraft. The venture enjoyed 30 percent French government financing, but Mooney withdrew in May 1991. Socata continued the program with the Finnish aircraft firm Valmet, and the TBM 700 won limited orders in the U.S. market.

Only Beech approached a full line of business aircraft, though it no longer produced small trainers. Since the majority of product liability suits involved single-engined and training models, a manufacturer needed the cushion of larger business aircraft to sustain production in single-engined models. Beech had that cushion and thus was able to offer a broad product line. Also, manufacturers were induced to concentrate on large executive aircraft because operators possessed greater maintenance resources, lessening the likelihood of accidents and consequent product liability suits. Liability insurance also was proportionately less costly for more expensive models.

Beech in 1991 offered the continually upgraded King Air C90 and Super King Air series, the Beechjet 400A, the Starship 2000, and the Model 1900. After closing the Selma plant in September 1986, Beech transferred Model 1900 production to Wichita. Beech delivered 255 Model 1900Cs between 1984 and 1991, and the type was largely responsible for Beech's improved earnings in 1988 and 1989, even in the face of the crisis in general aviation. The 1900C was succeeded by the improved Model 1900D, with a standup cabin, which first flew on March 1, 1990. The Model 1900D, while priced in the $5 million range, continued to sell. The piston-powered Bonanza and Baron also continued but constituted only a small percentage of Beech's total sales. May 1996 marked the milestone of more than 3,000 straight-tailed Bonanzas produced since their 1968 introduction, and the Bonanza series marked its 50th anniversary in 1997, a world record for continuous production of a basic design.

The Super King Air became the most successful and best-selling twin turboprop ever produced, with more than 2,000 of the series delivered from 1973. June 1996 marked the milestone of 5,000 King Air/Super King Air deliveries, including all military and export models. The export market remained strong, and almost 10 percent of industry sales were to the U.S. military. Beech achieved another major success when the Beech 400T won the Air Force Tanker Transport Training System (TTTS) order on February 21, 1990, over vigorous competition from the Learjet and the Citation S/II. Designated the T-1A Jayhawk, 180 were ordered for service from 1992.[5] Beech sales were second only to missiles and electronics among Raytheon business lines.

Max Bleck, president of Beech Aircraft, became president of parent company Raytheon on March 1, 1991. Arthur E. Wegner, formerly with United Technologies and a former president of Pratt & Whitney, became Beech chairman and CEO in July 1993. Olive Ann Beech, the most prominent woman executive in the history of the industry, died on July 6, 1993, at the age of 89. Frank Hedrick had died in 1984. Beech completed production of its 50,000th aircraft early in 1993, particularly noteworthy given its historical focus on the higher (and lower unit volume) end of the general aviation market.

Piper continued to contract operations with the market decline, consolidating remaining production at Vero Beach, where a new factory was completed in October 1986. The firm's brightest hope was the PA-46 Malibu turbocharged, six-seat executive model, which gained a strong market share.

The California industrialist and aviation enthusiast M. Stuart Millar purchased Piper on May 12, 1987, at a distress price, from Forstmann Little, which had just acquired Piper from the bankrupt Lear Siegler Corporation. Millar placed the company under his Romeo Charlie investment firm, in effect taking the company private.[6] Millar then rationalized the product line, built a strong order backlog, and resolved to fight crushing insurance costs by hiring a staff of lawyers to fight product liability suits in court. He thus hoped to reassure distributors and preclude future litigation, but by purchasing Piper, he also became potentially liable for every aircraft built by Piper over 50 years.

To revive the trainer market, Millar began production in 1988 of the two/four seat PA-28-161 Cadet, derived from the Warrior II. To hold down costs, he proceeded without adequate liability insurance.[7] He also resumed production of the veteran Super Cub in 1988 after WTA had withdrawn as licensee, and continued the license production agreements in Argentina, Poland, and Brazil. Major production activity was with the Cheyenne IIIA; the developed Malibu Mirage, which appeared in October 1988; the Seneca; and the Cadet. But as conditions worsened, only the Malibu Mirage remained in series production. Piper engineers also assisted with development of the Chilean ENAER Pillan military trainer, derived from the Cherokee. Millar was determined to expand aggressively, even with a backlog of liability suits.[8]

Another Millar effort was the LoPresti Aircraft Engineering Company, established in December 1987. Ownership was 75 percent by Millar and 25 percent by LeRoy LoPresti, formerly with Mooney. LoPresti also managed the venture. The intent was to produce a new version of the old Globe GC-1A Swift as the SwiftFury two-seat sportplane, but the venture closed in December 1990 due to financial problems. The PiperNorth operation, reestablished in November 1989 at Lock Haven with a Pennsylvania loan guarantee, also closed.

By the fall of 1989 Piper's problems were so severe that suppliers began to cut off credit, seriously disrupting production. The low-priced Cadet, serving as a loss leader, did not help cash flow.[9] The company desperately needed more sales of its Malibu Mirage, priced in the $500,000 range, but the cash crunch forced a two-week shutdown in February 1990. Millar again considered reopening the Lock Haven plant to produce both the Navajo and the SwiftFury, but financial conditions precluded the proposal.

By 1991 it was apparent that Millar's gamble was failing, as continued credit restrictions from suppliers limited the company's production capability and left it unable to fill orders. New investors were sought, but a prospective sale of Piper to Aerospatiale stalled over product liability concerns; any new owner faced potential product liability for more than 20,000 Piper aircraft in operation in the United States. A further difficulty was a series of seven Malibu/Mirage fatal accidents during 1989–1991. Investigations eventually exonerated the aircraft's structure, but that finding came too late as Piper, crushed by product liability awards and failing to find added financing, filed for Chapter 11 bankruptcy on July 2, 1991. The future of the Piper nameplate after 54 years looked dim.

A new investor, Stone Douglass, gained control from Stuart Millar by acquiring Millar's Romeo Charlie shares. Operations continued at a low level as the search continued for either a buyout or new financing. The company even briefly considered selling rights to Canada and restarting production there in order to escape U.S. product liability law; Canadian product liability law was more lenient. The eventual ownership transfer came at the end of 1994, however, to unsecured creditors led by engine supplier Teledyne Continental. Sales were hardly spurred by bankruptcy, but management continued to seek approval from creditors to reorganize and emerge from bankruptcy as a public firm.[10]

8—The Path to Recovery

On July 17, 1995, new Piper president and CEO Chuck Suma announced a successful restructuring as The New Piper Aircraft, Inc., owned by major creditors led by Newco Pac, Inc., and with investment bank backing. Piper assets were valued at $95 million. Production of established models, led by the Malibu Mirage, moved ahead. The PA-32 Saratoga and the PA-28 family also remained in production. The remaining Piper twin, the PA-34 Seneca IV, was an important factor and was succeeded by a refined Seneca V. Depending on market demand, the turbine-powered Cheyenne and Navajo also might be reinstated. Piper regained its former position as a strong competitor.

Fairchild, in San Antonio, continued with low-volume production of its Metro series. Some 1,000 had been produced by 1996, and orders for several military versions aided stability. Fairchild began development of a standup cabin version, largely to meet the challenge from its major competitor, the Beech 1900D.

Socata, the Aerospatiale general aviation subsidiary founded in 1966, in addition to producing the larger TBM 700, developed small single-engined designs. Product liability concerns having driven most American producers from that segment, Socata sensed an opportunity in consequence. The Socata Trinidad, Tobago, and Tampico made inroads into the U.S. market from the 1980s. In 1995 Socata also acquired rights to the former Grumman American/ Gulfstream Cougar light twin.

Even in the troubled environment, the entrepreneurial spirit that had always characterized the general aviation industry remained as active as any time in its history. New ventures appeared, producing either new designs or older models acquired from others, and aspiring to gain a market foothold whatever the current adversity. One such venture in single-engined aircraft was the American General Aircraft Corporation. In June 1989, investors led by James E. Cox, founder and president, purchased type certificates for single-engined Grumman American designs from Gulfstream Aerospace, which had ended production of the line in 1980. With an investment by Gulfstream, American General entered production at the Greenville, Mississippi, factory vacated by Boeing in 1990. Priced in the $100,000 range, a refined model of the fixed-gear AA-5B Tiger achieved some initial market success, but low sales forced the firm into a production suspension in 1993 and then into Chapter 11 in February 1994.

New investors acquired rights from Gulfstream to the Commander 112 and Commander 114 of the old Rockwell line in the summer of 1988. Production of the Commander 114 was revived by the Commander Aircraft Company at the Bethany, Oklahoma, factory. Gulfstream also sold twin-engined Aero Commander rights to Precision Aerospace Corporation of Everett, Washington, but no new production appeared. The company provided support for the large active fleet of twin-engined Aero Commanders.

American Champion was established by Jerry Mehlhaff in Rochester, Wisconsin, to revive Champion production. The corporation purchased rights for new-build production of derivatives of the veteran Aeronca Champion, including the Scout, Super Decathlon, and Citabria Explorer. Deliveries began in 1991, and in 1996 the sales total for all models reached 53. Bellanca remained marginally active with the Super Viking, effectively producing to order. Yet another Taylorcraft revival was attempted in November 1989, still involving the original 1930s design. That effort ceased in October 1992, apparently ending the Taylor name in the marketplace permanently. Gilbert Taylor, one of the major pioneers of light aircraft, died on March 29, 1988, at 89. The

B. D. Maule, founder-president, Maule Air, 1991 (Maule Air Inc.).

pioneer engineer Fred Weick, designer of the Ercoupe, died on July 8, 1993, at age 93.

Maule, possibly the last wholly family owned firm in the industry, maintained some 100 employees and output of 60–80 aircraft per year, and remained competitive with its MX-7 series. The Lunar Rocket was discontinued, but later models found steady demand. Many were equipped with floats. Belford Maule died September 2, 1995, aged 83, but the Maule family retained control of the company. The new Maule Comet, with fixed tricycle gear, was offered in the $75,000-$90,000 price range and bid to gain market share. Total production by the firm reached 2,000 aircraft in 1996.

The Ayres firm, also in Georgia and with about 500 employees, continued production of agricultural aircraft and of various aircraft and helicopter parts on which it subcontracted for larger firms. The basic Ayres model was in the $300,000 price range, at the higher end of the market, and turbine-powered models were even higher priced. Chairman and President Fred Ayres felt it was necessary to diversity from sole dependence on the agricultural market, and announced in 1996 the LM 200 Loadmaster light cargo aircraft, launched with an order from Federal Express for delivery starting in 1999. A simple and ungainly design with a large fuselage and fixed gear, the Loadmaster featured an innovative power arrangement of coupled turboprops driving a single nose-mounted propeller. Capable of transporting up to 7,500 pounds of cargo, the Loadmaster was intended to supplement the Federal Express fleet of Cessna Caravans, limited to 3,000 pound payloads.[11] The program carried major potential for Ayres, as FedEx anticipated a fleet of more than 200 Loadmasters eventually, and military sales were also anticipated.

In February 1995 Schweizer, which produced the original Grumman Ag-Cat for more than 30 years, sold rights to the design to a newly formed Ag-Cat Corporation in Missouri, a subsidiary of an aircraft modification center. The new firm planned to resume production with Schweizer providing assistance during the transition. That venture faded in 1997, however. Air Tractor continued as a strong presence in larger agricultural models, including turboprop powered versions priced up to $300,000.

Business Jet Survey

Business jets remained a basically sound segment of the general aviation field, although their use continued to be widely viewed as a luxury.[12] The business jet segment also was unquestionably the most dynamic and possibly the most competitive of general aviation. There were more firms competing in business jets than in any other aircraft category except for homebuilts. Major oil companies remained among the heaviest users of business jets, having numerous remote locations around the world requiring visits by executive and engineering teams. But by 1991, a recession year, the business jet market again experienced a severe contraction, with orders and deliveries reduced sharply from the rate of the immediate prior years. Perhaps reflecting overproduction, some 50 percent of the American business jet fleet was on the used aircraft market at any time. Many corporate-owned jets also were advertised for charter and periodically made available for humanitarian missions. Especially noteworthy was the Corporate Angel Network, founded in January 1982, which scheduled corporate aircraft to transport cancer patients to major medical centers for treatment. Specialized firms were established that acquired fleets of business jets for time-share ownership and use by companies, with fees paid on the basis of actual usage, a business concept with the potential for expanding overall demand. Cessna and others began to market business jets on that basis as well. But the business aircraft market, always cyclical, could not anticipate full recovery outside an overall economic recovery.

Presenting a further challenge, tax changes effective as of January 1991 as part of a federal deficit reduction package included the imposition for the first time of a luxury tax on certain aircraft categories. For general aviation, this involved a 10 percent tax on aircraft costing $250,000 or more unless it could be documented that the aircraft was employed 80 percent of the time for business use. Manufacturers and distributors attributed further declines in sales directly to this tax. Fortunately, it was repealed in 1993.

As with other market segments, the business jet field became seriously overcrowded. Competition was also strongly international, similar to the much larger commercial airliner sector, but U.S. producers still commanded about half the world market. International competitors included the Canadair Challenger, the Astra Jet series extending from the Rockwell Jet Commander, and British and French designs. Basic designs offered by the American industry included the Gulfstream IV, Sabreliner, Beechjet 400A (from Mitsubishi), the Citation series, and the Learjet series, including the Model 31A, the tip-tanked Model 35A, and the larger Model 60 replacing the Model 55. The oldest remaining business jet, the Sabreliner, finally ended production in 1989, but Sabreliner Corporation remained active with modification and product support for the more than 600 in service. The company also won a Service Life Extension Program (SLEP) contract from the Air Force for the Cessna T-37 fleet in August 1989.

Integrated Resources declared bankruptcy on February 13, 1990, and once again Learjet was on the auction block. Loss of the TTTS contract to Beech was a major setback for Learjet, which had developed a version of the Model 31 for the order. Learjet felt that its uncertain future was a negative factor in the competition, Gulfstream issued a letter of intent to purchase Learjet for $60 million, a relative bargain, but the letter expired unexercised on February 22, 1990, due in part to the TTTS loss. Then on April 9, 1990, approval was granted in bankruptcy court for the sale of Learjet to Bombardier of Canada for $75 million. A major challenge for Bombardier was the market perception that Learjet's models, despite continuous refinement, were the least advanced of the current business jets.[13] Learjet pinned major hopes on its new Model 45, announced in 1992 and sized between the Model 31 and the larger, long-ranged Model 60, which first flew in June 1991. The first completely new design since the original Model 23, the Model 45 was to replace the Model 35/36, and its more capacious cabin alleviated criticisms of narrow cabin space in earlier Learjet models.

Bombardier had expanded rapidly to offer business jets in the small, medium, and large segments, as well as regional airliners. In addition to the Learjet line and the Canadair Challenger, it acquired Short Brothers of Great Britain, the oldest continuously operating aircraft firm in the world. It then acquired de Havilland Canada from Boeing, in partnership with the Province of Ontario. The Challenger, incidentally, had begun life as the LearStar 600, which Bill Lear designed shortly before his death on May 29, 1978. Canadair purchased the design.

Cessna offered several Citation models. The popular straight-winged Citation II returned to production in 1987, but production of the Citation S/II ended in 1989. Its replacement, the further stretched and more powerful Citation V, first flew on August 18, 1987. While continuing the swept-winged Citation VI and VII, Cessna moved farther up the scale with the super mid-sized Citation X, the most advanced of the series yet developed, announced in 1990. Featuring improvements in aerodynamics and engines over the Citation VII, the Citation X made its first flight on December 21, 1993, and deliveries began in July 1996. The upgraded Citation V Ultra was offered from mid-1994, and the Citation V Bravo replaced the veteran Citation II from 1996.

Cessna also reentered the low end of the business jet segment with the new CitationJet, first flying on April 29, 1991, of the same dimensions as the original Citation I but one ton lighter owing to use of advanced materials and computer-aided design and manufacturing (CAD/CAM).[14] Initially priced at $2.5 million, low for business jets at the time, the CitationJet entered service in 1993 and sold briskly. A long series of CitationJet developments followed.

The successor venture of Edward J. Swearingen, Swearingen Aircraft, Inc., announced the small SA-30 Gulfjet project in October 1986, with production and marketing to be undertaken by Gulfstream through an agreement of October 1988. Production was planned at the old Aero Commander Bethany, Oklahoma, factory, but Gulfstream withdrew in August 1989, stating that the SA-30 did not fit its long-range plans. The name Gulfjet was dropped. Swearingen also had designed the SA-32T light turboprop military trainer.

In 1989 he obtained financial backing from the Jaffe Group investment firm, enabling him to complete the SA-32T. With dim prospects, the SA-32T faded, but production of the SA-30, now redesignated Swearingen-Jaffe SJ30, was planned in Delaware. The SJ30 made its first flight on February 13, 1991, and Swearingen stressed his design's superiority over the directly competitive CitationJet, with a price low enough to induce customers to move up from twin-turboprop models. As with the CitationJet, the SJ30 was powered by Williams/Rolls FJ44 engines but employed simpler technology. Jaffe then withdrew, however, leaving Swearingen to seek new backing, which he eventually obtained from Sino Aerospace of Taiwan. A new Sino-Swearingen Aircraft Company was formed, still in San Antonio, and production was planned for a new factory in Martinsburg, West Virginia, for which ground was broken in March 1996.

The highly publicized Beech Starship experienced various production and certification delays, many attributable to the composite structure, and first customer deliveries did not take place until 1991. The design encountered market resistance because of its $5 million price tag, equal to that for smaller jets, and a top speed that turned out to be significantly lower. Increased weight brought about by certification requirements did not help performance, and reaching the market during a serious recession in executive aircraft was another complication. Slow sales and rumored breakeven point of 500 aircraft raised widespread skepticism about the Starship's future. Despite criticism that it had simply misjudged the market, Beech maintained that it fully supported the program.[15] But with sales stalled, Beech finally announced in December 1994 that it would suspend Starship production, although holding open the option of revival if the market should recover. Only 53 had been built. Beech planned to continue the King Air series, however, as sales remained strong and there was no direct competitor.

The general aviation industry had been criticized for the lack of a technological revolution, but when it developed a model as advanced as the Starship, it encountered market failure. The Italian Piaggio P.180, with a similar canard configuration to the Starship, although of more conventional construction, also became a poor seller. Gates Learjet had invested some $40 million in the P.180 program during 1983–1986 but then withdrew with pessimism about market prospects.

Beech had never developed an original business jet, but its parent Raytheon purchased the business jet unit of British Aerospace Corporation for $372 million in August 1993. The sale was spurred by a BAe restructuring and consolidation similar in scope to that within the American aerospace/defense industry. The history of product line transfers between firms, including internationally, continued. Raytheon thereby gained a broader market presence with the BAe 125-800 and BAe 1000, larger than the Beechjet and marketed in

North America as the Hawker. Hawker was a legacy British aircraft company and a component of what became the giant British Aerospace. Raytheon also lessened its vulnerability to the declining military market, while benefiting from the Beech experience with the British design in the 1970s.

The acquisition initially became a new subsidiary, Raytheon Corporate Jets, but on September 15, 1994, Raytheon announced the combination of Beech and Corporate Jets into Raytheon Aircraft Company, headquartered in Wichita. Beech CEO Arthur Wegner became chairman and CEO of Raytheon Aircraft. Production of the business jets was sharply curtailed due to the weak market at the time, but was planned to resume at Wichita in 1997, as Raytheon transferred all jet production to Wichita. The Beech and Hawker units were integrated as business prospects appeared to improve.[16] The Beechcraft nameplate began to fade after more than 60 years. Raytheon Aircraft enjoyed a record year in 1995, with sales exceeding $2 billion. Employment expanded to over 10,000, and a priority was to modernize production facilities, many of which dated from the Second World War.

There was increasing emphasis in business jets with extended range capabilities, with Gulfstream, Bombardier (Canadair), and Dassault proposing models of 6,000–8000-mile range capability. But the even more ambitious and highly speculative Gulfstream joint venture with the Russian Sukhoi design bureau for a supersonic business jet ended in 1992. The supersonic business jet concept would reappear, however.

Gulfstream eventually experienced declining sales, which coincided with heavy development expenses for the larger and more advanced Gulfstream V. Concerns led Forstmann Little to intervene in the firm's management. There was widespread skepticism by investors about the prospects for such a large and expensive business jet, and a public stock offering in 1992 had to be withdrawn due to lack of market interest. Forstmann Little then bought out Allen Paulson in September 1992, with Paulson continuing to manage the company. But continued financial deterioration led to Paulson's reluctant retirement in October 1993, although he remained on the board.[17] Management deficiencies plus strong competition from Bombardier of Canada, further pressured the company. Theodore Forstmann, while primarily an investor, took the office of chairman and began to assemble a new management team. A particular achievement was in gaining concessions from major suppliers BMW Rolls-Royce, Honeywell, Textron, and Grumman.[18] His firm invested a further $250 million to complete development of the Gulfstream V, popularly known as the GV, while concurrently pursuing cost-cutting and downsizing. The Gulfstream IV, or GIV, with production past the 250 mark, continued alongside the Gulfstream V.

The GV was the largest and longest-ranged business jet yet developed by the American industry. While a major risk, with a $35 million price and an aggressive and direct competitor in the Canadair Global Express, the GV soon gained a backlog of more than 70 orders. Gulfstream revenues exceeded $1 billion in 1995, operations were profitable, and employment in Savannah exceeded 3,000, marking a complete turnaround after near-bankruptcy.[19] Continued favorable market prospects enabled a successful public offering in 1996 to raise more than $600 million. But a possible future threat was Boeing's announcement in 1996 of plans for an executive version of its new-generation Model 737 twin-jet airliner. A major milestone was delivery of the 1,000th Gulfstream in September 1997.

By 1995 the business jet segment had improved strongly, and new product development was especially active from that year. The Learjet Model 45 made its first flight on October 7 of that year, and deliveries began in 1997. The new model made extensive use of CAD/CAM in its development, and with a price in the $8 million range, bid to compete with larger business jets. The Gulfstream V made its appearance with a first flight on November 28. In 1995 Raytheon announced its first original business jet, the Premier I, for which development had begun in 1994. Somewhat larger than but still competitive with the CitationJet, the Premier employed elements of the advanced structure developed for the Starship. The move also indicated a major Raytheon commitment to the business jet field. Raytheon planned to follow the Premier I with larger models which would eventually succeed the Raytheon/Hawker 1000.

The Learjet Model 45 in its first test flight over Wichita, November 6, 1997 (Learjet, Inc., now Bombardier Business Aircraft).

New companies proposed lower-cost single-jet designs. Gaining attention was VisionAire, founded in 1988 in Missouri and working in facilities at Mojave, California. The company developed the Vantage low-cost single-engined business jet, featuring an all-composite structure, a forward-swept wing, and design refinements by Burt Rutan of Scaled Composites. Foreign competitors also developed new models.

Business jet marketing returned to an emphasis on cost savings for corporate users, in part due to the escalation in business-class airfares, but principally because corporate downsizing and consolidation required even more travel by hard-pressed executives. Still, business jet use remained a sensitive issue for most corporate owners; few were interested in publicizing their air fleets.

A Promising Recovery

Ironically, the decline and virtual destruction of the general aviation industry occurred during the Ronald Reagan administration, with its strongly pro-business tilt and expressed determination to recapture the spirit of unfettered free enterprise. But general aviation remained a significant factor in the national economy. Throughout the 1980s the size of the U.S. general aviation fleet remained in the 200,000 to 220,000 range, of which more than three-fourths were single-engined fixed-winged types.[20] In 1991 the average age of single-engined piston aircraft was 26 years.[21] By 1995 the average age of single-engined piston aircraft had increased to 29 years, the average age of turbine-powered business aircraft was 16 years, and for the overall general aviation fleet the average age was 26 years.[22] Thus for the long term, there were bright prospects for new production, simply to replace aging aircraft.

With civil demand depressed, the military market became even more critical for the larger general aviation firms. The business jet segment had benefited significantly, with the Learjet, Citation, Beechjet, and Gulfstream attracting substantial military orders. This was also true of the turbine-powered Metro and King Air. After the Navy ordered the Citation S/II as the T-47A to replace the older North American T-39 Sabreliner, the Army selected as its high-priority cargo/personnel transport the new Citation V Ultra as the UC-35A.

General Dynamics, reversing its acquisition of 1985, announced in October 1991 that it would dispose of the Cessna subsidiary. While Cessna remained quite profitable, General Dynamics determined that general aviation did not fit within its new strategic plan, which concentrated on its core technologies. In January 1992 Textron announced the purchase of Cessna for $660 million, which among other things linked Cessna and Lycoming engines, also a Textron company. That affiliation was short-lived, however, as Lycoming was sold to AlliedSignal in 1994. Textron also owned Bell Helicopter, and another unit was Avco, then a financial services firm but extending from the original Aviation Corporation of 1929, which had owned Stinson among other manufacturers. Raytheon/Beech had been an interested bidder for Cessna, but lost to Textron. Fear of antitrust actions also weighed against the acquisition.

The accepted rationale for ownership of general aviation manufacturers by large, financially strong corporations was that it would enable the firms to weather market downturns and maintain costly research and development programs that might otherwise be terminated. But the problems of Piper under different corporate parents, the frequent ownership changes for such firms as Aerostar, Mooney, Aero Commander, and Bellanca, and the experiences of Cessna with General Dynamics and Gulfstream with Chrysler, plus the experience of Rockwell-Standard/Rockwell International with several general aviation firms, combined to suggest that such ownership by a large, diversified corporate parent was not always beneficial to the firm or to the general aviation field. Furthermore, Beech earlier had been regarded as something of a drag on Raytheon, losing $9 million in 1987, for example.[23]

Both the Beech unit of Raytheon and the Cessna unit of Textron became strong contenders, along with several major military manufacturers, for the important Air Force/Navy Joint Primary Aircraft Training System (JPATS), for their new-generation trainer. The potential $6 billion contract attracted Beech at the outset, along with several other bidders, most in collaboration with designs of foreign partners. Cessna had not entered initially, but with lengthy delays in the selection process, entered a new twin-jet design based on the wing and engines of the CitationJet. The eventual winner, the turboprop Beech Mark II, was developed in collaboration with Pilatus of Switzerland from its established PC-9. It received the military designation T-6A Texan. The contract award, announced in June 1995, sparked vigorous protests from Textron, but the award remained with Raytheon. The combination of TTTS/T-1A production extending into 1997, and JPATS/T-6A orders enabled Raytheon to enjoy the cushion of military production, including strong export prospects, while awaiting a civil market recovery.

The most important step toward that recovery, long sought by the industry, was product liability reform. Legislative reform finally was realized with passage of the General Aviation Revitalization Act (GARA) signed into law by President Clinton on August 17, 1994. The law provided for an 18-year Statute of Repose, meaning that new aircraft are not subject to product liability claims after 18 years. Particularly encouraging for the industry was that by 1997–1998 the potential for new product liability lawsuits would drop significantly, since aircraft built during the high-production years of the late 1970s

8—The Path to Recovery

Signing ceremony of the General Aviation Revitalization Act (GARA, August 17, 1994, by President Clinton (White House photo office).

would then be excluded. Critics of the legislation maintained that the threat of product liability lawsuits led to more safety advances and innovation than would have been the case otherwise, but the law was hailed by the industry.

Russ Meyer announced immediately that he would reestablish production of the veteran Cessna models 172, 182, and 206, forecasting an output of some 2,000 annually. Needing increased capacity, Cessna announced construction of a new plant in Independence, Kansas, for the purpose. Cessna expected to expand its product offerings with market recovery, but such plans did not include revival of the piston-engined Golden Eagle and Chancellor, as turbine power was strongly favored for that class of aircraft. Nor would they include revival of the Skywagon, given the success of the Caravan.[24] With improving prospects for Cessna, Raytheon/Beech, and Learjet, the city of Wichita, which had suffered in the industry contraction, appeared to be on the verge of a long-awaited recovery.

Building on the recovery of the offshore oil service function, the market for larger general aviation helicopters also showed signs of vitality by 1995. Executive use of helicopters increased in a strengthening economy, and the international market was also a strong growth area. But civil helicopters remained the smallest segment of the overall aerospace industry. Production volume, while increasing, remained low. Helicopter use still was limited by cost; the leading small turbine helicopter, the Bell Model 206B Jet Ranger III, carried a base price at the time of some $750,000. Choice was widespread, however, with Bell, McDonnell Douglas, and several smaller manufacturers as factors. The improved Sikorsky S-76B, which appeared in 1988, was primarily for the export market, but a few domestic executive models were ordered.

Among smaller firms, Enstrom production remained sporadic; eleven were delivered from the Menominee, Michigan, factory in 1995. But in 1994 the company implemented an agreement for helicopter production in China, possibly enhancing its future. Robinson gained orders for 179 aircraft in 1995, encouraging given a base price of $135,000 for the two-seat model. Stanley Hiller's son Jeffrey repurchased the Rogerson-Hiller rights in 1993 with a view toward reviving production after several years of inactivity. Again relocated, this time to Newark, California, and backed by Thai investors, Hiller restarted production of the veteran UH-12E3. The first new production model first flew on June 2, 1995. Schweizer delivered 29 helicopters in 1995. Japanese businessman James Kimura had acquired Brantly type certificates in 1989, but a new Brantly International of Vernon, Texas, reacquired them in 1994 for further production. Little new production ensued, but the firm provided support for the existing fleet.

The Bell Model 230 medium twin ended production in 1995 and was succeeded by the greatly advanced Model 430, with a four-bladed rotor. It first flew on October 25, 1994. The Model 430 was a major stretch, with capacity for eight passengers, and prospects appeared promising despite being priced in the $4 million range. The new, smaller seven-seat Model 407, optimized for business use and priced at some $1.3 million, quickly gained strong orders, with 85 delivered during 1996. Intended to succeed both the JetRanger and LongRanger, and still powered by the Allison 250, the Model 407 featured a four-bladed rotor and a larger, roomier cabin.[25] All were produced at the BHC subsidiary, which continued as strong success. More than 1,500 BHC helicopters had been built though 1996, including 217 commercial helicopters in that year alone. The helicopter pioneer Arthur Young, who had begun with Bell in 1942, died in 1995, age 89.

In a bid to compete in the civil market, Kaman Corporation of Connecticut, the long-established military helicopter producer, developed the unusual K-MAX, which first flew on December 23, 1991. A single-seater with a narrow fuselage and combination skid-and-wheel landing gear, the K-MAX was configured to carry external cargo, either in slings or containers, as an "aerial truck." The K-MAX also featured an advanced intermeshing rotor blade system and was powered by a 1,500 shp Lycoming turboshaft, giving it a heavy lift capability. First deliveries were in 1994. Priced in the $3.5 million range, the K-MAX enjoyed encouraging domestic and export market prospects for a variety of industrial applications, especially logging.

The McDonnell Douglas Helicopter Company was renamed McDonnell Douglas Helicopter Systems in September 1994. The stretched MD 600, competitive with the Bell Model 430, was certificated for service from 1997. The most advanced model, the eight-passenger MD Explorer (originally MD 900), was launched in 1989, with first deliveries at the end of 1994. A multinational NOTAR development priced in the $3 million range, the MD Explorer featured major participation by Australia and Japan. The MD500 priced at some $700,000, the more powerful MD530, and the MD520 NOTAR continued.

Ironically, one potential downside to the recovery in general aviation manufacturing was that the kitplane segment, enjoying government regulatory support and increasing public acceptance, could be harmed by revitalized production of smaller single-engined factory models. Kit sales (see Table 8-1), already had leveled off in the 1990–1993 period after rapid growth during the 1980s. Kitplane construction had circumvented product liability lawsuits, but with legislative reform, certain factory-built aircraft could challenge the homebuilts on a value basis. The revived Cessna 172R, for example carried an initial price of $124,500 in 1996, making it more price competitive with four-seat kit models. Product development remained highly active, however, aided by the new Small Aircraft Certification Compliance Program of the FAA. The Cirrus Design SR20 and Stoddard-Hamilton GlaStar attracted particular attention.[26] Pioneer experimental aircraft developer Steve Wittman died April 27, 1995, age 91.

Table 8-1
Aircraft Kit and Plans Sales

Year	Kits	% Change	Plans	% Change
1990	1,147	N/A	2,560	n/a
1991	1,573	37	2,209	−14
1992	1,943	24	1,753	−21
1993	3,082	59	2,116	21
1994	4,085	33	2,831	34
1995	5,338	31	3,063	8
1996	5,713	7	2,645	−14
1997*	5,750	1	3,205	21
1998*	6,921	20	1,761	−45
1999*	7,751	12	1,606	−9

*Manufacturer's projections
SOURCE: *Kitplanes*, July 1997, p. 38.

Internationalization of the general aviation sector increased rapidly, although products of most producing nations maintained a clear national identity. Marketing had long been international, but development and production also were increasingly globalized. The activities of Bell in helicopters, Bombardier in business jets and commuter airliners, and widespread component sourcing between the two nations blurred the division between the U.S. and Canadian industries. Integration was increasing. The new Learjet 45 in particular benefited from its corporate linkages with Canadair and Short Brothers in its development, and had major components built in Canada and Northern Ireland. Production of the Sikorsky S-76 helicopter involved components from several countries.

In another manifestation of internationalization, Fairchild Aircraft acquired 80 percent of the German firm Dornier Luftfahrt GmbH on June 5, 1996. Fairchild Dornier planned to develop the German Models 226 and 326 commuters, larger than the 19-seat Metro II, to provide broader coverage of the commuter market. Daimler-Benz, parent of Dornier, had wanted to dispose of the company.

The agenda for the future of general aviation was encompassed within the term revitalization. Product liability reform had been the chief priority, but with success on that issue, attention turned to such matters as flight training, international harmonization of rules and standards, increased funding and greater autonomy for the FAA, and greater efficiency in certification matters.[27] By 1997 there were strong indications that the revitalization program was showing results. The number and variety of new general aviation aircraft was encouraging, and GAMA reported a record $3.1 billion in billings for 1996. The figure included fixed-wing aircraft only. Its member firms reported delivery of 1,132 aircraft for 1996, led by Raytheon, Cessna, Gulfstream, and Learjet.[28] Cessna, for example, introduced three new business jet models, CJ1, CJ2, and Encore, simultaneously at the 1998 NBAA exhibition. Business jet production had effectively tripled by value during the 1990s.

Perhaps portending a substantive response to the criticism of static technology in general aviation, NASA, already active in research on fuel-efficient engines and advanced propeller blades, announced that it would assist in development of new advanced-technology small aircraft engines. Following the landmark General Aviation Revitalization Act of 1994, the Advanced General Aviation Transport Experiments (AGATE) program, a consortium of NASA, the FAA, universities, and the general aviation industry, was established, also in 1994. With a goal of increasing the competitiveness of general aviation with land transport, including improved safety, affordability, and ease-of-use measures. AGATE concurrently undertook long-range development of advanced technology for fixed-wing light aircraft, including integrated design and manufacturing, ice protection, and airways system modernization. It was intended to stem the decline in general aviation innovation, and among other measures pursued the developed of composites in the structures of future general aviation aircraft.

One technological advance, affecting all aviation, was development of global positioning system (GPS) technology for navigation. From the 1990s Garmin GPS instrumentation became increasingly standard in business aircraft, as did "glass" cockpits, replacing older analog instruments.

The general aviation industry had endured a tumultuous time from the 1980s through the mid–1990s, but expansion and economic stability in the second half of that decade provided a basis for optimism for the longer term. Not only was the market for smaller piston singles recovering, but business jet demand and technological development in all segments of the industry were proceeding at a rapid pace.

9

The Industry Enters the New Millennium

The general aviation manufacturing industry entered the 21st century in a seemingly strong position, continuing the recovery of the late 1990s. Most forecasts were for continued strong growth, especially in business jets. For the year 2000, U.S. business jet output was valued at $10 billion, and a 2002 forecast was for sales of 5,600 new business jets worth $100 billion over the next decade, of which possibly 30 percent would be by fractional ownership.[1] Honeywell, the engine manufacturer, projected 7,700 new business jets worldwide over the 2004–2013 decade, and other optimistic forecasts appeared regularly. The majority of business jets worldwide were projected to be of U.S. manufacture. The corporate quest for greater efficiency and productivity was felt to spur demand, and the trend toward fractional ownership along with the prospect of an eventual supersonic business jet also were regarded as further stimuli.[2] The original fractional ownership firm, Executive Jet Aviation, had grown rapidly over its 35 years in business, and was acquired by famed investor Warren Buffett's Berkshire Hathaway group in 1998. Buffett had been a customer for several years, and was said to be impressed with the fractional ownership business model. The firm was renamed NetJets, Inc., in 2002.

Quite apart from developments in particular companies or specific aircraft categories, several further trends affected manufacturing, and all of general aviation, early in the new century. While most trends extended from long-existing conditions and situations, their combined effect strongly impacted the structure and market prospects of the industry.

One continuing concern was that the general aviation industry remained poorly understood by the public, which still tended to view the field as consisting largely of "private planes," and of bush and agricultural aircraft. GAMA, AOPA, and the NBAA made strenuous efforts to educate the public both as to the value of business use of aircraft and of the contribution of general aviation to the overall economy. A large segment of the public still regarded business jets as a luxury, however. Illustrative of the long-running controversy, chief executives of the Big Three auto manufacturers suffered public criticism after their 2008 testimony before Congress, asking for government funding support in the recession, when it was disclosed that all three had flown to Washington in their corporate jets even as their companies were on the verge of failure. A further concern was that many felt the new Obama Administration was unfriendly to the general aviation industry, despite its strong export performance and the 1.2 million jobs supported.

Changes in the Block Aircraft Registration Request (BARR) program, started in 2000 and jointly administered by the FAA and NBAA, presented a new problem. BARR prevented aircraft registrations and flight information from being disseminated over the Internet for aircraft still in route, a major concern of business flyers on the grounds of privacy and security. One example was that, if a corporation was considering the acquisition of another, and made flights to the target company's headquarters location, such information might become available to competitors and speculators. In 2009, however, the Department of Transportation removed BARR except in cases of legitimate security concern. Transportation Secretary Ray LaHood ruled that since civilian aircraft used open airways and ATC services, their operation was public information. Business aviation remained adamantly opposed. The overall issue of business-government relations in aviation remained complex and unresolved. One issue was that airlines felt the FAA should impose a user-fee scheme on general aviation to offset their support. General aviation opposed the measure, feeling that the current fuel excise tax system was the most equitable way to support the FAA.

The airliner hijackings and subsequent destruction by the terrorist attacks of September 11, 2001, in addition to causing a severe drop in general aviation aircraft demand, also threatened a potential catastrophe in that general aviation aircraft became viewed as a potential security threat. General aviation aircraft were prohibited post–9/11 from operating at Ronald Reagan National Airport in Washington, for example. With security improvements and effective lobbying from the industry, the director of the Transportation Security Administration (TSA), under the Department of Homeland Security, ruled in May 2005 that general aviation did not present a significant security threat, and operating restrictions eased. National Airport (DCA), among others, resumed general aviation operations.[3] The ruling reflected among other things the high degree of cooperation among GAMA, NBAA, EAA, and AOPA. Increasing environmental concerns required general aviation to make similar adaptations to those required of other sectors of aviation, with greater emphasis on fuel economy and more concern with emissions into the atmosphere. As in other sectors of the economy, there emerged also the concept of "green aviation." So-called "hush kits" for noisy engines of older business jets were increasingly installed. Another green trend was experimentation with diesel engines for smaller aircraft. Diesel technology had developed to the point that its application to aircraft was becoming economically and operationally feasible. Electric power for light aircraft also progressed beyond the experimental stage, with flying prototypes tested, and became regarded as a prospect for the future.

The AGATE program, never intended as permanent, was shut down in December 2001, to some extent a victim of 9/11. NASA, however, announced a new Small Aircraft Transportation System (SATS) program in 2005 to maximize the use of small aircraft and smaller airports.

A growing concern for all aviation was the increasing stress on the national airways system, coupled with the awareness that the air traffic control infrastructure was outdated. In response, the FAA developed the Next Generation Air Transportation System (NGATS) plan, resulting in passage of the VISION 100-Century of Aviation Reauthorization Act in 2003. The Act provided for capacity increases, safety improvements, and updated organization and business practices to handle air traffic that was projected to double in volume between 2006 and 2025. While of most immediate impact to commercial air carriers, the legislation would also affect general aviation, and was strongly supported by the industry. Soon known as NextGen, it became an umbrella term for modernization of the National Airspace System (NAS), and implementation would be by the FAA in partnership with the NBAA. That partnership signified that government did not maintain that it had all the answers and capability. The program was projected for completion in 2025, but adequate funding remained challenging in an era of massive budget deficits. The FAA provided conspicuous support for general aviation in other ways. In March 2001 it selected a team of universities with strong aeronautical programs to form the Air Transportation Center of Excellence for General Aviation Research (CGAR), to cooperate with the FAA in safety-related research and development. Embry-Riddle was selected as the lead university.

General aviation trends included development of new aircraft categories. Of special note was the Very Light Jet category, for small four or five seat jets not only for corporate use but for a projected boom in the air taxi market. Numerous Very Light Jet (VLJ) projects appeared for the anticipated market. Air taxi service had existed for decades, but relatively inexpensive small jets for that role, combined with on demand scheduling through the Internet, promised a major expansion. The very light jet concept, incidentally, was far from new, first manifested by the French Morane-Saulnier Paris four-seat model of 1954, a few examples of which remained. Another trend, especially for larger business jets, was the establishment of completion centers apart from the factory where "green" airframes would be fitted out to customer specifications. Hawker Beechcraft opened a large center in Little Rock, Arkansas, Learjet maintained its center in Tucson, Arizona, and Boeing had a total of seven centers for its Business Jets Division. Even Embraer opened a completion center in Melbourne, Florida, for its airframes manufactured in Brazil.

A promising new category came into being with FAA approval of Light Sport Aircraft (LSA), including a new Sport Pilot license for aviators, with standards less restrictive than for other licenses. The move toward making certification of sport pilots and light sport aircraft simpler had begun in the early 1990s. Regulations governing sport pilot and light sport aircraft, effective on September 1, 2004, were among the most far-reaching changes in general aviation since 1938. LSAs were restricted in weight, level flight speed, and stall speed, and sport pilots could be licensed with only 20 hours of flight training rather than 40 hours. The move spurred many firms to develop new aircraft for the market, under the classifications E-LSA for experimental and S-LSA for factory-built models. Sport pilots were allowed to fly only LSA models. The objective, of course, was to make licensing and flying more economical and accessible, and consequently to expand the market both for pilots and airplanes. Such older small models as the Cessna 150/152 did not qualify as LSAs, resulting in new models being developed by Cessna and several European firms, although they were slow in entering the market. As always, cost was a limiting factor, with some expressing doubt that the cost of flying would actually be much lower.[4] The original 1990s dream of a simple $50,000 factory-built LSA had long been abandoned, and it became evident that the most basic LSA models would carry six-figure prices.

A major and accelerating trend was the globalization of general aviation production. While globalization affected many industries and many product categories, it was particularly significant in aircraft production, and carried strong implications for general aviation. Significantly, Embraer of Brazil planned to shift complete assembly of its business jets at the Florida facility, while Cessna caused a stir when it announced that its Model 162 SkyCatcher LSA was to be assembled in China. Other manufacturers were also shifting production to China, which concurrently undertook a series of major acquisitions in the industry, beginning in 2009. First, China acquired Fisher Advanced Composite Components, a European aerostructures manufacturer, to fill a technological gap. In 2010 it moved to acquire Epic Air of Oregon, a kit aircraft supplier, and in 2011 Continental Motors from Teledyne, followed by Cirrus Design. There were indications of interest by China in undertaking licensed production of business jets. While private flying was virtually nonexistent in China, it was still regarded as possessing the greatest potential for general aviation growth in the world. The lack of growth in the U.S. market, combined with China's high economic growth rate, made business aviation a strong future growth sector, especially for business jets.[5]

Mexico became increasingly favored as a location for general aviation component production, and even production of complete aircraft was shifted to Mexico by certain producers. Bombardier announced that its new all-composite Learjet 85 would be assembled in a new plant in the city of Queretaro.[6] Labor costs averaging 30 percent under the United States, increasing availability of engineers, and proximity to the North American market attracted numerous manufacturing operations. Many suppliers likewise were attracted to Mexico, and the country worked to attract still more investors as part of its development strategy. Problems and concerns remained, however, including the need to import aluminum and certain specialized machinery, and worsening crime.[7]

After the shock of 9/11, general aviation production made a gradual but substantial recovery from 2002 through 2007, both in smaller single-engined models and in business jets. Total general aviation billings reached $15.2 billion in 2005, for example. Regardless of continuing economic challenges, an enduring strength of the American general aviation manufacturing industry was that it remained by far the most complete, most experienced, and most capable in the world. While American producers faced strong competition in certain business jet categories from Bombardier in Canada, Embraer in Brazil, and Dassault in France, and in certain lighter aircraft categories from competitors in Italy, Austria, Germany, Australia, and even Slovenia, no other country offered the infrastructure and the product range of the American industry. Although a small category, no other country sustained a specialized agricultural aircraft segment, for example.

Industry Survey

As with most producers, Piper's sales dropped sharply after 9/11. Piper continued its ownership odyssey. American Capital Strategies, which had previously invested $20 million in the New Piper Corporation in 1998, invested a further $34 million in July 2003, acquiring 94 percent of the company. Long-term investor Exeter Partners held the remaining 6 percent. New Piper was renamed Piper Aircraft, Inc., in September 2006. Then on May 1, 2009, ACS sold Piper to Impremis, an Asian investment company with offices in Bangkok, Singapore and Brunei, and largely funded by the government of Brunei. The acquisition carried with it among other things favorable portents for serving the growth of general aviation in Asia. Impremis appointed new management and expressed support for the new PiperJet project, but also carried out substantial layoffs. Impremis also committed Piper to remain in Vero Beach, as earlier the company had considered relocating, and the state of Florida had responded with incentives.[8] ACS gained $31 million on the sale to Impremis.

9—The Industry Enters the New Millennium

Piper's strongest market competitor was its PA-46 Malibu cabin class single-engined series. The piston-powered Malibu Mirage was joined by the turboprop-powered Malibu Meridian in 1999. Then Piper introduced the Matrix in 2006, essentially a Mirage without pressurization and priced considerably lower. (Piper later dropped the Malibu prefix, using only Mirage, Meridian, and Matrix as aircraft names.) Piper continued low-volume production of the Seneca V and its older single-engined models, but earlier had decided not to pursue an original light sport aircraft design.

Cessna experienced a difficult entry into the LSA market with its Model 162 SkyCatcher, powered by a 100 hp Teledyne Continental engine. The first prototype flew on October 13, 2006, but soon crashed, and the second suffered damage in another mishap. But Cessna announced strong backing of the program, and early orders were encouraging. Cessna took the unprecedented step of outsourcing assembly of the model to Shenyang Aircraft of China to control costs. But the initial price of $111,500 was regarded by most observers as difficult to maintain even with lower Chinese production costs, and the price was in fact raised soon after launch.

Another notable development was the Cessna NGP (Next Generation Piston) advanced four-seat model. With the industry long criticized for lack of a design revolution in small aircraft, Cessna responded with the NGP in 2005. Possibly intended as a response to the successful Cirrus series, the NGP featured a fully cantilevered high wing, somewhat reminiscent of the earlier Cardinal, and could have replaced the veteran 182 series. No production was undertaken, however. Cessna maintained low-volume production of its veteran Model 172 Skyhawk, Model 182 Skylane, and Model 206 Stationair models.

While Cessna's history, and to a great extent its reputation, had been built on smaller piston-powered aircraft, it had become the largest producer of business jets in the world. The CitationJet family remained the highest volume business jets in production. A successful addition to the family was the Citation Mustang, an "entry-level" light jet with a starting price under $3 million, which began development in 2002. After a first flight on April 23, 2005, deliveries began late in 2006. Demand held up in the recession, and total deliveries had reached 400 by 2012, a majority of which were exported. The CitationJet series expanded with the CJ2 and CJ3, succeeding the Citation Bravo, both announced in 2000, with deliveries beginning in 2003. The upgraded CitationJet CJ1+, in the $4 million range, came in June 2007, and the series ranged up to the eight/nine-seat CJ4, priced at almost $9 million. The midsize Citation Sovereign entered service in 2004, offering stronger competition in that segment. The flagship Citation X, considerably upgraded from its initial version, led the Cessna product line and was marketed as the fastest business jet in service.

In the meantime, Lancair in Oregon established an autonomous group from its kitplane lines in 1994 to develop the high-performance LC-40 Columbia business aircraft. The Columbia flew in 1996, and deliveries began in 2000. The type gained recognition, and after a brief production suspension in 2002, the company was renamed Columbia on July 18, 2005. Lance Neibauer exited the company in 2003, and the Columbia struggled in competition with Cirrus. With deteriorating finances, the firm declared bankruptcy in 2007. Cessna became an interested bidder, and acquired the assets of Columbia on December 4, 2007, for $26.4 million.[9] It intended to add the Columbia as a complement to its high-wing product line.

Cessna still faced serious competitive challenges, particularly from Embraer, which offered several directly competitive business jet models. Further, its parent Textron, Inc., was subject to recurring takeover rumors, with subsequent rumors of a possible spinoff of Cessna. The city of Wichita, still heavily dependent on general aviation, was reeling from the recession, and conditions were further complicated by Boeing's announcement of the closure of its long-running Wichita Division in 2007.

Mooney entered voluntary bankruptcy on July 27, 2001, although planning to maintain limited production while undergoing a financial reorganization. The company was revived on February 8, 2002, after Advanced Aerodynamics and Structures, Inc. (AASI), of Long Beach, California, acquired the position of Congress Financial Corporation. AASI, then developing its radically advanced A500 JetCruzer canard business aircraft, continued to operate the company as the renamed Mooney Aerospace Group, with Mooney Aircraft a subsidiary, and remained in Texas.[10] Production was restored from the spring of 2002, and Mooney cut prices in order to stimulate demand. The JetCruzer was eventually suspended as the company concentrated on Mooney. Then in May 2004, Allen Holding Finance bought Mooney Aircraft from its holding company, the former AASI, for $4 million, assuming all debt. Production of its veteran models continued at modest volume, gradually building up during the recovery years 2005–2008.

Of all primarily general aviation firms, Hawker Beechcraft probably faced the greatest number of challenges to its future in the new century. Following the series of organization changes in the 1990s, Raytheon Aircraft became increasingly autonomous, leading to the 2002 rebranding as Hawker Beechcraft. The company came under severe pressure in developing and bringing to market both the new Premier and the developed Hawker 400. The Premier, expected to appear on the market in 1998, was delayed until 2001, just before the 9/11–induced general aviation recession.

Hawker Beechcraft and its predecessors had been in the business jet field since 1963 with its marketing of the British de Havilland DH125, later redesignated HS125. Advanced developments extended through the Hawker 750, 850, 900, and 900XP, and ultimately to the long-range Hawker 1000, and the series possessed the distinction of being the longest-produced business jet models in the world. The series was marketed alongside the smaller Hawker 400. The Hawker 400 had a long history with Hawker Beechcraft after being acquired from Mitsubishi in the mid–1980s, where it was originally the MU-300 Diamond. Hawker Beechcraft had delivered more than 600 of the basic Hawker 400A and improved 400XP. In the meantime, Nextant Aerospace of Cleveland, Ohio, was established in 2007 to acquire used Hawker 400 airframes, then upgrade and resell them with new Williams FJ44 turbofans with FADEC replacing the original JT15D engines.

The redeveloped model, redesignated 400XT, attracted orders. Hawker Beechcraft responded with the new production 400XPR, thus competing with the Nextant upgrades, but with the 2008 recession orders slowed to a trickle. Hawker Beechcraft then announced a two-year production suspension of new business jet aircraft.

Product development continued. The planned replacement for the Hawker 1000 was the Horizon 1000, announced in 1996. Projected for service by 1999 but experiencing major delays, the Horizon 1000 did not fly until August 11, 2001. Classed as a super midsize, it bid to compete with the Gulfstream/Galaxy 200, Embraer Legacy 600, Bombardier Challenger 300, and Cessna Citation X. In 2002, with the corporate name change, the separate Beechcraft and Hawker brands were reinstated, with the Horizon again renamed Hawker 4000. With continuing delays, it was not certificated and placed in full production until June 2008, just in time for the steep recession. Despite a family resemblance to earlier models in the BAe/Hawker series, the Hawker 4000 was a new design. Components of early models had been built in the UK, but the Hawker 4000 was finished at the Little Rock, Arkansas, facility. Marketing began with a large order from NetJets, the former Executive Jet Aviation.[11]

James E. Schuster was brought in as president and CEO of then-Raytheon Aircraft in May 2001, and led a substantial recovery from 2002 to 2007. Raytheon had been considering the disposal of its aircraft interests for several years, however, and sold Hawker Beechcraft in 2007 into joint ownership by Onex of Canada and GS Capital Partners, a subsidiary of Goldman Sachs, for a price of $3.3 billion. In effect, the firm was taken private, and was officially renamed Hawker Beechcraft. Onex previously had become involved in aerospace with the acquisition of Spirit Aerosystems from Boeing. With the severe recession coming a year later there was a major loss in the value of Hawker Beechcraft. Demand was sharply off in all segments, and the investment proved to be a serious loss for Goldman Sachs, whose clients had also invested.[12] In the face of the decline Schuster retired, and Bill Boisture, with experience at British Aerospace and Hawker, and previously CEO of Gulfstream, was appointed to the position in March 2009. He was faced with managing probably more change than any other executive in the field.

The veteran Bonanza and Baron piston-powered models continued at low volume. The promising Premier was renamed Hawker 200, lending some consistency to Hawker Beechcraft's practice of numerical designations. That move did not last, however, as the company soon reverted to the established Premier name. Premier I and IA deliveries increased in the decade before the production suspension. The Super King Air series name had been dropped earlier, with all twin-turboprop models becoming King Air. The company planned to continue the series indefinitely. The long-running Model 1900 finally ended production in 2002.

Cirrus Design transformed completely to factory production with its high-performance SR20 fixed-gear model. The first SR20 delivery came in 1999, and the model became a strong competitor in its segment. In August 2001 the Arcapita investment firm, headquartered in Atlanta, Georgia, but owned by Middle Eastern investors, took a 58 percent holding in Cirrus Design.[13] Despite Muslim control and operating under Islamic business principles, the arrangement remained stable after 9/11. Production of the SR20 and larger SR22 even increased during the 2008 recession, but Cirrus suspended its LSA project due to market conditions. Cirrus aircraft were noteworthy for their Ballistic Recovery System (BRS), which deployed a parachute in the event of an in-flight emergency to lower the aircraft safely to the ground. Cirrus also tested its Vision SJ50 prototype VLJ, but faced a serious financing challenge. Founder Alan Klapmeier needed $120 million to complete development and bring it into service, but major financing for a new jet design was difficult in the recessionary environment. Owners then attempted to spin off the Vision SJ50 into a standalone company, with separate financing, which Alan Klapmeier would manage after stepping down as chairman of Cirrus. Whether the planned initial price of $1.3 million could be maintained was in serious question.[14] But he strongly believed that the Vision SJ50 could replace veteran twin-engined propeller models, such as the Beech Baron, that he regarded as obsolete.[15] Brother Dale Klapmeier remained with the company as vice chairman.

The originally Swearingen SJ30, while widely regarded as a sound design, endured a long, torturous journey toward production and service. After the withdrawals of Gulfstream and Jaffe, Swearingen teamed with a Taiwanese partner in 1997 to form Sino Swearingen Aerospace, with most manufacturing to be undertaken at its new plant in Martinsburg, West Virginia, with final assembly and fitting out at Swearingen headquarters in San Antonio. To enhance its competitiveness in the small jet segment, the design was stretched into the SJ30-2 in 1996. In the meantime, however, the originally projected price of some $2 million had tripled to $6 million, and development still was not completed. The process finally appeared to be at the point of success by 2001, ten years after the first flight of the then Swearingen-Jaffe prototype.

9—The Industry Enters the New Millennium

With the new West Virginia plant, production was expected to begin in 2002 after certification.[16] Sino Swearingen had been forced to halt development in 2001 after a cash crunch, but certification was finally achieved in November 2005. Then came a further setback as Taiwan Aerospace withdrew in 2007, after only a few aircraft were completed, again leaving the SJ30-2 with doubtful prospects.

Certain new ventures appeared strongly promising but still ran aground. Adam Aircraft Industries, of Englewood, Colorado, was formed in 1998 by millionaire businessman Rick Adam and partners. Goldman Sachs was an early investor. The company developed an innovative push-pull twin-boom model, designed by Burt Rutan, for the high-performance executive market. The concept emphasized the advantages of centerline thrust for a twin-engined model, being powered by two 350 hp Continental engines, and was configured for six seats. Originally designated M-309, for Rutan's 309th design, it was later named the Carbon-Aero, referring to its composite construction. The first prototype, again renamed the A500, flew on July 11, 2002. Base price was initially projected at $895,000, but soon rose to more than $1.2 million. The model still attracted serious attention, and was joined by the A700 AdamJet, of the same twin-boom configuration but powered by rear-mounted Williams FJ33 jet engines, and potentially a competitor in the emerging VLJ category. It was projected to cost $2.3 million.[17] A serious capital shortfall, however, forced the company to cease operations on February 11, 2008, after only a few models had been completed. Russian investors then purchased Adam for $10 million with a plan to recertify the A700. But with the development and financing challenges during a severe recession, they disposed of Adam in spring 2009 to another American entrepreneur, Thomas Hsueh, who studied plans to redesign and reestablish the aircraft in production if market prospects warranted. Those few owners of the A500 worried how their aircraft could be supported over the long term.

The highly publicized Eclipse VLJ had a long and troubled history, extending first from optimistic projections of a large air taxi market that would demand fleets of low-priced VLJs. The concept appeared so promising initially that VLJ models were planned at various points by Cirrus, Piper, Diamond, Visionaire, and Stratos in addition to Eclipse. Vern Raburn, a former Microsoft executive and veteran pilot, envisioned such a small jet design and founded the company in Albuquerque, New Mexico, in May 1998, making it a contemporary of the ill-fated Adam firm. He enjoyed the backing of several major investors, most importantly Bill Gates of Microsoft. Harold A. Poling, formerly CEO of Ford, was chairman. The Eclipse was developed in partnership with Williams, and was powered by two small Williams EJ22 jets. The Eclipse 500 prototype flew on August 26, 2002, but the Williams engine experienced development problems in addition to delivering inadequate power.

It was abandoned in November 2002 and more powerful PWC CJ610Fs were substituted. The Eclipse with the new engines flew on December 31, 2004, and production was planned from that point. The Eclipse had been originally projected to sell for some $850,000, but after development delays and the engine change the price escalated sharply. After certification, production went ahead in 2006 with optimistic advertising, with Eclipse claiming 2,500 orders at one point.

Even as Eclipse production moved forward, skeptics of the premise remained, including the author and most prominently *Flying*, the leading general aviation journal, both as to a realistic price and the development of a large jet air taxi market.[18] The original promoter of the concept, DanJet, projected a computerized reservation system that would bring trips, aircraft, and crews together efficiently, so that operations could be profitable with only one or two passengers per trip. When the Eclipse reached the market late in 2006, the price had risen to $2.1 million, not far below that of the entry-level Cessna Citation Mustang. Further, a large air taxi market never developed, and major orders from two air taxi operators were cancelled as they ceased operations in 2008 with the recession. Eclipse had projected a breakeven point of 600 units, but only 259 Eclipses were completed before a production shutdown. Many completed airframes still lacked full equipment, and the selling price was well below cost. In early 2008, as problems mounted, the European Technology and Investment Research Center (ETIRC), headquartered in Luxembourg but principally Russian-owned, became the majority investor. Vern Raburn was removed as CEO in July 2008, replaced by chairman Paul Pieper from ETIRC.[19] Raburn had been criticized for not being more forthcoming about mounting problems at Eclipse. With cash draining rapidly, the company declared Chapter 11 bankruptcy in November 2008, possibly the biggest general aviation failure in history. Eclipse secured additional financing to meet the remaining payroll, but still went into Chapter 7 liquidation. A revival soon was attempted by ETIRC, which briefly considered producing the Eclipse in Russia, but the attempt ended.

A onetime potential rival to the Eclipse, the Visionaire Vantage, powered by a single turbojet, first flew on November 16, 1996, but the company suffered bankruptcy and was liquidated in March 2003. A successor Eviation LLC acquired the rights and was established on October 2, 2003, to pursue a twin-engined development of the VA-10 Vantage. That venture faded as well. Another venture, Safire Aircraft Corporation of West Palm Beach, Florida, was incorporated in February 1998 to develop the SA-26 small business jet. To be powered by two small jet engines, the SA-26 was projected to enter the market in 2004, but that effort ended before production.

Learjet, while owned by Bombardier, retained production in Wichita, with airframes finished at its completion center in Tucson, Arizona. The company reached a milestone with delivery of the 2,000th Learjet in August 1999. Learjet suffered a sharp drop in sales after 9/11, and undertook large-scale layoffs in Wichita in 2002. The Model 40 and Model 45 remained market factors, and the older and larger Model 60 was succeeded by the developed Model 60XR, with a redesigned interior and advanced avionics, which entered service in 2006. Learjet remained a significant competitor in the middle range of the business jet market, although its designs were regarded as somewhat dated.

Gulfstream, after years of instability, was financially strong again in the late 1990s. General Dynamics, reentering the business jet market after its disposal of Cessna in 1992, acquired Gulfstream on July 31, 1999, for $4.8 billion. The new ownership proved stable, and Gulfstream remained a major force in the larger business jet market. Its leadership in the high end of the business jet market continued with the introduction of the G550 in September 2003, succeeding what had been the GV. The GIV continued as the redesignated G450. Potentially of greater significance was development of an even larger business jet, the G650. First planned in 2003, the program was approved by parent General Dynamics in May 2005, and formally announced in 2008. It was regarded as the most ambitious project for Gulfstream (and predecessor Grumman) since the Gulfstream II in 1965, and was the largest, most advanced and highest performance model ever developed by Gulfstream. While of similar configuration to earlier Gulfstreams, the G650 was in fact a completely new design. The model cost $1 billion to develop to the point of service entry, and was priced in the $65 million range. The program remained on strong footing despite the economic reverses coming soon after its appearance on the market.

The midsize Gulfstream G250, still built in Israel and fitted out in the U.S. completion center, succeeded the older G200, originally the Galaxy marketed by Galaxy Aerospace. General Dynamics had acquired Galaxy Aerospace and its product line in 2001. While a major advance ever the G200, the G250 faced a depressed market and weak orders. In September 2011 it was redesignated G280 out of consideration for the increasingly critical Chinese market, where 280 was considered a more amenable number sequence in Chinese culture. G200 production ended in December 20, 2011, after 14 years, with delivery of the 250th and last at the Dallas completion center. The G550 enjoyed a continuing global military market for electronic warfare versions, and Gulfstream enjoyed strong coverage in the luxury jet sector, with its product line of the G150, G280, older G450 and G550 long-range models, and the new G650.

In the very large and long-range business jet segment, the Boeing Business Jets division made strong progress, aided by the growing market perception that long-range business jets were essential to reach distant markets such as the Middle East, China, and India. The first Boeing BBJ, a hybrid adaptation of the 737–700 and 737–800 new-generation models, and a joint venture of Boeing and General Electric, was announced in July 1996. In fact, the venture was first suggested by GE CEO Jack Welch to Boeing CEO Phil Condit, and GE became the first customer for the Boeing BBJ. The first delivery was on October 29, 1998, and 114 were delivered by 2007. Known as the BBJ 1, it was joined by the BBJ 2, based on the 737–800, and by the longer-ranged BBJ 3, based on the 737–900ER. Boeing's airliner competitor Airbus also competed in the large business jet market.

Despite daunting development costs, technological challenges, and a dubious market, the dream of a supersonic long-range business jet persisted. The Aerion firm of Reno, Nevada, founded in 2002 and headed by veteran aviation executive Brian Barents, announced its SBJ concept in 2004. Target price was $80 million, and the company claimed serious customer interest, but development still lagged.

The small but significant agricultural sector was led by the veteran producer Air Tractor of Olney, Texas. Air Tractor had produced more than 2,000 aircraft by 2002, and maintained a small but steady delivery rate of some 60 per year, primarily of its AT-402 and larger AT-502 turbine-powered models.

Ayres, while continuing the large agricultural line it had acquired in 1977, heavily staked its future on the Loadmaster specialized cargo aircraft, with backing by Federal Express as the major customer. A first flight was originally projected for 1999, but Ayres, lacking full engineering resources, in 1998 acquired 93 percent control of the veteran Czech aircraft firm Let Kunovice. Let's experience in transport development was valuable in the design and development of the Loadmaster, and Fred Ayres felt that ownership would enable him to better control of the overall project. The Loadmaster still fell seriously behind schedule, however, and in a further complication, Let Kunovice went bankrupt in 2000 when its primary banker cut off credit. Unable to secure a definite delivery date, and frustrated with delays, FedEx cancelled its order in June 2000, leading to a production shutdown. FedEx briefly considered financing the firm, but withdrew. GATX, the major creditor, foreclosed on August 7, 2001, and Ayres entered Chapter 11 bankruptcy in November 2001.[20] The Loadmaster prototype was never completed. Among other setbacks, the United States had been planning to use Ayres agricultural aircraft in drug suppression in Colombia, but that prospect ended with the Ayres shutdown.

The successor Thrush Aircraft, Inc., was formed on June 30, 2003, with rights to the agricultural aircraft line. Businessman Payne Hughes purchased the assets and restarted production. The product line was modernized, with the Model 710 powered by the PWC PT6A and the Model 510 powered by the GE H80 turboprop, a developed version of the Czech Walter engine. The smaller Thrush 400, powered by the legacy R-1340 radial piston engine, was also offered. Operations gained stability. President Larry Bays expressed pride in that Thrush aircraft operated around the world, and were particularly useful in renewed drug suppression efforts in Latin America.[21] The Thrush Model 710 was also modified into an armed patrol and surveillance model by Iomax, at its Mooresville, North Carolina, facility. It was noteworthy that all Air Tractor, Ayres, and Thrush agricultural models originated with and extended from the designs of Leland Snow. Current Thrush models contained a high component of steel in their structure to handle the stressful loads required, and agricultural aircraft had progressed impressively, both in technology and capability, since the early days of modified Stearman trainers in the role.

Maule Air production was sustained at low volume throughout the decade. An order from the Civil Air Patrol in 2000 was significant. June Maule, who had led the company after the death of her husband, died in 2009, but control remained with the Maule family. The company celebrated its 50th anniversary in Moultrie, Georgia, in 2011. The MX-7, with 180 hp, and the more powerful M-7 continued. A new M-9 offered an increase in capacity. Further, the original Maule M-4 was revived in the upgraded Jetasen II version.

Innovation and new market attempts, always marking the industry, continued regardless of unfavorable economic conditions. Groen Brothers had been established in Salt Lake City in 1986 to develop a modern gyroplane concept. While the concept was not new, extending from the experiments of Cierva in the 1920s, the brothers felt that technical advances could make it safer and more stable than earlier autogyros. The small Groen SparrowHawk model first flew on February 4, 1997. The fledgling firm initially sought financing from Saudi Arabia and China, offering to share production with those nations, but deals eventually collapsed. Investors were hard to attract after the collapse of the tech bubble and the terrorist attacks of 9/11, but the brothers persisted. The craft was marketed as valuable for police and anti-terrorist op-

The Ayres (later Thrush) Turbo Thrush S2R-T34, a powerful agricultural aircraft (photograph by Gary Blockley, courtesy Thrush Aircraft).

The Ayres (later Thrush) Turbo Thrush S2R-G10, with the P&W Canada PT6A engine (photograph by Gary Blockley, courtesy Thrush Aircraft).

erations. While unable to hover as a helicopter, it would be much cheaper to buy and operate. The kit was priced at $32,000 while a fully assembled model was around $65,000, while a competing small factory-built helicopter would cost $500,000.[22] American Autogyro, Inc., was formed in December 2002 as a subsidiary of Groen to develop the Hawk, but was merged into the parent in November 2004. Jay Groen died in 2006, but his brother David continued. Groen was also working for FAA certification for its larger Hawk 4.

Quest Aircraft Company was formed in Sandpoint, Idaho, in 2001, to build and market its Kodiak bush airplane, designed by Tom Hamilton. Turboprop-powered and of rugged construction, the Kodiak was somewhat competitive with the Cessna Caravan and was intended to replace such veteran bush aircraft as the Canadian Beaver and Otter. The Kodiak first flew on October 16, 2004, and began to find customers in its narrow segment. Some 24 were delivered in 2009, and the U.S. Fish and Wildlife Service was a customer.

Aviat of Wyoming continued with its successful Husky, serving both as a sportplane and small utility or bush aircraft. It had acquired rights to the legacy Globe Swift and Monocoupe 110 designs, but did not move ahead with production of either. Aviat continued to offer the Pitts S-2C sportplane as a complete aircraft, and the Christen Eagle II as a kit. CubCrafters, Inc., of Yakima, Washington, was the latest in a long series of ventures to sustain the original Piper Super Cub, beginning deliveries in 1999. Of particular note was that the Super Cub qualified as a light sport aircraft. The line expanded with the Top Cub, a high-performance model, and the Carbon Cub kit model. Another veteran design, the originally Meyers 200, went through several ownership changes, including MICCO, a venture of the Seminole tribe of Florida. Production was intended at Fort Pierce, Florida, but operations moved to Bartlesville, Oklahoma, in 2007, after being acquired by a Chinese owner, LanShe Aerospace, in March 2003. American Champion of Rochester,

Wisconsin, continued as a low-volume producer of its veteran but respected products. Several versions of the Citabria, Decathlon, and Scout were offered, and the classic Champ qualified as an LSA.

While very small, another venture indicative of continuing entrepreneurship and innovation in general aviation was Waco Classic Aircraft Corporation of Battle Creek, Michigan, begun in the 1980s as Classic Aircraft Corporation by Dick Kettles, a fixed-base operator. Kettles updated the original 1930s Waco YMF-5 biplane and placed it in low-rate production as a sportplane. Kettles later sold the company to veteran pilot Peter Bowers, who maintained production of the YMF-5 at a basic price of $450,000. In 2011 Bowers reintroduced the small Great Lakes 2T-1A-2 biplane as well, also modernized with a new engine and contemporary construction materials, at a price of some $240,000.

Alexandria Aircraft of Alexandria, Minnesota, holding the Bellanca nameplate but never a major market factor, evidently became inactive after 2005. The Socata TB line, for some time a factor in the American light single-engined market, also exited in 2005. Commander Aircraft, operating as a subsidiary of Aviation General since 1998, maintained low-volume production of the Commander single-engined line until bankruptcy on December 27, 2002. It reorganized under a new corporate structure on July 5, 2003, but again failed, entering Chapter 7 liquidation on January 14, 2005. Attempts to sell the assets were unsuccessful. Fairchild Dornier suffered bankruptcy in 2002, but a successor firm continued to provide support for the D328 executive transport and commuter airliner. The exit of Fairchild Dornier also marked the exit of the Fairchild nameplate from aircraft.

Homebuilt/Kitplane Developments

One trend in the kitplane or homebuilt sector was the development and marketing of larger and higher-performance models for kit construction. While most kits were for small and simple single-seat and two-seat sport and aerobatic airplanes, more sophisticated models for business use were increasingly available. For example, Aircraft Investor Resources, Inc. (AIR), established in 2004 in Bend, Oregon, and marketing under the name Epic Aircraft, designed an ambitious six-seat turboprop-powered business model, the LT. It was originally produced as a kit, priced from $895,000 to more than $1 million. After legal difficulties resulting in Chapter 11 bankruptcy in 2009, the kit model was discontinued in 2010. CAIGA of China originally bid $4.3 million for the company, but was required under a court order to partner with LT Builders Group, consisting of LT owners. Epic was afterward acquired by the Russian Engineering LLC firm in March 2012. The firm subsequently developed the factory-built Epic E1000 and pursued certification. Base price was expected to be $2.75 million.

Another ambitious model was the Lancair Evolution, a five-seat model with computer-assisted design and composite construction. Including the PT-6 turboprop engine and complete instrumentation, the kit was priced at more than $1 million. A lower-priced piston-powered model, still pressurized, was added later. The Evolution marked the culmination of Lance Neibauer's work on high-performance kit designs. Beginning with two-seaters, he felt encouraged by AGATE to develop larger and more innovative designs. In addition, there was the new Legacy high-performance two-seat kit model. The high-performance fixed-gear LC40 Columbia, developed by Neibauer, appeared in 1998 under its own nameplate, as mentioned previously. The Columbia had struggled to compete with Cirrus, but the design survived with Cessna. Under new ownership, the Evolution also survived and appeared promising. Other trends included the development of kitbuilt helicopters and amphibians.

Table 9-1
Homebuilt Aircraft C of A's Issued

Year	Total
1995	1,040
1996	1,016
1997	786
1998	848
1999	760
2000	913
2001	1,437
2002	1,204
2003	907
2004	958
2005	1,081
2006	911
2007	1,614
2008	836
2009	855
2010	941

SOURCE: Experimental Aircraft Association, *Report to Homebuilders*, 2012, p. 2.

9—The Industry Enters the New Millennium

While comprehensive and reliable statistics were sometimes difficult to obtain, it was quite clear that the homebuilt sector was large and growing. The EAA *Report to Homebuilders* for 2011 reported a figure of some 33,000 registered homebuilts in the United States, with more in other countries. That total constituted some 15 percent of the U.S. single-engined piston fleet.[23] The report also emphasized the well-developed supporting infrastructure for homebuilt aircraft, and mentioned that the segment showed the most consistent growth of any in general aviation, even in the recession. While there were still concerns over the homebuilt accident rate, the fleet was growing by an average of 1,000 aircraft per year.

Table 9-2
U.S. Experimental Aircraft Fleet, 2000–2013

Year	Amateur-Experimental	Exhibition Built	Experimental Light-Sport	Other	Total
2000	16,739	1,973	—	1,694	20,406
2001	16,736	2,052	—	1,633	20,421
2002	18,168	2,190	—	1,578	21,936
2003	17,028	2,031	—	1,491	20,550
2004	19,165	2,070	—	1,565	22,800
2005	19,817	2,120	—	1,691	23,628
2006	19,316	2,103	—	1,629	23,048
2007	19,538	2,101	—	1,589	23,228
2008	19,767	2,096	—	1,501	23,364
2009	20,794	2,063	5,077	1,562	29,496
2010	21,270	2,029	4,878	1,485	29,662
2011	n/a	n/a	n/a	n/a	n/a
2012	18,843	1,923	4,631	1,317	26,715
2013	17,503	1,908	4,157	1,350	24,918

SOURCE: FAA Survey.

The following survey highlights the major active kit manufacturers active early in the new century. Aero Designs, Inc., of San Antonio, Texas, offered the low-wing Pulsar XP. The Pulsar's status became unclear, however, as a Pulsar Aircraft Corporation acquired rights and moved assembly to the Republic of El Salvador. Avid Aircraft, Inc., of Caldwell, Idaho, offered the Rotax-powered Flyer Mark IV and the Lycoming-powered Magnum. Bede of Medina, Ohio, operating as Bedecorp LLC, still was engaged in development of small single- and two-seat kitplanes, most of low-wing configuration. Stoddard-Hamilton, which after continuing financial problems had declared bankruptcy on July 17, 2000, was succeeded by separate companies, Glasair and GlaStar, to produce developed Hamilton fiberglass designs. The Glasair two-seat design was offered in taildragger, tricycle, and retractable gear options. Next came the developed Glasair IIS in 1990, and further developments. The two companies then were merged in 2005, still in Arlington, Washington. Glasair offered the Super II low-wing side-by-side seating model, and the Glasair III high-performance model. GlaStar models were high-wing. All models were of predominantly fiberglass construction, and Glasair continued to emphasize expedited construction for its kits. By 2013 total kit production of the Glasair I, II, and IV exceeded 1,800.

Frank Christensen's sport design, the Christen Eagle, competed with the Stits S-2A. He was a major contributor toward making kit construction feasible to the masses. Although retired, his kits remained available through Aviat. Randy Schlitter's Rans of Hays, Kansas, continued as a significant kit producer, with some models qualifying as LSAs. More than 1,500 of the Rans S-6 were flying. Rans continued to develop an extensive line of light aircraft Perhaps the most notable kitplane industrialist was Richard VanGrunsven, whose Van's, Inc., founded in 1974, was recognized as the oldest continuously operating kitplane producer in the United States. His production record, at over 7,600 kits delivered by 2011, was definitely the highest. His initial RV-1

The RANS S-7S Courier, a representative homebuilt aircraft of 2018 (courtesy RANS Designs, Inc.).

was developed from the Stits design, but subsequent designs up to the RV-14 were original. (The RV designation was from his initials.) His models encompassed both tandem seating and side-by-side seating, and still featured aluminum construction rather than composites. He moved operations to Aurora, Oregon, in 2001. Most established kit models were still actively produced.

Kitfox Aircraft LLC, of Homedale, Idaho, began in 1984 as Denney Aerocraft Company, established by Dan Denney. He sold rights to a new Skystar Aircraft Corporation of Nampa, Idaho, in July 1992, which continued production of his designs. The company then underwent an employee takeover in 2000. It reported a total of 5,000 kits sold by August 2005, led by the Kitfox IV, but declared bankruptcy that year. The company continued as Kitfox Aircraft with the Kitfox IV and further developments. Most qualified as LSAs. The Sequoia Falco, while a highly regarded design, earned a reputation as time-consuming to construct, and continued at low volume. Liberty Aircraft, of Melbourne, Florida, manufactured the Liberty XL-2, from the British-designed Europa sport model, and won FAA certification in 2006. The company attracted Kuwaiti investment in 2004, and later a Chinese owner. Some 100 kits had been produced by 2009, and new production was essentially to order.

Zenith Aircraft Company, of Mexico, Missouri, offered a broad product

The RANS S-21 Outbound, a representative homebuilt aircraft of 2018 (courtesy RANS Designs, Inc.).

line, with some 2,700 kits sold by 2002. It began in 1992 with designs acquired under license from the Canadian engineer Chris Heintz, who founded a company in Ontario in 1974. Zenith, an anagram of Heintz, undertook continuous development of the designs, marketed as Zenair, and included the CH701 two-seat high-wing sport model, the four-seat CH 801, the CH750 LSA, and the CH650 low-wing sport model. All except the CH801 potentially qualified as LSAs. Sebastian Heintz became manager, succeeding his father, who remained active in the field. Aircraft Manufacturing and Development (AMD) of Eastman, Georgia, established in 1999, offered three aircraft designs, the Alarus CH2000 light two-seat trainer, the Zodiac CH601 light sport aircraft, and the Patriot 150 high-winged two-seat LSA, which was not available as a kit, but only as a complete ready-to-fly model. While originally owned by the Heintz family, and producing designs similar to those of Zenith, the company was later owned by local interests. Sonex was founded in 1999 in the EAA city of Oshkosh, Wisconsin. It built advanced all-metal, high-performance, low-wing single-place designs for kit construction. While small in volume, Sonex won increasing respect, and developed a single-jet powered model.

Veteran designer and executive LeRoy LoPresti died on August 7, 2002, of injuries suffered in a fall, at age 73. Curtis Pitts, the pioneer aerobatic experimenter and homebuilt designer, died June 10, 2005, age 88.

Helicopter Survey

American civil helicopter producers faced increasingly strong European competition, especially from Eurocopter and AgustaWestland. Russian helicopters, benefiting from Western engine and electronics technology, also were becoming a potential market factor. The helicopter sector probably faced a more severe threat from European competitors than any other general aviation sector, as some felt that Europe had exceeded American investment in the field. In fact, Europe began to out produce North America in turbine helicopters, and Eurocopter enjoyed 40 percent of the world market for civil helicopters as compared to 17 percent for Bell.[24] European helicopters were increasingly competitive in the oil service field as well. U.S. production remained strong, however. In 2004 Bell delivered a total of 109 of its civil models, from the 206 through the 412, while Sikorsky delivered 25 S-76 and 4 S-92 models.[25] Some production records were conspicuously impressive. By 2010 Bell had delivered more than 6,300 of the Model 206 of all variants since production began in 1967. Production of the Model 206, along with the Models 427 and 430, finally ended in 2010. The advanced Model 430, carrying eight passengers, enjoyed a relatively brief production life, as it had only been introduced in the mid–1990s. The Model 206 series remained widely used for emergency medical service (EMS), among other roles. Air Medical Group Holdings (AMGH) for example, reported a fleet of 155 Bell helicopters. The Model 206B-4 LongRanger remained in limited production.

Bell continued to offer a broad range of civil helicopters. New models included the Model 412EP medium twin, an advanced development of its classic Huey military series, which became a competitor. Bell also developed the new Model 429 GlobalRanger, first flying on February 27, 2007, with advanced rotor blades, offered in both corporate and EMS configurations. It was a significant technical advance over the veteran LongRanger, Model 427, and earlier models, and was priced in the $5 million range. Boeing and Bell had collaborated on development of the early XV-15 tiltrotor for years. Boeing withdrew in 1998, but Bell partnered with Agusta of Italy on the civil tiltrotor model for executive use, redesignated Bell/Agusta BA609. Then Bell withdrew in 2011 after development delays and rising costs, and the program became no longer American. Agusta still pursued certification, although it was delayed beyond 2014.

MD Helicopters experienced ownership changes following the merger of McDonnell Douglas into Boeing in 1997. A proposed merger of the helicopter operation with Bell Helicopters was prohibited by antitrust considerations, and the firm was sold to Dutch investors in 1999. With continued competitive pressures, sales declined and production ended in 2005. Investor Lynn Tilton, after two successful decades on Wall Street in investment banking and collateralized debt obligations, founded the global investment firm Patriarch Partners in 2000. Her firm engaged in venture capital operations by rescuing troubled industrial firms, with the announced goal of keeping jobs in the United States. She acquired MD Helicopters in 2005, with a goal to turn the firm around rather than to bring about a quick sale. She worked with suppliers and customers to revive current models, and faced a particular challenge in reviving the deteriorating supply chain. Tilton moved her firm's headquarters to Arizona, but shifted much helicopter production to Mexico. MD also operated as a Women's Business Enterprise, attracting government support under that program.[26]

While traditionally a military firm, Sikorsky increasingly turned its attention to the larger civil helicopter segment. The Model S-76 remained a strong contender in the global civil market, particularly for offshore oil platform service. More than 800 S-76s of all variants up through the S-76++ had been delivered by 2011. Sikorsky had launched the even larger S-92 in June 1995, both for military and business roles. The model was also heavily globalized, with components produced in Japan, China, Taiwan, Spain, and by Embraer of Brazil. First flight was December 23, 1999, and the first models entered service in 2004. S-92 orders remained steady both for executive transportation and oil platform service. The Schweizer (formerly Hughes)

The Sikorsky S-76 in Emergency Medical configuration, circa (Igor I. Sikorsky Historical Archives © November 2018).

Model 300 was to be built by a Shanghai/Sikorsky joint venture announced in February 2002. Sikorsky then acquired Schweizer as a wholly owned subsidiary in August 2004. Sikorsky began transferring production of the Schweizer models to its Coatesville, Pennsylvania, factory.

While the rotary-wing market was dominated by turbine-powered models, Enstrom and Sikorsky-owned Schweizer, in addition to Robinson, remained factors. Enstrom gained an order for 30 TH-480B trainers from the Japan Ground Self-Defense Forces, and its prospects improved with the attraction of Chinese investment. Robinson, while a small firm, enjoyed steady demand for its helicopters. It provided strong competition in the segment, especially in pricing. The Kaman K-Max civil model ended its limited production run in 2003, although subject to revival if demand warranted.

The light helicopter pioneer Stanley Hiller, Jr., died in California April 20, 2006, at 82, and R. J. Enstrom, also a light helicopter pioneer, died in 2007, age 89.

The time from the late 1990s to 2008 had seen many setbacks to general aviation producers. Once-promising aircraft developers as Ayres, Adam, and Eclipse suffered bankruptcy, while others struggled to gain a foothold in the marketplace. Even so, many established designs reemerged under new corporate names, such as Thrush, and under new ownership, such as Piper, Cirrus, Mooney, Hawker Beechcraft, and the former MD Helicopters. Entrepreneurship, the characteristic that had marked general aviation from its beginnings, remained strong. Despite the market upheaval and the altered operating environment brought about by 9/11, rapidly increasing globalization, and regulatory changes, the industry had made heartening progress overall in the first decade of the 21st century. Demand and deliveries increased steadily during the middle of the decade. But just as the future appeared brighter, and optimism prevailed throughout the industry, the sudden and unanticipated recession of 2008–2009 led to yet another trauma. Overall business declined sharply, even threatening the survival of long-established firms as well as damaging the prospects of promising new contenders.

10

Again, Crisis and Recovery

There had been substantial progress in the general aviation industry from the late 1990s to 2008, both in technological innovations and overall industry stability, but in that year the most severe economic contraction since the Great Depression struck. Just as general aviation was beginning to enjoy stronger demand and renewed prosperity, the Great Recession of 2008 and beyond confronted the industry with its greatest crisis since the product liability crisis of the 1980s. Always sensitive to economic conditions, the general aviation aircraft market suffered immediately and severely. Demand for many types of aircraft virtually collapsed, as large corporations and other business users that might otherwise have renewed or expanded their fleets instead cancelled or postponed purchases. Many manufacturers imposed production suspensions for certain models, followed by substantial employee layoffs. The impact was deeper and longer lasting than the crisis following 9/11, and affected almost all segments of the industry, but was felt most severely in the business jet segment. In addition, ever-increasing development costs and an overcrowded market acted to severely restrict commercial prospects of numerous models. Several promising new designs were suspended or cancelled entirely, and certain long-established firms faced diminished futures, if not extinction. By 2012–2013 the overall economy was showing signs of improvement, but the general aviation aircraft market still lagged. While most maintained optimism for an eventual recovery, the date for its realization was pushed farther out.

Most marketing and development emphasis remained on the high-dollar business jet field, while the prospects for a return to high-volume production of light single-engined aircraft remained dubious. The major problem was that the industry still was unable to develop and market an affordable light personal or business aircraft. With two-seat LSA models priced at $150,000 and up, and larger piston single-engined models costing from $300,000 to more than $900,000, factory-built airplanes remained out of reach of all but the truly wealthy. It was already well established that the escalating prices of factory-built aircraft had led directly to the rise of the kit industry. The affordability problem was of long-term duration, of course, extending back more than 80 years. While technological improvements and innovations were significant cost factors, sharp price rises, well over the rate of inflation, still dampened the overall market potential.

Regulatory changes were felt by many to further complicate the prospects for a strong general aviation market recovery. After years of study, the FAA in 2014 imposed a requirement that all general aviation aircraft, except for the smallest, be equipped with Automatic Dependent Surveillance-Broadcast (ADS-B) equipment by the year 2020, as a key component of the overall NextGen system transformation. Such equipment would be required for all aircraft operating in controlled airspace, and would enable all aircraft to broadcast their positions and flight data to all others in the area. While ADS-B unquestionably would be a major advance in air safety and operating efficiency, retrofit costs were projected to be very high, in turn imposing a considerable economic challenge to owners, especially of smaller and older aircraft. Initial estimates were that the upgrades could cost from $5,000 to $40,000, depending on the model of aircraft, a disturbing prospect for most owners. The NBAA along with other general aviation organizations supported NextGen, but also expressed concern over the cost impact of the mandate.

Another issue with the FAA included plans to assess user fees on general aviation operations. Legislation introduced in 2016, the Aviation Innovation, Reform, and Reauthorization (AIRR) Act, included a provision to privatize the air traffic control system, financed by user fees. General aviation organizations were united in their opposition to burdensome fees. The AIRR evolved into a 2018 law reauthorizing the FAA for another five years, which was supported by the industry.

Beyond such specific measures, the safety record of general aviation remained a public concern. While flight safety was paramount for manufacturers, owners, and pilots, and numerous safety advances had been made, general aviation still was regarded as less safe than other aviation sectors, and that perception was borne out by crash statistics. The NBAA emphasized the point that many accidents were in the nature of ground damage rather than occurring in flight, yet it was undeniable that general aviation accidents and fatalities greatly exceeded those of scheduled commercial services. Private flying fatalities of such high-profile figures as John F. Kennedy, Jr., John Denver, and famed test pilot Scott Crossfield reinforced the public perception of unsafe operations. The most frequently determined reason for general aviation fatalities was Loss of Control (LOC), leading to questions about the adequacy of flight training. The issue remained contentious. A possibly favorable result was that there was increasing emphasis on development of safety innovations, particularly on flight controls.

Industry Survey

Regardless of negative events and market challenges largely attributable to the Great Recession, product development and competitive undertakings continued at a high level throughout the industry, as Table 10-1 describes.

Table 10-1
U.S. General Aviation Production by Major Category

Year	Pistons	Turboprops	Business Jets
2000	1,980	415	752
2001	1,792	422	784
2002	1,721	280	676
2003	1,896	272	518
2004	2,051	319	592
2005	2,465	375	750
2006	2,755	412	887
2007	2,675	465	1,137
2008	2,119	538	1,317
2009	963	446	874
2010	889	368	767
2011	898	526	696
2012	908	584	672
2013	1,030	645	678
2014	1,129	603	722
2015	1,056	557	718
2016	1,019	582	667
2017	1,085	563	676

SOURCE: *2017 Annual Report*, p. 25. Washington, D.C.: GAMA, 2017. From 2011, figures include agricultural airplanes, new piston manufacturers, and some helicopters.

The PA-47 PiperJet, Piper's first jet design, was launched after years of study and aimed at the projected VLJ market. Powered by a single tail-mounted engine, the PiperJet made its first flight in July 2008, and attracted strong interest. The prototype used the basic cabin of the Malibu series, but the design soon was recast with a larger cabin, renamed Altaire, and was projected to reach the market in 2014 at a price of $2.4 million. Then Piper's new Asian owners, facing the continuing recession and dubious market prospects, announced the suspension of the Altaire on October 24, 2011, although development was on schedule. More than 200 Piper employees had worked on the program. Piper briefly entered the LSA market by undertaking license production of a Czech design that it marketed as the PiperSport. While a low-wing model, it was competitive with the Cessna SkyCatcher. But the program was suspended in January 2011 after some 40 were completed.

The Piper nameplate celebrated its 75th anniversary in 2012. The cabin-class single-engined models extending from the original Malibu remained Piper's most important line and were continuously upgraded. The turboprop Meridian was redesignated M600 and M500, the former being the high-performance version, and the Mirage became the M350. All, including the Matrix, were refined, with the M600 gaining a completely new wing. With a price in the $3 million range, the M600 effectively succeeded the Altaire. The legacy Arrow and Archer lines were offered as trainers, as was the Seminole for twin-engined training.

The fortunes of Mooney during the 2008–2010 recession served to illustrate the overall business decline for the industry. In 2007, a boom year, Mooney delivered 79 aircraft. But in 2010 it delivered only two, and in 2011 it delivered none. Employment dropped from 480 to nine. Then named Mooney Aviation Company and under private ownership, the company's management acknowledged that it simply lacked the capital to restart production, although several aircraft were on the line in various stages of completion. Successive owners over the decades had not stabilized the company. The firm continued to support the active fleet of some 7,000 Mooneys, and prices of used Mooney models appeared to hold up well. A challenge for the firm in attaining any long-term viability was its aged production facilities; the plant basically dated from the 1950s, with little automation.[1] In 2013 Mooney again came under new ownership, being acquired by the Chinese Meijing Group, and renamed Mooney International Corporation. Led by CEO Jerry Chen, the group invested substantial capital and acquired new production facilities. Production was resumed in 2014 for both the established M20 Ovation and Acclaim series, and more advanced developments were announced. Then, late in 2014, Mooney announced two new three-seat small models of composite construction. The M10T had diesel power and fixed gear, while the M10J featured retractable gear and higher power.

In size reminiscent of the original Mite of 1948, the new models retained the classic Mooney configuration, but were designed in California under contract rather than in-house. New president Vivek Sarena, an experienced aeronautical engineer, replaced Jerry Chen in 2016. Production of established models moved ahead, but the small M10 models were suspended.

Cessna, the leading business jet producer by production volume with its dominance in smaller models, announced a plan to move up the scale with the Columbus, the largest and most ambitious model it had ever conceived. The new model was announced in February 2008, after earlier being presented as the Large Cabin Concept aircraft in 2006. But development then was suspended in April 2009 and cancelled in September 2009,due to the severe recession.[2] Still committed to the larger business jet segment, Cessna in 2010 announced the new Citation Ten, succeeding the long-produced Citation X, heretofore its largest aircraft and still marketed as the fastest business jet. The Citation Ten also indicated Cessna's intention to end the use of roman numeral designations, but that was soon reversed as customers preferred the traditional designations, and the design again became Citation X. The new Citation X was considerably refined over the earlier version, largely unchanged since 2002, being longer, with winglets, new engines and avionics, and a refurbished interior. As the Citation Ten, it made its first flight on January 17, 2012, and specified maximum cruising speed was Mach 0.92.[3] Certification came in mid–2013.

Cessna's business overall fell sharply in the 2008–2010 recession, with output falling to 50 percent of the 2008 peak. Production of several models was suspended, and massive layoffs were carried out at all Cessna factories and support facilities. Cessna was particularly affected in that its product line consisted principally of small and medium-sized business jets, always more vulnerable to economic contractions. It was announced on May 2, 2011, in the depths of the business decline, that Jack Pelton, CEO since 2001, had retired, likely a victim of the recession. New product announcements continued, however, first with the Citation M2, sized between the light Mustang and the CitationJet series and featuring more advanced FJ44 engines, with a $4.2 million base price. Basically an upgrade of the CJ series, the M2 effectively replaced the low-end CitationJet CJ1+, which was discontinued after less than six years. M2 deliveries began in 2013.

Further manifesting its strong belief in an eventual business jet market recovery, Cessna pursued an ambitious development program. Late in 2011, two new designs were announced. First was the Citation 680A Latitude, developed from the Sovereign at the higher end of the midsize segment, and sized between the Citation XLS and Sovereign. The improved Sovereign+ remained the pacesetter in the midsize category, with impressive design refinements and avionics, but the Citation Latitude was expected to be an even more significant technological advance. The Latitude featured the widest, most spacious cabin in the line and became virtually a new design. It was announced for service from 2014, priced at $14.9 million. The program received a boost with a major order from NetJets soon after its announcement. Cessna followed the Latitude with announcement of the larger Citation Longitude, effectively replacing the cancelled Columbus. Price was projected in the $25 million range, and it entered flight testing after 2015.[4] The Longitude was to be powered by the advanced French Silvercrest engine. With a flurry of design activity, Cessna offered more comprehensive coverage of the business jet market than ever before, with the Mustang, M2, CitationJet series, Sovereign+, Citation XLS+, revised Citation X, and the new designs.

Cessna announced further new developments, including most impressively the completely new Hemisphere, its largest business jet ever, with a 4,500-nautical mile range and a price above $35 million. Unveiled in October 2015, it bid to compete with the newest Gulfstream models. In another category, Cessna in July 2016 announced the Denali, a single-engined executive model powered by the new GE Catalyst advanced turboprop (ATP), of similar configuration to but larger than the successful Pilatus PC-12. With a price around $4.8 million, it would be a strong competitor in its category, and was projected to enter the market late in 2019. Delays with both the aircraft and the engine delayed flight testing into 2020, however.

Prospects were not so encouraging at the low end of Cessna's product line. Deliveries of the SkyCatcher LSA began in 2008 against a backlog of 850 announced orders, but as expected the base price was raised to $149,000 for 2012. Cessna also announced that it would undertake more finishing out of airframes in Wichita. New Cessna CEO Scott Ernest then publicly stated in October 2013 that the Model 162 SkyCatcher had no future. Orders had declined sharply after the strong launch, and marketing and production were suspended in mid–2014 after only some 200 had been delivered. Cessna concluded that the program could not become profitable, and the once-promising LSA category appeared almost moribund.

It remained noteworthy that by 2014 Cessna had produced more than 48,000 of the basic Model 172, later Skyhawk, since 1955. Also noteworthy was that the Independence, Kansas, plant that had begun production only in 1997 reached the milestone of 9,000 single-engined piston airplanes produced on March 4, 2010. Cessna had originally projected the 10,000 mark would be reached earlier in the new century, but with weak demand it was not attained until 2014. The Independence plant was built when Cessna had no excess capacity in Wichita, but with market disruptions and declining demand for the Skyhawk, that factory was faced with excess capacity as well. Skyhawk and Skylane production had been suspended for some time as well. Cessna transferred some Citation and TTx production work to Independence, and the Model 182 and Model 206 remained in low-volume production. Another major milestone was delivery of the 2,000th Caravan in September 2010. The first Caravan delivery was in 1985, demand remained steady, and the type was certified in 100 countries. In 2016 Cessna announced transfer of Caravan production to Independence also, freeing capacity for the new Longitude.

After the Columbia acquisition, Cessna faced the difficulties of managing a remote operation, and decided to close the Oregon plant in 2009. Production of the line was moved to Independence, helping alleviate its excess capacity. The move coincided with Cessna's suspension of the large Columbus. Cessna undertook numerous refinements, renamed the designs the Corvalis 350 (normally aspirated) and Corvalis 400 (turbocharged), and marketed the high-performance, low-winged, fixed-gear singles as complements to its traditional high-winged models. The Corvalis effectively replaced the cancelled NGP in the product line. Cessna planned to produce components for the Corvalis at its facility in Chihuahua, Mexico. But coming in the face of the severe recession, and with several delays due to structural issues, Cessna suspended the Corvalis until 2012. By 2013 the design reemerged, was recertified, redesignated the T240, and renamed once again as the Cessna TTx. Powered only by the turbocharged engine, it reentered production, with numerous updates.[5] The basic model dated back more than 20 years from Lance Neibauer and the Lancair ES. The new TTx was positioned as a direct competitor to the Cirrus series, but Mexican-produced components suffered from quality control issues. The TTx market simply did not develop, however, with only 17 models delivered in 2017, and Cessna announced the end of the program, on which it had invested millions.

Cessna scaled back its once-ambitious plans for manufacturing in China. Not only was the production arrangement for the SkyCatcher over, but discussions with AVIC to co-produce the Sovereign and new Latitude were suspended. Arrangements for assembly of the Caravan, a model with strong applicability in China, and the Citation XLS+ business jet model, still moved ahead with CAIGA. CAIGA had announced a plan to develop its own small business aircraft, the TP150, based on the Epic LT high-performance kitplane, although China's plan to acquire Epic had been reversed in 2010.[6] CAIGA instead purchased the Epic design for future development.

Bend, Oregon, adversely affected by Cessna's move of the former Columbia plant, worked to regain production in general aviation with kit producer Epic Aircraft. Epic acquired the former Cessna factory, but declared bankruptcy in 2008. After reorganization, Epic resumed development of its high-performance kitplane business aircraft model, the Epic 1000, which reentered the market in 2018.

Hawker Beechcraft announced in December 2010 that it would remain in Wichita, after considering an offer, including financial incentives, from Baton Rouge, Louisiana, to relocate there. The city of Wichita had responded with an incentive package. Hawker Beechcraft had cumulative losses of $1 billion for 2009–2011, and while emphasizing cost cutting, there was little optimism for a profit in 2012. CEO Bill Boisture publicly expected 2012 to be a tough year. The Hawker 4000, in the overcrowded super midsize segment, and the King Air line were perhaps more vulnerable to an economic downturn than larger models. In addition to large operating losses, the company carried a major debt burden, and pushed through a restructuring, resulting in among other things major job losses.[7] As with many aviation firms, Hawker Beechcraft considered relationships in China. AVIC, already owning Cirrus, announced interest in developing two new business jets with a foreign partner. Hawker Beechcraft was a prime candidate for the deal, although competing with IAI, Bombardier, and Cessna for such an affiliation. China regarded the advanced technology of the Hawker 4000 as highly desirable.

Despite all efforts at stabilization, the continuing severe recession and Hawker Beechcraft's heavy debt burden resulted in a long-rumored declaration of bankruptcy, coming on May 3, 2012. The event immediately brought up the question of a sale of the company. Several U.S. buyers were discussed, and there was considerable surprise when Hawker Beechcraft announced, on July 9, 2012, an agreement to be purchased by Superior Aviation Beijing of China for $1.8 billion. While the established AVIC and its general aviation component CAIGA had been active in the field, little was known about Superior, a much smaller firm. There was also the immediate concern about transfer and control of military technology, although Hawker Beechcraft Defense Company would not be included in the sale.[8]

With bankruptcy coming in its 80th anniversary year, there was much reflection about the long decline of the Beechcraft brand. In particular, its problems were attributed to the massive loss involved with the Starship, serious delays and slow sales of the 400A, the Premier, and the new Hawker 4000, plus loss of military contracts. Since its sale by Raytheon, Hawker Beechcraft also lacked the support of a large corporate parent such as Textron or General Dynamics. It appeared likely that certain long-established models would be discontinued or sold. Not long after, in October 2012, and with little surprise in the aviation community, the negotiations with Superior Aviation were ended. Hawker Beechcraft was left as a standalone company working through Chapter 11. Renamed Beechcraft, Inc., the company shed some $2.5 billion in debt through bankruptcy, and engaged in discussions with new bidders about acquisition of certain of its aircraft lines. The future of many of its business jet models was cloudy, but the company remained determined to develop both new piston-powered and turbine-powered models. The independent Beech would continue its veteran piston and turboprop lines as it pursued new models, but might discontinue or sell its business jet models. The new King Air 250, with numerous improvements, was announced in October 2010 as successor to the King Air 200, and was widely regarded as the best of a long line of King Airs. Noteworthy was the delivery of the 7,000th model of the basic King Air twin-turboprop series, extending back to 1964, in October 2012. The Bonanza celebrated its 65th anniversary also in 2012.

The subsidiary Hawker Beechcraft Defense Company controlled T-6B Texan production for the Air Force and other military customers. Deliveries began in 2000 and were completed by 2011 with more than 700 delivered. Export sales continued to Greece, Israel, Iraq, Morocco and others, and the T-6C variant for the Navy was produced through 2014. Mexico also ordered the T-6C. The Air Force requirement for a light armed reconnaissance aircraft (LARA) led to Hawker Beechcraft teaming with Lockheed Martin with a T-6B development designated AT-6 for the contract. The Air Force later deferred its LARA program, but continued with a requirement for a similar Light Air Strike (LAS) aircraft for use by Afghan forces. The loss of the contract award in 2011 to Embraer of Brazil, partnered with Sierra Nevada Corporation, a Nevada-based high-technology firm, for a version of its Super Tucano trainer, led to vigorous protests. Hawker Beechcraft filed suit against the award in Court of Federal Claims, carrying major implications both for the company and for the city of Wichita.[9] Hawker Beechcraft had been emphasizing the military market pending a civil market recovery. At a time of serious losses, the one bright spot had been the military trainer line, along with continuing demand for military versions of the King Air series. The MC-12W Liberty intelligence, surveillance, and reconnaissance (ISR) version of the King Air 350 was extensively employed.

Beechcraft appeared to be on the rebound with the announcement on December 26, 2013, of its acquisition by Textron. The announced price of $1.4 billion for what had become Beech Holdings carried a major loss to previous owners Onex and GS Capital Partners. Among other things, the acquisition combined two of the three most iconic names in general aviation (the third being Piper). Textron announced it had been interested in Beech for some time, especially after the declaration of bankruptcy in 2012. The immediate task was to determine the product fit with Textron's existing fixed-wing manufacturer, Cessna, and it appeared that there was considerable logic to the combination. Cessna had no equivalent to the King Air line, nor did it have direct competitors to the low-wing, retractable gear Bonanza or twin-engined Baron. The respected Hawker 4000 and Premier models came with the acquisition, but their production was already suspended and the future for both appeared doubtful. The old Hawker models extending from the British originals already were ended. The Beech nameplate was to be maintained, but it would clearly take some time to integrate operations into Textron.[10] With the acquisition, Bill Boisture departed the company and Cessna CEO Scott Ernest was named head of the new Textron Aviation subsidiary, formed in March 2014 to control fixed-wing production. Cessna was the surviving company with regard to management, but marketing of the two lines remained separate. Textron had built a strong aviation identity, also owning Bell Helicopters and Lycoming. Beech sales had been approximately $1.8 billion in

2013, and the company had already downsized substantially before the acquisition. Further layoffs appeared likely, but at last Beechcraft had gained strong financial backing, and product support for some 36,000 Beech and Hawker models in service was also assured. There was a real prospect that new models could appear under the Beechcraft nameplate.

While separate from Textron's general aviation activities, Textron AirLand, a joint venture of Textron and independent investors, revealed the experimental Scorpion light combat aircraft in 2014. The aircraft had been developed largely in secret, making extensive use of Cessna's jet design technology, and attained its first flight after the remarkably brief development time of two and one-half years. There was no U.S. military requirement, but Textron actively marketed the design to overseas customers, emphasizing its much lower operating costs over established combat jets. Potential missions included intelligence, surveillance, and reconnaissance (ISR) in addition to strike and maritime patrol. Powered by twin Honeywell engines of 8,000 pounds thrust each, it promised performance up to contemporary military standards. Textron also planned to offer a trainer version of the Scorpion for the long-delayed advanced trainer requirement of the U.S. Air Force, but then decided it did not meet the trainer specification. As of 2018 the Scorpion had attracted no orders.

Gulfstream, its product line principally at the higher end of the business jet market, perhaps was less affected by the great recession than others. The prototype of its new G650 first flew in November 2009, but its fatal crash during a test flight in early 2011 was a major setback for the program. The G650 quickly moved back on schedule for type certificate approval, however, and deliveries began in 2012. Most encouraging was the strong order backlog for some 200 G650s in advance of service entry.[11] With the G650 under way, Gulfstream began considering eventual successors to the long-running G450 and G550 programs, and undertook its secret Project P42 in 2008 to develop such new models. Gulfstream made a public announcement in October 2014, in advance of the annual NBAA convention, of two advanced models, the G500 and G600. While similar in configuration to existing Gulfstream models, and building on G650 technology, the new models were clean-sheet designs. With higher performance than their predecessors but more economical in operation, and providing expanded interior room, the new models were planned to eventually replace the G450 and G550. Gulfstream announced that the older models were to remain in production as long as they were supported by market demand. In-service dates were projected as 2018 for the G500 and 2019 for the G600. Both were to be powered by new PWC 800-series engines rather than the long-serving BR725, and Gulfstream planned to produce a higher percentage of the total airplane in Savannah than before.[12]

The Gulfstream G280 flight deck (© Gulfstream Aerospace Corporation, reproduced with permission).

The Gulfstream G650 interior (© Gulfstream Aerospace Corporation, reproduced with permission).

The Gulfstream G650 production line (© Gulfstream Aerospace Corporation, reproduced with permission).

Gulfstream still faced strong competition in the high-end field from the Bombardier 5000 and 6000 series, the French Falcon 900, and especially from the new and very advanced Falcon 8X. Supporting the dynamic high-end field were new-technology large business jet engines developed by GE, with its Passport model, and by SNECMA of France with the Silvercrest, in addition to those in the PWC line. All threatened the once-dominant position of Rolls-Royce, although the Silvercrest encountered developmental delays.

Aerion, with its supersonic business jet project, was determined to ease the U.S. prohibition on flying supersonically over land, first by technological changes to hush the sonic boom, and second by lobbying Congress for relaxation of the law. Gulfstream, rumored at times to be considering the supersonic field, still did not announce any such plans, leaving the concept to Aerion. Aerion gained significant financial backing by billionaire investor Robert Bass, and revamped its original twin-engined design, redesignated as AS2 with three engines and a reduced noise footprint. It entered into a technical partnership with Airbus for the project.[13] With noise regulation still a concern, Aerion worked to develop quiet supersonic flight, and revised its projected in-service date from 2021 to 2025.

Table 10-2 Billings (in millions) for General Aviation Airplane Shipments by Type, Manufactured Worldwide, 2000–2017

Year	Grand Total	Piston	Turbine
2000	13,496	512	12,984
2001	13,868	541	13,327
2002	11,778	483	11,295
2003	9,998	545	9,453
2004	12,093	692	11,401
2005	15,156	805	14,350
2006	18,815	857	17,958
2007	21,837	897	20,940
2008	24,846	945	23,901
2009	19,474	442	19,032
2010	19,715	415	19,300
2011	19,042	441	18,600
2012	18,895	428	18,467
2013	23,450	571	22,879
2014	24,499	635	23,864
2015	24,129	601	23,528
2016	21,092	661	20,432
2017	20,197	718	19,479

SOURCE: *2017 Annual Report*, p. 16. Washington: GAMA, 2017.

In a major and surprising move, the AVIC unit of China Aviation Industry Corporation announced plans to acquire Cirrus Design on March 2, 2011. In part reflecting the potential of general aviation in China, the move also would give China greater access to the U.S. market for future product offerings. The cash infusion from AVIC gave Cirrus further resources to develop the Vision SJ50, and in turn provided AVIC access to Cirrus technology. The merger was completed with China Aviation General Aircraft Co., Ltd. (CAIGA) as renamed, in June 2011. The merger enabled continuation of existing and new programs. Production remained in the United States, but assembly in China would move ahead with market growth. AVIC had established strong links with the U.S. industry in recent years, including a joint venture with GE in avionics. The issue of technology transfer appeared, however, with attendant national security concerns.[14] Finally, it was announced that the Cirrus Vision SJ50 had secured the necessary financing for production approval, with service expected in 2015 at a price approaching $2 million. Doubts were still expressed by some over the market prospects, in that potential buyers might find better value with, for example, a used Cessna Mustang as opposed to a new Vision SJ50. But the Vision entered the market with substantial orders, and was the top of the Cirrus line. Prospects appeared encouraging and orders mounted.

The Cirrus SR20 was ordered by the Air Force for training at the Air Force Academy. Designated T-53A, 25 were ordered for delivery during 2010–2012, replacing the Diamond T-52A. Cirrus marked delivery of its 5,000th aircraft in 2011, as Dale Klapmeier became president and CEO. With continuing strong and stable demand, Cirrus deliveries reached 7,000 in 2018.

After ending his attempt to form a separate company for the Vision SJ50, Alan Klapmeier departed for a venture to acquire and develop the Farnborough F1 Kestrel high-performance single-turboprop business aircraft from Great Britain, acquiring rights from the bankrupt firm. A new factory was planned at a closed air force base in New Hampshire. Klapmeier anticipated that the Kestrel would underprice the competitive TBM 700, but financing remained a challenge.

After the withdrawal of Taiwan Aerospace, the long-gestating SJ30 program cast about for a new investor, and the Emivest investment firm of Dubai took ownership in 2008, just in time for the severe recession and business jet market decline. The model was renamed the Emivest SJ30, but then the new owners declared bankruptcy in 2010 after having invested $90 million in the program. Afterward, Chinese interests considered an investment, but withdrew in 2011. Finally, Metalcraft Technologies (MTI) of Cedar City, Utah, a major supplier, bought the venture, including debt, from bankruptcy court. All activity was transferred to Utah. MTI established an affiliated company, SyberJet Aircraft, to complete development and to market the SJ-30-2 as the SyberJet. Some production was under way in 2012, and the SyberJet was regarded as the fastest and longest-ranged in its class. Still, after more than 20 years in development, its future appeared dubious in an increasingly overcrowded market. Development continued as the SyberJet was relaunched under its current owner MSC Aerospace of Cedar City, Utah, descended from the old Metalcraft. All affiliates were grouped under MSC Aerospace. SyberJet had purchased rights and assets for only $20 million and was free from debt. Certification had been planned for 2015, with production to follow, but that target experienced still further delay. The developed SJ30x, with more powerful engines and advanced avionics, was projected for certification in 2017, but that date passed. Late in 2019, a further developed SJ30i was announced, to enter service after further testing. The evident demise of the competitive Beech Premier could enhance market prospects.

Further new entries appeared in the business jet segment. Honda Aircraft Company, a wholly owned subsidiary of automotive giant Honda Motor Company, developed its innovative HA-420 HondaJet for the smaller or "entry level" executive jet market. Honda claimed its overwing mounted twin jets enhanced performance and fuel efficiency. A new factory was built in Greensboro, North Carolina, for production. First flight of the production-standard model was on December 20, 2010, but production was delayed, with first deliveries deferred beyond the early target date of 2013. Honda originally developed its proprietary HF118 small turbofan for the model, but unsatisfactory performance led to the collaboration with GE as Honda Aero Engines. The developed engine became the HF120, in the 2,000 lb. thrust category, from 2004, but the HF120 encountered development delays as well. Initially located at GE's Lynn, Massachusetts, plant, HF120 production was transferred to Greensboro. The HondaJet carried an initial price in the $4.5 million range, and Honda claimed more than 100 orders.[15] After further delays, there was discernible progress by 2014. The Type Inspection Authorization (TIA) finally came in early 2016, and the HF120 engine was also certified, so that customer deliveries were under way.

The Eclipse story took a more positive turn in 2009 with the announcement of a new firm, Eclipse Aerospace, formed by existing Eclipse owners and operators led by businessman and pilot Mason Holland. Eclipse Aerospace purchased assets of the original Eclipse for $40 million, incidentally the only bid, with the goal of eventually restarting production. The first objective was to provide parts and support to sustain the Eclipse 500 fleet that had reached service before the shutdown. Additional equipment needed to bring the fleet up to full operating specifications was acquired. The undertaking received a major boost when Sikorsky announced that it had taken a 42 percent minority investment in the new firm and would help support the venture. The Eclipse engine supplier, Pratt & Whitney, was a sister firm of Sikorsky under United Technologies. Sikorsky had acquired control of PZL Mielec, a legacy Polish aircraft firm, in 2007, and major components would be built that Polish factory, with final assembly in the original Albuquerque factory. Recognized as a sound basic design, the upgraded and refined Eclipse 550 moved toward production, fitted with more advanced electronics but not requiring a new type certificate. It was projected to reach the market in 2013 at a base price of $2.9 million.[16] Volume, at least initially, was expected to be modest, and as was so common with restructured programs, production was delayed.

In something of a surprise, the holding company ONE Aviation was formed in February 2015, combining Eclipse Aerospace and Kestrel, with Alan Klapmeier as CEO of both operating companies. Deliveries of the Eclipse 550 were projected to reach some two dozen for 2015, although the company struggled to sell even that modest number. The Kestrel awaited financing as priority went to the Eclipse. ONE Aviation also announced developments of the Eclipse, first with the lengthened Eclipse EA700, with more powerful Willams FJ33 engines. It was projected to replace the earlier Eclipse, but financing uncertainties made prospects cloudy. On October 11, 2018, Alan Klapmeier sent the firm into Chapter Eleven bankruptcy. While cutting staff, he kept development progressing with an even more advanced Eclipse 550, and the EA700 evolved into the Eclipse Canada. One future possibility was acquisition by Chinese interests.

Of most importance to Learjet's future was the new Model 85, announced in October 2007, which while retaining classic Learjet lines was a clean-sheet design. Sized between the midsize and super-midsize categories, and priced at some $17 million, the Model 85 bid to compete with the most advanced business jets ever developed. Of all-composite construction, it was to be assembled at the new factory in Queretaro, Mexico, with deliveries originally projected for 2013. Learjet also announced a major expansion of its Wichita factory, with financial support from the State of Kansas. Continuing its product development, Learjet announced the Models 70 and 75 in 2012, to succeed the Models 40 and 45. Both were refined developments of the older models and would replace them in the market.

While the Learjet 85 program experienced development delays, not uncommon with new models, it appeared to be on the point of flight testing when on January 15, 2015, Learjet's owner Bombardier announced that it had halted the program, concerned over weak demand and an overall negative forecast for growth in the overcrowded super midsize segment. Massive cash outlays required were another concern, but some observers believed that the suspension was symptomatic of deeper problems at Bombardier. Layoffs loomed for some 1,000 workers in both Queretaro and Wichita. While announced as a suspension, it appeared doubtful that the program would be revived in the near future.[17] With Bombardier's increasingly severe problems, including delays in its new long-range models, the Learjet line itself might be sold. A new U.S.-based corporate parent might help ensure its future. Only the Models 70 and 75 remained in the current Learjet product line.

The year 2011 marked 15 years of Boeing Business Jets, and the original BBJ 1, 2, and 3 had been joined by BBJ versions of the 757, 767, 777, and new 787, and even by BBJ versions of the jumbo 747 and new 747–8. Demand remained steady, even in a recession. While Boeing usually did not announce the identities of customers, orders for the executive version of the 747–8 were assumed to be for heads of state. Boeing reported total orders for 205 of all variants by mid–2011. Some 15 models of the 787 were ordered by private customers, and a new industry effectively was created to finish out large airliner airframes to customer specifications. Continuing development, Boeing announced in 2012 that it would offer BBJ versions of its advanced 737 MAX airliner from 2017. Airbus remained a potent competitor with Boeing in the segment.

Table 10-3 Worldwide Business Jet Shipments (in units) by U.S. Manufacturer, 2004–2017

Year	2004	2005	2006	2007	2008	2009	2010	2011	2012
Boeing Business Jets									
All models	3	4	13	7	6	5	12	8	12
Bombardier Business									
Learjet 40/45	39	49	56	57	48	33	16	24	24
Learjet 60/XR	9	18	15	23	26	13	12	19	15
Learjet 70/75	—	—	—	—	—	—	—	—	—
Cirrus Aircraft									
SF50	—	—	—	—	—	—	—	—	—
Emivest									
SJ30-2	—	—	—	—	—	—	—	—	—
Gulfstream Aerospace									
G200/G280	22	26	42	59	68	19	24	21	1
G300 thru G650	56	63	71	79	88	75	75	78	83
Honda Aircraft									
HA420 HondaJet	—	—			—	—	—	—	—
ONE Aviation									
Eclipse 500	—	—	1	98	161	—	—	—	—
Eclipse 550	—	—	—	—	—	—	—	—	—
Textron (Beechcraft)									
Premier 1/A	37	30	23	54	31	16	11	11	3
Hawker 400/XP	28	53	53	41	35	11	12	1	—
Hawker 750	—	—	—	—	23	13	5	7	—
Hawker 800/XP	50	58	8	—	—	—	—	—	—
Hawker 850/XP	—	—	56	35	15	3	1	9	—
Hawker 900/XP	—	—	—	32	50	35	28	22	17
Hawker 4000	—	—	—	—	6	20	16	10	12
Textron (Cessna)									
Citation Mustang	—	—	1	45	101	125	73	43	38
CitationJet 1-4, incl. M2	53	89	134	156	164	75	59	87	84
Bravo	—	25	21	18	—	—	—	—	—

Year	2004	2005	2006	2007	2008	2009	2010	2011	2012
Encore /+	24	13	12	23	28	5	5	4	—
Excel	23	—	—	—	—	—	—	—	—
Citation XLS/+	32	64	3	82	80	44	22	27	31
Sovereign/+	9	46	57	65	77	33	16	19	22
Citation X	15	14	12	17	16	7	3	3	6

Year	2013	2014	2015	2016	2017
Boeing Business Jets					
All models	7	10	11	4	7
Bombardier Business					
Learjet 40 and 45	1	—	—	—	—
Learjet 60/XR	10	1	—	—	—
Learjet 70/75	18	33	32	24	14
Cirrus Aircraft					
SF50	—	—	—	3	22
Gulfstream Aerospace					
G200/G280	23	33	34	27	30
G300 thru G650ER	121	117	120	94	90
Honda Aircraft					
HA420 HondaJet	—	—	2	23	43
ONE Aviation					
Eclipse 550	—	12	7	8	6
Textron (Beechcraft)					
Hawker 4000	6	—	—	—	—
Textron (Cessna)					
Citation Mustang					
Citation 1-4 incl. M2	75	92	97	92	88
Citation XLS/+	31	22	21	18	18
Sovereign/+	13	28	18	11	9
Latitude	—	—	16	42	54
Citation X/X+	—	9	6	4	4

SOURCE: *2017 Annual Report*, GAMA, pp. 17–18. Washington: GAMA, 2017.

Agricultural aircraft, while a small segment, gained in importance. The two survivors in a field that once had included entrants by Piper, Cessna, and Grumman were Air Tractor and Thrush. Both continued to thrive, with Thrush delivering 51 aircraft in 2013 and AirTractor delivering 174. More than half were exported. Leland Snow died on February 22, 2011, at age 80. He was a lifelong physical fitness enthusiast and collapsed during a morning run. He had started his company at age 21. Jim Hirsh succeeded to the position of CEO of AirTractor. The U.S. fleet of agricultural aircraft was estimated at over 3,000, leading to optimism for a steady replacement demand. Some projected the future employment of Unmanned Aerial Vehicles (UAV) for agricultural applications, however, constituting a potential threat to piloted agricultural aircraft.[18]

The Air Tractor AT-802, the most capable in the line, won an order for ten of the specialized AT-802U military light attack models from the United Arab Emirates (UAE). They were delivered 2010–2011, after being outfitted by the modification firm Iomax with underwing and fuselage hard points for a variety of weaponry plus surveillance hardware. The order eventually reached 24 aircraft. The AT-802 was also finding a role in firefighting. A Spanish company ordered a fleet of the modified AT-802F as the Fire Boss, adding that role to crop spraying and light attack. The Fire Boss was deployed against numerous forest fires in Spain and other areas of Europe.

Another encouraging sign for smaller firms was steady demand for the Quest Kodiak utility aircraft, with 30 Kodiaks delivered in 2014. Quest Aviation was acquired in February 2015 by Setouchi Holdings of Japan, further increasing the globalization of the general aviation industry. Other small firms such as Aviat in Wyoming and American Champion in Wisconsin continued their respected veteran designs. CubCrafters offered the upgraded XCub to supplement its established CarbonCub.

A significant development in the homebuilt or kit field was formation of the Aircraft Kit Industry Association (AKIA) in 2012, a move supported by the FAA. Fifteen manufacturers and suppliers were founding members, and the number quickly grew to 26. Among other things, this represented the maturing of the long-established sector. Association leaders included Dick VanGrunsven of Vans, John McBean of Kitfox, and Jeremy Monnett of Sonex. Goals included supporting manufacturers, enhancing aviation education for youth, increasing the number of active pilots, and enhancing the love of flying for all.

The compilation of aggregate production statistics for kit models remained difficult. There was no central repository of information on the industry, and some manufacturers were rather reluctant to provide numbers. There was also uncertainty about the completion rate for purchased kits. Regardless, there was general agreement that the field was growing significantly.

Vans announced in 2014 that it had delivered its 1,000th RV-12 kit, for example. One innovation was that CubCrafters, which offered the Carbon Cub kit model in addition to its factory-built line, began a Builder Assist program, allowing customers to come to their Yakima, Washington factory and fabricate parts for their airplane, speeding completion while keeping within the 51 percent rule. CubCrafters then would assemble more of the airplane, with the customer returning to complete final assembly and certification, expediting the build process while still offering the savings of home construction. At the high end of the kit line, Lancair, builder of the high-performance Evolution model, went into liquidation in 2016, although some 70 were flying. The high-performance Evolution line continued as a separate spinoff company, but the smaller Legacy model was ended. Lancair then announced the Mako, powered by a turbocharged 350 hp piston, which as a kit could match the Cirrus at perhaps half the price. The PT6A turboprop-powered Evolution was priced at $1.5 million, and Lancair offered a Builder Assist program to speed up construction.

In something of an interaction between the kit field and the LSA category, certain producers were spurred to petition for exemptions on LSA weight restrictions to bring more designs under the category, enhancing the market potential. The new Icon Aircraft won an exemption on the LSA weight limit in 2010 so that its Icon A5 2-seat sport amphibian, with its heavier airframe, could fall within the LSA category. The aeronautical engineer and designer Jim Bede died on July 9, 2015, at age 82. Over a 50-year career he had developed many innovative small aircraft designs, but was less successful in production.

Civil Helicopter Developments

In the highly competitive civil helicopter field, Robinson production continued strong. Deliveries of all models totaled 356 in 2011, representing a significant recovery from the 2008–2010 recession. Business was increasing for the turbine-powered Model R66, with more than 100 orders reported at launch. A factory expansion was required for the new model, and first delivery was in October 2010. The introductory base price was $790,000, and Robinson aspired for the R66 to replace the veteran Bell 206 in the light turbine-powered segment. Frank Robinson retired in 2010 at age 80, after having driven development of the R66, and was succeeded by his son Kurt. Kurt Robinson continued the established business model of designing and marketing helicopters priced at half the competition. By 2010 the Robinson production total reached 10,000 helicopters over more than 30 years, and the success of the R66 carried favorable portents for the future. Deliveries of the

Frank Robinson with his helicopters, August 2009 (Robinson Helicopter Company).

R66 turbine model reached 500 in 2014, a scant three and one-half years after certification.

    Development continued apace, with new models being announced by several producers, in part to meet strong competition from Europe. Bell made intensive efforts to expand and strengthen its position in larger civil helicopters, announcing in February 2012 the Model 525 Relentless, its most ambitious civil project to date, to meet European competition. Classed as a "super medium" in size, powered by twin 2,000 hp CT7–2FI turboshafts driving a composite five-blade main rotor and four-blade tail rotor, the Model 525 was intended for the growing offshore oil service sector as well as for executive use, and could accommodate up to 20 passengers in high-density configuration. Bell's 407 and 429 Global Ranger models were capable performers, but were regarded as too small for the critical offshore oil platform service function. The largest civil helicopter ever developed by Bell, with an estimated $500 million development cost, the 525 was positioned as a strong competitor to new Airbus (formerly Eurocopter, renamed in 2014) and AgustaWestland models. While somewhat resembling a stretch of the Model 429, and building on that model's commercial success, the 525 was a completely new design. It was projected to fly in 2014.[19] First flight did not occur until more than a year later, however, and the crash of a prototype also delayed the program. Service entry was pushed into 2020, if not later. The Relentless would also compete with the large Sikorsky S-92, both in oil service and executive transportation.[20]

10—Again, Crisis and Recovery

The successful Canadian Mirabel plant reached the production milestone of 4,000 helicopters in January 2012. Bell had studied a new small helicopter model for years, and the success of the R66 further spurred Bell to develop a competitor and successor to the long-running Model 206 program that ended in 2010. More than 4,400 of the older Model 206s were in service, but most were aging and would require eventual replacement. The Model 505 JetRanger X was formally announced in February 2014. While externally rather similar to the Model 206, the Model 505 was a completely new design incorporating the latest technology, and Bell announced a target price of just over $1 million, competitive with the R66 and with Enstrom. The Model 505 was intended for three principal roles, utility, executive/passenger transport, and law enforcement, although military roles could appear later. While major emphasis in the industry had been on larger helicopters, more profitable for the manufacturers, smaller models gained increased attention.

Sikorsky had long considered a new-generation model of its long-running S-76 series. After protracted development, the advanced S-76D was announced in 2005, in part a response to the successful AgustaWestland AW139, and offered higher performance for the same price as the predecessor S-76C++. Certification was finally attained in October 2012 and deliveries began against a strong order backlog of some $500 million. S-76D airframes were manufactured by Aerovochody in Czech Republic and by Changhe in China, following the globalized production arrangement of its larger stablemate the S-92. A victory for Sikorsky was that a specialized version of the S-92 was selected as the new presidential helicopter in that long-delayed program, for service from 2017. While a firm program, the VH-92 presidential helicopter still had not entered service by 2019.

Sikorsky also competed in the small helicopter segment with its formerly Schweizer models, the S-300 and S-400 series. Sikorsky ended the line and closed the plant in 2012. Brantly was acquired by Qingdao Helicopters in 2007, with production of its small models moved to China. Its competitor Enstrom received a potential boost to its fortunes by being acquired by Chungqing Helicopter Investment Company in December 2012, the latest in a series of ownership changes. The move came under the Chungqing General Aviation Group, and appeared to enhance prospects for sales to China. Its factory in Menominee, Michigan, underwent a major expansion, and its established TH180 trainer, 280FX piston-powered model, and turbine-powered Model 480 continued. MD Helicopters under Patriarch Partners struggled to gain civil market share, but did secure an order for 12 military models from Afghanistan.

Charles Kaman, noted helicopter engineer and founder of the company bearing his name, died January 31, 2011, at age 91.

The Future: An Assessment

The general aviation industry has experienced a turbulent history. Long-term success for aircraft manufacturers has been elusive, with production suspensions, development cancellations, and bankruptcies all too common. If any single conclusion emerges, it is that attaining and sustaining profitability in general aviation aircraft production has been exceptionally difficult. The three essential facets of the industry, development, production, and marketing, must be combined for success. Many companies and many promising designs have failed due to production, certification, and financing problems, and certain sound designs simply could not compete in the market. Further, the broad economy must be operating at a level sufficient to support strong demand for new aircraft. With globalization, the world economy is equally important to the industry, as American aircraft are marketed not only domestically but in the global marketplace. As we draw this account to a close, a major question remained that of a strong market recovery after the severe recession of 2008–2010. Earlier confident projections that a recovery would be realized by 2012 were not borne out, and a recovery to perhaps the level of 2007 remained uncertain. One factor in favor of that recovery was a decline in the number of business jets offered for sale in the secondary market, portending increased demand for new production. The North American market remained the largest for business jets, with roughly 60 percent of world demand, as well as the largest for all general aviation aircraft. Europe was second, and the Middle East and Latin America were growing in importance. The BRIC (Brazil, Russia, India, and China) countries were growing markets. Russia and China in particular had been regarded as poised for major growth, but increasing political tensions threatened those prospects. Honeywell's forecast was for prolonged weak business jet production, but the Teal Group, a leading aviation consulting firm, reported that 7,889 business jets with a value of $143.4 billion were produced from 2000–2009, and forecast a total of 10,285 business jets with a value of $184.1 billion to be produced from 2010 to 2019.[21] At the 2013 NBAA convention, major business jet makers forecast double-digit gains for 2014. It could be viewed that the business jet market had indeed made a complete recovery by that year. Sales had declined 50 percent since the crisis of 2008, but GAMA reported a strong overall increase in general aviation aircraft sales for 2013, with 2,256 aircraft delivered for $23.4 billion. The year 2009 marked the first year that more than 50 percent of U.S.-produced business jets were exported. Another point of optimism was that demand for business jets had increased in every year from 2010 to 2014, with demand growing especially in the Middle East and Asia. Also favorable for the longer term was that about 60 percent of new jet sales were replacements for existing aircraft, and the inventory of used aircraft has diminished. Overall business flying hours increased as well.[22] But business jet orders still remained sluggish in 2016–2017, pushing a full market recovery even farther out.

Table 10-4
General Aviation Exports ($000)

Year	Units	% of Total	$ Billings	% of Total
2001	505	19.2	$2,380.6	27.5
2002	372	16.8	1,980.9	25.4
2003	336	15.7	1,218.2	18.9
2004	333	14.1	1,419.6	20.8
2005	557	19.5	2,585.9	29.8
2006	891	28.3	4,395.5	42.4
2007	1,142	34.8	4,587.0	38.4
2008	1,161	37.7	5,863.8	43.9
2009	732	46.2	4,612.7	50.8
2010	689	51.6	4,867.8	61.8
2011	486	40.0	4,585.8	50.7
2012	720	47.7	4,791.1	59.8
2013	691	42.8	5,616.9	50.7
2014	696	42.7	5,419.2	46.4
2015	524	32.9	5,431.2	45.3
2016	453	29.6	4,451.3	38.5
2017	541	33.9	4,347.9	41.1

SOURCE: *2017 Annual Report*, GAMA, p. 23. Washington, D.C., GAMA, 2017.

One significant factor in business jet demand and utilization was the continuing strong growth of leasing and fractional ownership firms. NetJets, Inc., the largest factional ownership firm, continued to dominate. In common with other operators, however, NetJets declined in the recession as companies cut back flying hours, but had largely recovered by 2013. With a fleet of more than 600 business jets of all sizes, NetJets could order in numbers sufficient to impact the overall industry, and continued to modernize and replace its fleet.[23] Certain manufacturers also established leasing subsidiaries for their models, and Delta Air Lines operated a business jet charter service. In addition to overcoming economic reverses, NetJets faced a conflict with the Internal Revenue Service, which ruled that flights on fractionally owned aircraft were equivalent to commercial airliner flights for which tickets were taxed, that passengers owed tax on their flights, and assessed NetJets a large sum. NetJets eventually prevailed over the IRS on the issue.

Business jet production volume, the dominant sector by value of general aviation, remained far below its peak years. Further, those firms focused on smaller jets, such as Cessna, had suffered more in the recession. On that point, market analysts widely noted that if the business jet market were divided into halves by price, with the dividing line at $25 million, historically both halves had risen and fallen in close lockstep with the overall economy. In the recent recession, however, demand in the lower half plummeted, while the upper half retained its strength, the inference being that smaller, less expensive business jets were operated by smaller corporations, less able to withstand downturns. Fractional operators also have helped sustain the demand for larger jets, and larger corporations, likely to operate high-end business jets, have more ability to withstand economic downturns than small companies using smaller aircraft.[24] It should be remembered, however, that business jets, as is the case with almost all general aviation aircraft, are essentially a discretionary purchase, and as such are postponable and even cancellable. General aviation is anything but a recession-proof industry.

The sharp decline in the price of oil in 2016 further complicated the demand picture. The market for oil and gas platform service helicopters was also negatively impacted. Many international customers of business jets were damaged by the oil price decline, with sales of higher end business jets, previously viewed as recession-proof, negatively affected. There were announced cuts in production across the industry, and there were rising numbers of used business jets offered for sale. Major international competitors such as Bombardier, Embraer, and Dassault also cut production. The apparent recovery in 2012–2015 led to overproduction, and optimistic demand forecasts for the latter years of the decade were tempered. An emerging view was the business jet sector had been in a long-term recession from 2008. With new product development and technological innovation continuing apace, the question emerged of whether new and more advanced products would stimulate demand.

General aviation manufacturers have been further handicapped by overall erratic economic growth and financial instability. Potential customers are almost inevitably inhibited if they doubt the ability of the manufacturer to survive. The Adam and Eclipse firms provided unfortunate illustrations. Long-established manufacturers also were criticized for design conservatism, but innovative new entrants then faced failure by inability to attract sufficient capital for sustainability. Furthermore, although having grown over time, general aviation has never attained the status of a "hot" industry, and lacked the degree of political influence of the much larger military, commercial, and space sectors of the aerospace industry. It is unquestionably the least appreciated, most misunderstood sector of aviation. The tendency of the general public to still use the term "private plane," to regard corporate jet use with suspicion, and to misunderstand or fail to recognize business aviation, remains. Yet its value and importance to the economy are beyond question. While dominated by business flying, general aviation has long since expanded to include such important missions as fighting forest fires, aerial crop seeding and spraying, reforesting clearcut areas, wildlife study, infrared photography to detect plant disease, law enforcement and traffic reporting, and medical and missionary support to remote areas in developing countries. A strength was that the industry still was strongly characterized by risk-taking and innovation, important to any vibrant industry and to the national economy. The industry needs more Bill Lears, Burt Rutans, LeRoy LoPrestis, Frank Robinsons, and Dick VanGrunsvens.

Quite apart from general aviation activities, it was also recognized that the industry was an important component of the defense industry. General aviation manufacturers had long been subcontractors on military aircraft, and military versions of certain general aviation aircraft had long been ordered by the armed forces for national security purposes, and this would continue as the first century drew to a close. General aviation manufacturers developed and adapted aircraft for military flight training, observation, and light strike, even adapting agricultural aircraft for that purpose. Employment of versions of general aviation helicopters for military roles, and of military helicopters adapted for civil use, had a long history.

The production volume enjoyed in the 1970s for general aviation aircraft is unlikely to be restored. In particular the market for factory-built single piston-powered light aircraft, historically the foundation of general aviation, was very low. In 2018 only 954 such models were produced worldwide, leaving the homebuilt or kit sector to fulfill what demand remained.[25] The VLJ market, once optimistically projected into the thousands, came forcefully down to earth, with future output probably little more than 100 aircraft per year. The LSA market, also once viewed with high optimism, appeared to be severely diminished. It seemed ironic that the small single-piston segment, that once practically defined general aviation, appeared to possess the weakest growth prospects. Cessna, Piper, Beech, Cirrus, Mooney, Aviat, and others pursued market share in what was not really a growth sector. The long-running Skyhawk, Skylane, and Stationair models were essentially produced to order.

A reasonable estimate for factory-produced fixed-wing general aviation aircraft worldwide, from LSAs to Boeing BBJs, is something on the order of 4,000 per year, a figure that will of course fluctuate with overall economic conditions. Kit aircraft production will also grow, but overall civil helicopter demand seemed weak. A point of optimism is that there were some 211,000 registered civil aircraft (apart from scheduled airliners) in the United States in 2018, and some fifteen percent of the fleet consisted of experimental, or homebuilt, aircraft. There were also some 36,000 aircraft of all types in Canada. As the overall fleet ages, replacement needs will gain in importance in stimulating new production. As the American general aviation fleet is some 90 percent of the world general aviation fleet, most new production will come from U.S. manufacturers. Another long-term concern, however, is that the number of private pilots in the United States has declined, from 243,000 in 2001 to 162,000 in 2017, both figures not including recreational and sport pilots. Further, most of those pilots were older. Leaders in the general aviation industry emphasized increased pilot training to maintain the civilian pilot numbers. Increasing expense of flying and flying training remained a major challenge.

The perception of those active in general aviation remained that the FAA was overly bureaucratic and restrictive, yet it was a positive that the LSA category and Sport Pilot programs were established. General aviation also supported green aviation measures. The Small Airplane Revitalization Act of 2013 provided for increased safety measures and reduced certification costs for light aircraft. The Act also provided for revisions to FAA Part 23 that would expedite the certification process for new designs.

In favor of the industry's future is that by 2015 it had largely carried out a major, fundamental restructuring in response to economic, competitive, and technological changes. Major producers such as Cessna, Learjet, and Gulfstream had somewhat stabilized under larger corporate parents. The acquisition of Beechcraft by Textron also was positive. While effectively forced, the restructuring is largely complete and should result in an overall stronger industry sector, albeit with fewer producers. The only major American-owned business jet producers remaining were Cessna and Gulfstream. The conclusion was inescapable, however, that the business jet field still was seriously overcrowded, especially when factoring in such global competitors as Bombardier, Dassault, Embraer, and Learjet and new entrants such as Honda. Nonetheless, it is impressive that the major competitors were still investing heavily in new model development. It is also impressive that business jet designs, once fully encompassed within the small, midsize, super midsize, and large categories, have proliferated to the point that those categories are no longer adequate. The available range of models constitutes virtually a continuum in size and capability, ranging from VLJs to the Boeing 747-8.

Even though business aircraft remain a discretionary purchase, the existing general aviation fleet eventually will need replacement. Recent legal and regulatory reforms and infrastructure improvements have been important, if not essential, to the growth of general aviation. That replacement requirement and continuation of the entrepreneurial spirit which has characterized the field are probably even more important. The continuing competitive spirit, combined with industry restructuring, expanded international markets, and continued technological development, provides a basis for guarded optimism for the future of the industry and for the growth of general aviation.

Chapter Notes

Chapter 1

1. Tom Crouch, "General Aviation: The Search for a Market," in E. M. Emme (ed.), *200 Years of Flight in America: A Bicentennial Survey*, Univelt, San Diego, 1977, p. 113.
2. Alexander Klemin, "Investing in Aviation," *Scientific American*, February 1929, p. 149.
3. Roger Bilstein, *Flight Patterns*, University of Georgia Press, Athens, 1983, p. 67.
4. Herm Schreiner, "The Waco Story. Part I: Clayton Brukner & the Founding Years," *American Aviation Historical Society Journal*, vol. 25, Winter 1980, p. 282.
5. John T. Nevill, "The Story of Wichita," *Aviation*, November 1930, p. 291.
6. *Ibid.*, December 1930, p. 355; and Frank Joseph Rowe and Craig Miner, *Borne on the South Wind*, Wichita Eagle and Beacon Publishing Company, Wichita, KS, 1994, p. 67.
7. Edward H. Phillips, *Cessna: A Master's Expression*, Flying Books, Eagan, MN, 1985, p. 35.
8. Edward H. Phillips, *Travel Air: Wings Over the Prairie*, Flying Books, Eagan, MN, 1982, p. 7.
9. William H. McDaniel, *The History of Beech*, Beech Aircraft Corp., Wichita, KS, 1982, p. 12.
10. Rowe and Miner, op cit., p. 97.
11. Mitch Mayborn and Peter M. Bowers, "A History of the Stearman Aircraft Company," in *Stearman Guidebook*, Flying Enterprises Publications, Dallas, 1973, pp. 4–5.
12. Phillips, *Travel Air*, p. 44.
13. Paul R. Matt, *Alfred Victor Verville*, vol. 18: *Historical Aviation Album*, Corona Del Mar, CA, 1987, pp. 93–94.
14. John W. Underwood, *The Stinsons*, Heritage Press, Glendale, CA, 1969, p. 29.
15. *Aircraft Year Book, 1929*, Manufacturers Aircraft Association, New York, p. 74.
16. "Fairchild Company Buys Control of Kreider-Reisner," *Wings of Industry*, April 15, 1929, p. 1.
17. *Jane's All the World's Aircraft, 1929*, Sampson Low, Marston and Co., London, p. 269; and *Aircraft Year Book*, 1929, p. 75.
18. "Cessna Airplane Factory is Located at Wichita," *Aviation and Aeronautical Engineering*, December 1, 1916, p. 294.
19. Phillips, op cit., pp. 32–33.
20. *Ibid.*, p. 32–33 and 38; and Nevill, op cit., December 1930, p. 354.

Chapter 2

1. David B. Stevenson, "Charles Healy Day and His New Standards," *American Aviation Historical Society Journal*, vol. 41, Fall 1996, p. 207.
2. Grover Loening, *Takeoff into Greatness: How American Aviation Grew so Big so Fast*, Putnam, New York, 1968, p. 172.
3. Crouch, op. cit., pp. 122–123.
4. Bilstein, op. cit., pp. 68–69.
5. *Aerospace Facts and Figures, 1959*, Aerospace Industries Association, Washington, D. C., pp. 6–7.
6. Richard P. Hallion, *Designers and Test Pilots: The Epic of Flight* series, Time, New York, 1983, pp. 40–41.
7. Robert H. Rankin, "The Genius of Giuseppe," *Flying*, February 1953, pp. 36–37 and 60–61.
8. Hallion, op. cit., pp. 42–45.
9. Rankin, p. 61.
10. *Jane's All the World's Aircraft*, 1929.

11. Paul R. Matt, *Aeronca: Its Formation and First Aircraft*, *Historical Aviation Album*, vol. 10, Corona Del Mar, CA, 1971, p. 227.
12. Bilstein, op. cit., p. 70.
13. Matt, *Aeronca*, op. cit.
14. Devon Francis, *Mr. Piper and His Cubs*, Iowa State University Press, Ames, 1973, pp. 16–17, 22, and 41.
15. William F. Trimble, *High Frontier: A History of Aeronautics in Pennsylvania*, University of Pittsburgh Press, Pittsburgh, 1982, p. 183; and "Count the Cubs," *Fortune*, June 1940, p. 113.
16. Bill Wright, *Rearwin*, Sunflower University Press, Manhattan, KS, 1997, pp. 63–65.
17. Chet Peek, *The Spartan Story*, Three Peaks Publishing, Norman, OK, 1994, pp. 18–21.
18. Randolph F. Hall, "Cunningham-Hall Aircraft Corp. Story," *American Aviation Historical Society Journal*, vol. 16, Summer 1971, p. 90.
19. Trimble, op. cit., p. 174.
20. Frank Kingston Smith, *Legacy of Wings: The Story of Harold F. Pitcairn*, J. Aronson, New York, 1981, pp. 26 and 29.
21. Trimble, op. cit.
22. James J. Horgan, *City of Flight: The History of Aviation in St. Louis*, Patrice Press, Gerald, MO, 1984, p. 302.
23. Frederick W. Roos, "Curtiss-Wright St. Louis," *American Aviation Historical Society Journal*, vol. 35, Winter 1990, p. 305.
24. McDaniel, op. cit., p. 9.
25. Roos, op. cit., p. 293.
26. Phillips, *Cessna*, pp. 85–86.
27. McDaniel, op. cit.
28. *Aviation*, May 1933, p. 148.
29. Genevieve Brown, *Development of Transport Airplanes and Air Transport Equipment*, Air Technical Service Command, Wright Field, OH, April 1946, p. 67.
30. Horgan, op. cit., p. 321.
31. *Jane's All the World's Aircraft*, 1942, p. 209.
32. Bob Whittier, "Light Plane Heritage," *EAA Experimenter*, December 1993, pp. 31.
33. Chet Peek, *The Pietenpohl Story*, Three Peaks Publishing, Norman, OK, 2006, p. 50.
34. Eugene L. Vidal, "Low-Priced Airplane," *Aviation*, February 1934, pp. 40–41.
35. Joseph J. Corn, *The Winged Gospel: America's Romance with Aviation*, Oxford University Press, New York, 1983, pp. 98–100.
36. William F. Trimble, "The Collapse of the Dream: Lightplane Ownership and General Aviation in the United States after World War II," in William F. Trimble (ed.), *Pioneers and Operations*, vol. 2: *From Airships to Airbus: The History of Civil and Commercial Aviation*, Smithsonian Institution Press, Washington, D. C., 1995, p. 129.

Chapter 3

1. Crouch, op. cit., p. 117; and Roger Bilstein, *Flight in America*, Johns Hopkins University Press, Baltimore, 1984, p. 109.
2. Trimble, *High Frontier*, p. 185. "Count the Cubs," *Fortune*, June 1940, gives a figure of 523 for that year.
3. Trimble, *High Frontier*, p. 185
4. Chet Peek, *Taylorcraft: The Taylorcraft Story*, SunShine House, Terre Haute, IN, 1992, p. 24.
5. *Ibid.*, p. 43; and Donald Ross, *An Appraisal of Prospects for the Aircraft Manufacturing Industry*, White, Weld, and Co., New York, 1940.
6. Francis, op. cit., pp. 46–59.
7. William G. Cunningham, *The American Aircraft Industry: A Study in Industrial Location*, Lorrin L. Morrison, Los Angeles, 1951, p. 68.
8. John C. Swick, *The Luscombe Story: Every Cloud Has a Silvaire Lining*, SunShine House, Terre Haute, IN, 1987, pp. 65–68.
9. Smith, Frank K., op. cit., p. 301.
10. Trimble, *High Frontier*, p. 209.
11. McDaniel, op. cit., pp. 24–28.
12. Phillips, *Cessna*, pp. 99–104.
13. "Stubborn Cessna Toiled Day, Night," *Aviation Pioneers*, Wichita Eagle-Beacon Publishing Co., Wichita, KS, 1987, p. 5.
14. Kenneth D. Wilson and Thomas E. Lowe, "Lloyd C. Stearman, 1898–1975," *American Aviation Historical Society Journal*, vol. 36, Summer 1991, p. 90.
15. Crouch, op. cit., p. 123.
16. Underwood, op. cit., pp. 72–74.
17. Almarin Phillips, *Technology and Market Structure: A Study of the Aircraft Industry*, Heath Lexington, Lexington, MA, 1971, p. 92.
18. Bill Gunston, *One of a Kind: The Story of Grumman*, Grumman Corp., Bethpage, NY, 1988, p. 24.

19. *Of Men and Stars: A History of Lockheed Aircraft Corporation, 1913-1957*, Chapter 5, Lockheed Aircraft Corp., Burbank, CA, 1957, p. 8.
20. James R. Wilburn, "Social and Economic Aspects of the Aircraft Industry in Metropolitan Los Angeles during World War II," unpublished Ph.D. dissertation, UCLA, 1971, pp. 11–12; and letter, Robert E. Gross to Courtlandt S. Gross, March 31, 1957, Gross Papers, Box 13, Library of Congress.
21. Carl J. Peterson, *The CallAir Affair*, privately published by the author, 1989, p. 16.
22. Cunningham, op. cit., p. 175.
23. William Wagner, *Ryan, The Aviator*, McGraw-Hill, New York, 1971, p. 178.
24. Grover Loening, *Aviation and Banking*, Chase National Bank, New York, October 1938, p. 10.
25. Alfred Goldberg (ed.), *History of the United States Air Force*, Van Nostrand Co., Princeton, NJ, 1974, p. 118.
26. Francis, op. cit., pp. 75 and 82.
27. Underwood, op. cit., pp. 66–67.
28. "Beechcraft Takes Off on the Wings of a Jet," *Business Week*, February 25, 1956, p. 180.
29. McDaniel, op. cit., pp. 51–58.
30. Phillips, *Cessna*, pp. 119–121.
31. Trimble, *High Frontier*, p. 183.
32. Swick, op. cit., p. 89.

Chapter 4

1. Wright, *Rearwin*, op. cit., pp. 197–200.
2. Phillips, *Cessna*, p. 121.
3. Lew Townsend, "Lightplane Mergers: Beech, Cessna, Lear Didn't Get Together," *Wichita Eagle-Beacon*, Wichita, February 10, 1990, pp. 1F and 8F.
4. *Aerospace Facts and Figures, 1959*, p. 7.
5. *Aircraft Fact and Figures, 1957*, Aircraft Industries Association, Washington, D.C., p. 7, states 1,417. Retired General Echols, in his speech to the AIA in 1947, mentions a figure of 1,330 military aircraft produced for 1946, the same figure quoted by Robert E. Gross of Lockheed.
6. George Bryant Woods, *The Aircraft Manufacturing Industry: Present and Future Prospects*, White, Weld, and Co., New York, 1946, p. 46.

7. *Aircraft Year Book, 1946*, Aircraft Industries Association, Washington, D.C., p. 235; and Crouch, op. cit., p. 126. Joseph T. Geuting, Jr., manager of the Private Aircraft Council, made such an estimate.
8. Bilstein, *Flight in America*, p. 195.
9. John Foster, Jr., "The Personal Plane Sales Target," (survey for Parks Air College), *Aviation*, January 1944, pp. 116–117.
10. *NACA-Industry Conference on Personal Aircraft Research*, Langley Memorial Aeronautical Laboratories, Langley Field, VA, September 20, 1946.
11. Woods, op. cit.
12. Edward T. Austin, *Rohr: The Story of a Corporation*, Rohr Corp., Chula Vista, CA, 1969, pp. 41–42.
13. Richard Thruelson, *The Grumman Story*, Praeger, New York, 1976, pp. 225–226.
14. Herbert Solow, "North American: A Corporation Deeply Committed" *Fortune*, June 1962, p. 164.
15. Wagner, op. cit., p. 226.
16. "Experiment at Republic," *Fortune*, February 1947, p. 167.
17. "New Planes for Personal Flying," *Fortune*, February 1946, p. 126.
18. *General Aviation Statistical Databook, 1990-1991*, GAMA, Washington, D. C., p. 4.
19. Peek, op. cit., p. 167.
20. Trimble, *High Frontier*, p. 244.
21. Hall, op. cit., p. 167.
22. Wright, *Rearwin*, p. 213.
23. Swick, op. cit., p. pp. 106–107 and 152.
24. Rowe and Miner, op. cit., pp. 159–160.
25. McDaniel, op. cit., pp. 67 and 118; and Frank E. Hedrick, *Pageantry of Flight: The Story of Beech Aircraft Corporation*, Newcomen Society, New York, September 28, 1967, p. 23.
26. Trimble, *High Frontier*, p. 244; and Francis, op. cit., pp. 139–141.
27. Francis, op. cit., pp. 142–148.
28. Underwood, op. cit., p. 76.
29. Trimble, *High Frontier*, p. 244; and Francis, op. cit., pp. 139–141.
30. Francis, op. cit., pp. 151–161.
31. Thruelson, op. cit., p. 226.
32. Jay P. Spencer, *Vertical Challenge: The Hiller Aircraft Story*, University of Washington Press, Seattle, 1992, p. 54.
33. Gerard P. Moran, *Aeroplanes Vought, 1917-1977*, Historical Aviation Album, Temple City, CA, 1978, pp. 130–133.
34. Nicholas M. Williams, "The Aero Commander 520," *American Aviation His-*

torical Society Journal, vol. 35, Spring 1990, pp. 20–25.
35. Corn, op. cit., p. 140.
36. *Aviation Facts and Figures, 1953*, Aircraft Industries Association, Washington, D. C., pp. 140–141.

Chapter 5

1. Cunningham, op. cit., pp. 196–197.
2. *Aviation Facts and Figures*, 1959, p. 86.
3. George Hardie, Jr., "The Long Road Back: The American Airmen's Association," *Sport Aviation*, June 1986, pp. 35–37.
4. Keith Beveridge, *Kitplanes*, July 1997, p. 33.
5. Gordon Baxter, "Mooney," *Flying*, September 1997, p. 258.
6. Thomas J. Harris, *The Magic of Aero Design*, Newcomen Society, New York, May 10, 1962.
7. Williams, op. cit., p. 37.
8. Petersen, op. cit., pp. 18–23.
9. *Janes's All the World's Aircraft*, 1967–68, p. 272.
10. Francis, op. cit., p. 181; and Kent Misegades, "Genesis of a Classic," *Sport Aviation*, January 2010, pp. 43–48.
11. Trimble, *High Frontier*, p. 261.
12. *An Eye to the Sky*, Cessna Aircraft Company, Wichita, KS, 1962, pp. 66, 262.
13. *Flight International*, vol. 91, June 29, 1967, p. 1074.
14. "Beechcraft Takes Off on the Wings of a Jet," pp. 178–180.
15. Hedrick, op. cit., p. 32.
16. Gunston, op. cit., pp. 74–75.
17. David A. Brown, "Aero Commander Management Shifts Set," *Aviation Week & Space Technology*," July 19, 1965, pp. 20–21.
18. "Aero Commander Plans to Market Full Single-Engine Aircraft Line," *Aviation Week & Space Technology*, March 2, 1964, p. 36.
19. Andy Aastad, "The Birth of Enstrom Helicopters," *Rotor*, Summer 2007, pp. 58–60.
20. *Aviation Week & Space Technology*, April 13, 1964, p. 28.
21. Crouch, op. cit., p. 126.
22. "500 Largest Industrial Corporations," *Fortune*, June 15, 1968, pp. 188–204.
23. "A Look at America's Newest Volume Industry in 1970," internal study, Cessna Aircraft Company, Kansas Aviation Museum papers, circa 1960.
24. McDaniel, op. cit., p. 135.
25. Robert J. Serling, *The Jet Age: The Epic of Flight* series, Time, New York, 1982, p. 112; and Richard Rasche, *Stormy Genius*, Houghton Mifflin, Boston, 1985, pp. 223–226.
26. Jeffrey Ethell, *NASA and General Aviation*, NASA, Washington, D. C., 1986, p. 14.
27. Rasche, op. cit., pp. 226 and 253.

Chapter 6

1. *Ibid.*, p. 289; and Townsend, op. cit., p. 8F.
2. Crouch, op. cit., p. 111.
3. Ethell, op. cit., pp. 4, 11.
4. *General Aviation Statistical Databook, 1990-1991*, p. 4.
5. "Crosswinds," *Forbes*, November 1, 1968, p. 4.
6. "A House Divided at Piper," *Business Week*, March 16, 1974, p. 94.
7. Francis, op. cit., pp. 219–223.
8. *Aviation Week & Space Technology*, April 19, 1970, pp. 67–69; and Trimble, *High Frontier*, p. 283.
9. Erwin J. Bulban, "Piper, Swearingen Study Link; Latter Developing Business Jet," *Aviation Week & Space Technology*, July 26, 1971, p. 19.
10. "A House Divided at Piper," p. 94.
11. Richard J. Levine, "An Attack Aircraft That's Cheap, Good, Gets Cold Shoulder," *The Wall Street Journal*, May 30, 1974, p. 1.
12. Roger Bilstein, *Flight in America*, rev. ed., Johns Hopkins Press, Baltimore, 1993, p. 292; and Ronald G. Green, *Brazilian Government Support for the Aerospace Industry*, U.S. Department of Commerce, March 1987, p. x.
13. David M. North, "Piper Gears for Strong Market Assault," *Aviation Week & Space Technology*, November 20, 1978, p. 97.
14. McDaniel, op. cit., p. 364; and *The Wall Street Journal*, October 4, 1973, p. 9.
15. McDaniel, op. cit., p. 366.
16. *Ibid.*, p. 429.
17. G. Christian Hill and Barbara Eisenberg, "Dangerous Planes: Testimony, Documents Indicate 4 Beech Models Had Unsafe Fuel Tanks," *The Wall Street Journal*, July 30, 1971, pp. 1, 23.
18. McDaniel, op. cit., p. 465.
19. *Janes's All the World's Aircraft*, 1976–1977, p. 254.

20. Barry Bluestone, Peter Jordan, and Mark Sullivan, *Aircraft Industry Dynamics: An Analysis of Competition, Capital, and Labor*, Auburn House, Boston, 1981, p. 11.
21. Ethell, op. cit., p. 653.
22. *Flying*, May 1991, p. 12.
23. "Crosswinds," p. 46.
24. McDaniel, op. cit., p. 425.

Chapter 7

1. Warren J. Alverson, "The Shaky Case for the Company Jet," *Business Horizons*, Fall 1972, p. 87.
2. "500 Largest Industrial Corporations," *Fortune*, May 5, 1980, pp. 274–299.
3. *General Aviation Statistical Databook, 1990–1991*, p. 8.
4. Office of Aerospace, *A Competitive Assessment of the U.S. General Aviation Aircraft Industry*, Executive Summary, U.S. Department of Commerce, Washington, D. C., June 1986, p. x.
5. Erwin J. Bulban, "Raytheon, Beech Move Toward Merger, *Aviation Week & Space Technology*, October 8, 1987, p. 24.
6. McDaniel, op. cit., p. 509.
7. Ruth Simon, "Flying on a Wing and a Half," *Forbes*, July 13, 1987, p. 350; and "Why Beech Is Floating on Cloud 9," *Business Week*, March 19, 1990, p. 129.
8. Ian Goold, "Waxing Mooney," *Flight International*, November 29, 1986, pp. 105–106.
9. "British Aerospace Lawsuit Forces Fairchild to Seek Chapter 11 Protection," *Aviation Week & Space Technology*, February 19, 1990, p. 20.
10. "Potential Buyers Express Interest in Fairchild," *Aviation Week & Space Technology*, July 23, 1990, p. 34.
11. David M. North, "Gulfstream Terminates Production of Turboprop Commander Line," *Aviation Week & Space Technology*, January 28, 1985, p. 24.
12. "For Gulfstream, the Sky May Not Be the Only Limit," *Business Week*, February 26, 1990, p. 48.
13. *Interavia*, August 8, 1985, p. 845.
14. Ronald J. Wanttaja, *Kitplanes*, 2nd E, McGraw-Hill, New York, 1996, p. 7.
15. *Ibid.*, pp. 22–24.
16. Author's Interview with Danny Hiner, Vice President, Production, Aviat, November 21, 1997.

17. Experimental Aircraft Association, statistical reports, from FAA figures.
18. Timothy K. Smith, "Liability Costs Drive Small-Plane Business Back into Pilots' Barns," *The Wall Street Journal*, December 11, 1991, p. A1.
19. Office of Aerospace, *A Competitive Assessment of the U.S. Civil Helicopter Industry*, U.S. Department of Commerce, Washington, D.C., April 1998, p. 68.
20. McDaniel, op. cit., p. 383.
21. Author's Interview with Stan Green, former vice president and general counsel of GAMA, May 27, 1992.
22. "Pulling Out of a Nose-Dive," *Economist*, June 18, 1988, p. 90.
23. Timothy K. Smith, op. cit., p. A1.
24. Office of Aerospace, *A Competitive Assessment of the U.S. General Aviation Aircraft Industry*, p. 534.
25. *Jane's All the World's Aircraft*, 1989–1990, p. 29.
26. "Pulling Out of a Nose-Dive," p. 90.
27. L. J. Truitt and S. E. Tarry, "The Rise and Fall of General Aviation: Product Liability, Market Structure, and Technological Innovation," *Transportation Journal*, Summer 1995, p. 61.
28. Office of Aerospace, *A Competitive Assessment of the U.S. General Aviation Aircraft Industry*, p. 22. The four firms involved were Beech, Cessna, Gulfstream and Learjet.
29. Truitt and Tarry, op. cit., pp. 53, 61, and 65.
30. Timothy K. Smith, op. cit., p. A10.
31. "Against the Law," *Economist*, June 10, 1989, p. 66.
32. *General Aviation Statistical Databook, 1990–1991*, p. 4.
33. General Aviation Manufacturers Association, news release, January 16, 1992.

Chapter 8

1. Office of Aerospace, *A Competitive Assessment of the U.S. General Aviation Aircraft Industry*, p. 10.
2. *Jane's All the World's Aircraft*, 1990–1991, p. 475.
3. Truitt and Tarry, op. cit., p. 61.
4. *Jane's*, 1990–1991, p. 393.
5. "Against the Law," p. 66.
6. "Why Beech Is Floating on Cloud 9," pp. 128–129.

7. "Piper May Still Be Carrying Excess Baggage, *Business Week*, June 12, 1989, p. 76.
8. "Pulling Out of a Nose-Dive," p. 91.
9. "Piper May Still Be Carrying Excess Baggage," p. 76.
10. "Without Cash, Piper May Have Trouble Keeping Its Nose Up," *Business Week*, March 5, 1990, p. 32; and Edward A. Phillips, "Piper Lays off 170 Employees, Reduces Aircraft Production," *Aviation Week & Space Technology*, July 23, 1990, p. 32.
11. James T. McKenna, "Piper Creditors to Vote on Reorganization Plan," *Aviation Week & Space Technology*, May 22, 1995, p. 24.
12. Scott Thurston, "FedEx Deal Could Put Small Firm 'on the Map,'" *Atlanta Journal/Constitution*, December 1, 1996, p. R6.
13. Eric Weiner, "For Now, the Ultimate Status Symbol Still Sells," *The New York Times*, September 30, 1990, p. C4.
14. G. Pierre Goad, "Salvaged Units Help Bombardier Sell Jets," *The Wall Street Journal*, April 26, 1990, p. B11.
15. *Flying*, June 1991, p. 110.
16. John R. Wilke, "Beech's Sleekly Styled Starship Fails to Take Off with Corporate Customers," *The Wall Street Journal*, September 29, 1993, p. B1.
17. Paul Proctor, "Raytheon Restructures Merged Aircraft Units," *Aviation Week & Space Technology*, June 5, 1995, p. 58.
18. Anthony Bianco, "Gulfstream's Pilot," *Business Week*, April 15, 1997, p. 68.
19. *Ibid.*, p. 69
20. Scott Thurston, "Overhauled Gulfstream Preparing to Go Public," *Atlanta Journal/Constitution*, September 3, 1996, p. C4.
21. *General Aviation Statistical Databook, 1990–1991*, p. 24.
22. *Ibid.*, p. 111.
23. *General Aviation Statistical Databook, 1996*, GAMA, Washington, D.C., p. 11.
24. "Why Beech Is Floating on Cloud 9," pp. 128–129.
25. Rod Simpson, "From Beagles to Beechjets: General Aviation Defined," *Air International*, October 1995, p. 207.
26. Paul Proctor, "Helicopter Sales Buoyed by Strong Economics," *Aviation Week & Space Technology*, February 3, 1997, pp. 54–56.
27. Edward H. Phillips, "Advanced Kit-Builts Dominate EAA Show," *Aviation Week & Space Technology*, August 15, 1994, p. 50.
28. *Annual Industry Review*, GAMA, Washington, D.C., 1997, p. 1.

Chapter 9

1. *Ibid.*, p. 5.
2. Paul Jackson, Foreword, *Jane's All the World's Aircraft, 2000–2001*, p. 17; and "Biz-Jet Market to Approach $100 Billion, Analysts Say," *Aviationnow.com*, May 7, 2002, pp. 1–2.
3. Richard Aboulafia, "Quest for Corporate Efficiency Helps Buoy Business Jet Market," *Aviationnow.com*. Report, May 15, 2001, pp. 1–6.
4. 2011 NBAA *Business Aviation Fact Book*, p. 30; and GAMA news release, May 25, 2005.
5. Earl Downs, "Sport Pilot at Five," *Sport Aviation*, September 2009, pp. 46–51.
6. Andrew Galbraith, "Small Jet Makers Flock to China," *The Wall Street Journal*, April 17, 2012, B6.
7. Nicolas Casey, "The New Learjet... Now Mexican Made," *The Wall Street Journal*, July 29, 2011, B 1–2.
8. *Ibid.*
9. *Flying*, July 2009, p. 21.
10. "Cessna Completes Columbia Acquisition," *Flying*, February 2008, p. 17.
11. Angela Kim, "AASI Moves to Buy Mooney Aircraft," *Aviationnow.com*, February 8, 2002, pp. 1–2.
12. Jon Lake, "Hawker 4000," *Air International*, January 2011, pp. 69–73.
13. David Collogan, "Raytheon Seeking Buyer for Wichita Aircraft Maker," *Aviation Week & Space Technology*, July 31, 2006; and Joseph C. Anselmo, "Equity Groups Finalize Raytheon Aircraft Purchase," *Aviationnow.com*, March 27, 2007, p. 1.
14. David Markiewicz, "High Finance Firm Keeps Profile Low," *Atlanta Journal-Constitution*, November 15, 2009, D1, 8.
15. Frances Fiorino, "Vision Plan," *Aviation Week & Space Technology*, July 6, 2009, p. 30.
16. *Ibid.*
17. "Sino Swearingen Launches Production in Martinsburg," *Aviationnow.com*, March 13, 2002, pp. 1–2; and Dave Collogan, "With TC in Hand, Production Certificate Is Next Objective for SJ-30-2," *Aviationnow.com*, November 15, 2005, pp. 1–2.
18. Mary Lou Pickel, "Jets Small, Hopes

Big," *Atlanta Journal-Constitution*, January 20, 2004, E1, 4; and William Garvey, Ed., "Russian Investors Purchased Bankrupt Adam Aircraft," *Aviation Week & Space Technology*, August 17, 2009, p. 46.

19. J. Lynn Lunsford, "Tech Pioneer's New Business Jet: Seats Six for $850,000." *The Wall Street Journal*, July 12, 2002, B1, 4; J. Lynn Lunsford, "Bucking Skeptics, One Man Tries Selling Tiny Jets," *The Wall Street Journal*, May 6-7, 2006, A1, 5; Andy Pasztor, "Jet Maker Eclipse Files for Chapter 11," *The Wall Street Journal*, November 26, 2008, B1, 4; and J. Mac McClellan, "What Went Wrong With Eclipse?" *Flying*, March 2009, pp. 11-14.

20. Fred George and Frances Fiorino, "After Vern," *Aviation Week & Space Technology*, August 4, 2008, pp. 36-37; and Editorial, "Vern Raburn's Legacy," *Aviation Week & Space Technology*, August 4, 2008.

21. Dave Hirschman, "FedEx Cancels Loadmaster, Imperiling Firm," *Atlanta Journal-Constitution*, June 30, 2001, F3.

22. "South Georgia Company Proud of Its Crop-Dusting Planes," *Atlanta Journal-Constitution*, May 8, 2005, F3; and J. Mac McClellan, "The Lowest Flying Job Anywhere," *Sport Aviation*, August 2012, pp. 26-36.

23. Ann Keeton, "Wright Brothers Saw Airplane; Groen Brothers See Gyroplane," *The Wall Street Journal*, September 14, 2005, B3A.

24. Experimental Aircraft Association, *Report to Homebuilders 2011*.

25. *Jane's All the World's Aircraft*, 2005-2006, p. 15.

26. Daniel Michaels, "Helicopters Soar Overseas," *The Wall Street Journal*, January 2, 2004, A7.

Chapter 10

1. Liz Moscrop, "Highflier Rebuilds Broken Companies," *Financial Times*, October 19, 2010, p. 3.

2. William Garvey, "Hanging On," *Aviation Week & Space Technology*, February 6, 2012, p. 23.

3. Graham Warwick and Darren Shannon, "Corporate Casualties," *Aviation Week & Space Technology*, May 4, 2009, p. 36.

4. Robert Goyer (news item), *Flying*, March 2012, p. 15.

5. "Cessna Launches Latitude," *Flying*, December 2011, p. 16.

6. Robert Goyer, "Cessna TTx," *Flying*, April 2014, pp. 44-50.

7. Bradley Perrett, "Rescaled Ambitions," *Aviation Week & Space Technology*, April 7/14, 2014, pp. 62-63.

8. David Kesmodel and Nathan Hodge, "Hawker Sees Tough Year for Business Jets," *The Wall Street Journal*, January 31, 2012, B7; Mike Spector, "Hawker Nearing Chapter 11," *The Wall Street Journal*, May 3, 2012, B1-2.

9. William Garvey and Kerry Lynch, "White Knight, Red Flag," *Aviation Week & Space Technology*, July 16, 2012, pp. 40-41; Peter Sanders, "Hawker Woos Military as Sales Sink," *The Wall Street Journal*, January 31, 2012, B1-2; Joseph C. Anselmo, Michael Bruno, and Robert Wall, "Last Chance," *Aviation Week & Space Technology*, January 2, 2012, pp. 31-32; and Roxana Hegeman, "Air Force Temporarily Halts Work on Contract after Hawker Beechcraft Lawsuit," *Canadian Business*, June 23, 2012, pp. 1-2.

10. Kerry Lynch, "Beechcraft Rebound," *Aviation Week & Space Technology*, January 13, 2014, p. 28.

11. Fred George, "Gulfstream G650," *Business & Commercial Aviation*, October 2010, pp. 82-84.

12. Fred George, "Next-Gen Gulfstreams," *Aviation Week & Space Technology*, October 20, 2014, pp. 45-47; and Robert Goyer, "Gulfstream Launches All-New Jets," *Flying*, December 2014, pp. 46-51.

13. J. Scott Trubey, "Jet Maker Focusing on Sound Barrier," *Atlanta Journal Constitution*, January 4, 2015, pp. D1, 4.

14. Norihiko Shirouzu, "China to Buy U.S. Plane Maker," *The Wall Street Journal*, March 3, 2011, B1

15. William Garvey, "HondaJet Progresses," *Aviation Week & Space Technology*, January 3, 2011, p. 32.

16. Graham Warwick, "Eclipse Redux," *Aviation Week & Space Technology*, June 18, 2012, pp. 43-44.

17. Jon Ostrower and Paul Vieira, "Bombardier Shelves Its New Learjet," *The Wall Street Journal*, January 16, 2015, B4.

18. William Garvey, "Up on the Farm," *Aviation Week & Space Technology*, March 24, 2014, p. 16.

19. Pia Bergqvist, "Bell Goes Relentless," *Flying*, April 2012, p. 20.

20. Jon Lake, "Ringing in the Changes," *Air International*, October 2014, pp. 90–93.

21. Richard Aboulafia, Teal Group, quoted in William Garvey and Michael A. Taverna, "New Dawn," *Aviation Week & Space Technology*, May 5, 2010, pp. 46–47; and Joseph C. Anselmo and William Garvey, "Prolonged Pain," *Aviation Week & Space Technology*, October 10, 2011, pp. 54–55.

22. Doug Cameron and Chelsey Dulany, "Demand on Rise for Gulfstream, Cessna Jets," *The Wall Street Journal*, January 29, 2015, B6.

23. Jon Ostrower, "NetJets Readies a Big Order," *The Wall Street Journal*," June 12, 2012, B2; and Jon Ostrower and Robert Wall, "Political Winds Buffet Business Jets," *The Wall Street Journal*, October 20, 2014, B7.

24. Joseph C. Anselmo and William Garvey, "The Haves and Have Nots," *Aviation Week & Space Technology*, October 18, 2010, pp. 52–55.

25. General Aviation Manufacturers Association, *2018 Annual Report*, p. 15.

Bibliography

Articles, Monographs and Reports

Aboulafia, Richard. "Quest for Corporate Efficiency Helps Buoy Business Jet Market," *Aviationnow.com*, May 15, 2001, p. 1.

"Aero Commander Plans to Market Full Single-Engine Aircraft Line," *Aviation Week & Space Technology*, March 2, 1964, p. 36.

"Against the Law," *Economist*, June 10, 1989, p. 56.

Alverson, Warren J. "The Shaky Case for the Company Jet," *Business Horizons*, vol. 15, April 1972, pp. 79–88.

Anselmo, Joseph C., and William Garvey. "The Haves and Have Nots," *Aviation Week & Space Technology*, October 18, 2010, pp. 52–55.

"At 20, Corporate Angel Network Is Poised to Grow," *Business & Commercial Aviation*, November 2000.

"Aviation Pioneers," *Wichita Eagle-Beacon*, 1987. Reprint of a series of articles on Kansas aviation history published in the *Eagle-Beacon*, beginning October 8, 1984.

"Beechcraft Takes Off on the Wings of a Jet," *Business Week*, February 25, 1956, pp. 178–186.

Bianco, Anthony, and William C. Symonds. "Gulfstream's Pilot," *Business Week*, April 14, 1997, pp. 64–76.

"BizJet Market to Approach $100 Billion, Analysts Say," *Aviationnow.com*, May 8, 2002, pp. 1–2.

"British Aerospace Lawsuit Forces Fairchild to Seek Chapter 11 Protection," *Aviation Week & Space Technology*, February 19, 1990, p. 20.

Brown, David A. "Aero Commander Management Shifts Set," *Aviation Week & Space Technology*, July 19, 1965, pp. 20–21.

Burner, David L. "GAMA Agenda: Address to General Aviation Manufacturers Association," February 10, 1995.

Casey, Nicolas. "The New Learjet...Now Mexican Made," *The Wall Street Journal*, July 29, 2011, B 1–2.

"Cessna Airplane Factory is Located in Wichita," *Aviation and Aeronautical Engineering*, December 1, 1916, p. 294.

Clark, Pilita. "Hopes Fade for Early Start to Recovery," *Financial Times*, October 19, 2010, Corporate Aviation Special Report, pp. 1, 4.

"Count the Cubs," *Fortune*, June 1940, pp. 77–81; 114–118.

Crouch, Tom. "General Aviation: The Search for a Market," in Eugene M. Emme (ed.), *200 Years of Flight in America: A Bicentennial Survey*, Univelt, San Diego, 1977, pp. 111–135.

Department of Commerce. *A Competitive Assessment of the U. S. General Aviation Aircraft Industry*, June 1986.

"A Divided House at Piper," *Business Week*, March 16, 1974, pp. 94–97.

Downs, Earl. "Sport Pilot at Five," *Sport Aviation*, September 2009, pp. 46–51.

"Experiment at Republic," *Fortune*, February 1946, pp. 123–125; 164–172.

"Fairchild Company Buys Control of Kreider-Reisner," *Wings of Industry*, April 15, 1929, p. 1.

Fiorino, Frances. "Banner Year," *Aviation Week & Space Technology*, February 18, 2008, p. 96.

"For Gulfstream, the Sky May Not Be the Only Limit," *Business Week*, February 26, 1990, p. 48.

Foster, John, Jr. "The Personal Plane Sales

Target" (survey for Parks Air College), *Aviation*, January 1944, pp. 116–117 and 364–368.

Galbraith, Andrew. "Small-Jet Makers Flock to China," *The Wall Street Journal*, April 17, 2012, B6.

Garvey, William. "Up on the Farm," *Aviation Week & Space Technology*, March 24, 2014, p. 16.

Garvey, William, and Kerry Lynch. "White Knight, Red Flag," *Aviation Week & Space Technology*, July 16, 2012, pp. 40–41.

Garvey, William, and Michael A. Taverna. "New Dawn," *Aviation Week & Space Technology*, May 10, 2010, pp. 46–47.

Geisse, John H., and Samuel C. Williams. *Postwar Outlook for Private Flying*, Report to Assistant Secretary of Commerce W.A.M. Burden, 1943.

George, Fred. "Gulfstream G650," *Business & Commercial Aviation*, October 2010, pp. 82–83.

George, Fred, and Frances Fiorino. "After Vern," *Aviation Week & Space Technology*, August 4, 2008, pp. 36–37.

Goad, G. Pierre. "Salvaged Units Help Bombardier Sell Jets," *The Wall Street Journal*, April 26, 1990, p. B11.

Goold, Ian. "Waxing Mooney," *Flight International*, November 29, 1986, pp. 105–106.

Goyer, Robert. "Gulfstream Launches All-New Jets," *Flying*, December 2014, pp. 46–51.

———. "Hawker 4000," *Flying*, November 2011, pp. 40–47.

———. "New Eclipse," *Flying*, February 2011, pp. 42–49.

Gustafson, David. "Tom Hamilton and the Glasair," *Flyingmag.com*, June 1, 2012, p. 1.

———. "Van's Aircraft and the RV Nation," *Flyingmag.com*, May 15, 2012, p. 1.

Hall, Randolph F. "Cunningham-Hall Aircraft Corporation Story," *American Aviation Historical Society Journal*, Summer 1971, pp. 90–97.

Hardie, George, Jr. "The Long Road Back," *Sport Aviation*, June 1986, pp. 35–37.

Harris, Thomas J. *The Magic of Aero Design*, The Newcomen Society, New York, May 10, 1962 (Monograph).

Hedrick, Frank E. *Pageantry of Flight: The Story of Beech Aircraft Corporation*, The Newcomen Society, New York, September 28, 1957 (Monograph).

Hill, G. Christian, and Barbara Isenberg. "Dangerous Planes: Testimony, Documents Indicate 4 Beech Models Had Unsafe Fuel Tanks," *The Wall Street Journal*, July 30, 1971, pp. 1 and 23.

Hirschman, Dave. "Carrying the Load," *Atlanta Journal-Constitution*, September 10, 2000, Q1, 5.

———. "FedEx Cancels Loadmaster, Imperiling Firm," *Atlanta Journal-Constitution*, June 30, 2001, F3.

———. "Gulfstream Seeks Military-Sales Boost," *Atlanta Journal-Constitution*, August 22, 2002, H1, 4.

Hubler, Mark. "High Economy," *AOPA Pilot*, February 2001.

Keeton, Ann. "Wright Brothers Saw Airplane: Groen Brothers See Gyroplane," *The Wall Street Journal*, September 14, 2005, B3A.

Kesmodel, David, and Nathan Hodge. "Hawker Sees Tough Year for Business Jets," *The Wall Street Journal*, January 31, 2012, p. B7.

Klemin, Alexander. "Investing in Aviation," *Scientific American*, February 1929, pp. 148–153.

Lake, Jon. "Hawker 4000," *Air International*, January 2011, pp. 69–73.

———. "Ringing in the Changes," *Air International*, October 2014, pp. 90–93.

Levine, Richard J. "An Attack Aircraft That's Cheap, Good, Gets Cold Shoulder," *The Wall Street Journal*, May 30, 1974, p. 1.

Lunsford, J. Lynn. "Bucking Skeptics, One Man Tries Selling Tiny Jets," *The Wall Street Journal*, May 6–7, 2006, A1, 5.

———. "Tech Pioneer's New Business Jet: Seats Six for $850,000," *The Wall Street Journal*, July 12, 2002, B1.

Matt, Paul R. Aeronca: Its Formation and First Aircraft, vol. 10: *Historical Aviation Album*, 1971, pp. 270–286.

———. Alfred Victor Verville, vol. 18: *Historical Aviation Album*, 1987, pp. 88–96.

Markiewicz, David. "High Finance Firm Keeps Profile Low," *Atlanta Journal-Constitution*, November 15, 2009, pp. D1, 8.

Mayborn, Mitch, and Peter M. Bowers. "A History of the Stearman Aircraft Company," Stearman Guidebook, *Flying Enterprises Publications*, Dallas, 1973, pp. 4–5.

McClellan, J. Mac. "The Lowest Flying Job Anywhere," *Sport Aviation*, August 2012, pp. 26–36.

———. "What Went Wrong with Eclipse," *Flying*, March 2009, pp. 11–14.

McKenna, James T. "Piper Creditors to Vote on Reorganization Plan," *Aviation Week & Space Technology*, May 22, 1995, p. 24.

Michaels, Daniel. "Helicopters Soar Overseas," *The Wall Street Journal*, January 2, 2004, A7.

Misegades, Kent. "Genesis of a Classic," *Sport Aviation*, January 2010, pp. 43–48.

Moscrop, Liz. "Highflier Rebuilds Broken Companies," *Financial Times*, October 19, 2010, p. 3.

Nevill, John. "The Story of Wichita," *Aviation*, September 1930, pp. 166–170; and December 1930, pp. 353–357.

"New Planes for Personal Flying," *Fortune*, February 1946, pp. 124–129; 154–158.

North, David M. "Piper Gears for Strong Market Assault," *Aviation Week & Space Technology*, November 20, 1978, p. 97.

Office of Aerospace. *A Competitive Assessment of the U. S. Civil Helicopter Industry*, Department of Commerce, April 1998.

Ostrower, Jon, and Robert Wall. "Political Winds Buffet Business Jets," *The Wall Street Journal*, October 20, 2014, B7.

Pasztor, Andy. "Jet Maker Eclipse Files for Chapter 11," *The Wall Street Journal*, November 26, 2008, B1, 4.

Perrett, Bradley. "Rescaled Ambitions," *Aviation Week & Space Technology*, April 7/14, 2014, pp. 62–63.

Phillips, Edward H. "Advanced Kit-Builts Dominate EAA Show," *Aviation Week & Space Technology*, August 15, 1994, pp. 50–51.

_____. "Piper Lays Off 170 Employees, Reduces Aircraft Production," *Aviation Week & Space Technology*, July 23, 1990, p. 32.

Pickel, Mary Lou. "Jets Small: Hopes Big," *Atlanta Journal-Constitution*, January 20, 2004, E1, 3.

Piper, W. T., Jr. *From Cubs to Navajo: The Story of Piper Aircraft Corporation*, The Newcomen Society, New York, April 23, 1970 (monograph).

"Piper May Still Be Carrying Excess Baggage," *Business Week*, June 12, 1989, p. 76.

Pope, Steven. "Those Amazing RVs," *Flying*, October 2011, pp. 56–61.

"Potential Buyers Express Interest in Fairchild," *Aviation Week & Space Technology*, July 23, 1990, p. 34.

Proctor, Paul. "Helicopter Sales Buoyed by Strong Economics," *Aviation Week & Space Technology*, February 3, 1997, pp. 54–56.

_____. "Raytheon Restructures Merged Aircraft Units," *Aviation Week & Space Technology*, June 5, 1995, pp. 58–59.

"Pulling Out of a Nose-Dive," *Economist*, June 18, 1988, pp. 90–91.

Rankin, Robert H. "The Genius of Guiseppe," *Flying*, February 1953, pp. 36–37 and 60–61.

Roos, Frederick W. "Curtiss-Wright St. Louis," *American Aviation Historical Society Journal*, vol. 35, Winter 1990, pp. 293–305.

Sanders, Peter. "As Aviation Jobs Take Off, Wichita Frets Its Future," *The Wall Street Journal*, October 12, 2009, p. A5.

_____. "Hawker Woos Military as Sales Sink," *The Wall Street Journal*, January 31, 2012, B1–2.

Schneider, Charles E. "Piper Faces Fiscal, Internal Hurdles," *Aviation Week & Space Technology*, October 19, 1970, pp. 67–69.

Schreiner, Herm. "The Waco Story, Part 1: Clayton Brukner and the Founding Years," *American Aviation Historical Society Journal*, vol. 25, Winter 1980, pp. 281–299.

_____. "The Waco Story, Part 2: Expansion with the 'F' Series, *American Aviation Historical Society Journal*, vol. 29, Fall 1984, pp. 214–227.

Shirouzu, Norihiko. "China to Buy U. S. Plane Maker," *The Wall Street Journal*, March 3, 2011, B1.

Simon, Ruth. "Flying on a Wing and a Half," *Forbes*, July 13, 1987, pp. 350 and 355.

Simpson, Rod. "From Beagles to Beechjets: General Aviation Defined," *Air International*, October 1995, pp. 205–209.

Smith, Timothy K. "Liability Costs Drive Small-Plane Business Back into Pilots' Barns," *The Wall Street Journal*, December 11, 1991, pp. A1 and A10.

"Sino Swearingen Launches Production in Martinsburg," *Aviationnow.com*, March 13, 2002, p. 1.

Solow, Herbert. "North American: A Corporation Deeply Committed, *Fortune*, June 1962, pp. 145–149 and 164–182.

"South Georgia Company Proud of Its Crop-Dusting Planes," *Atlanta Journal-Constitution*, May 8, 2003, F3.

Stevenson, David B. "Charles Healy Day and His New Standards," *American Aviation Historical Society Journal*, vol. 41, Fall 1996, pp. 200–219.

Thurston, Scott. "After Recovery, Jet Maker Hits Cruising Altitude," *Atlanta Journal-Constitution*, May 16, 1999, Q11.

_____. "FedEx Deal Could Put Small Firm 'on the Map,'" *Atlanta Journal-Constitution*, December 1, 1996, p. 86.

———. "Overhauled Gulfstream Preparing to Go Public," *Atlanta Journal-Constitution*, September 3, 1996, p. C4.

Townsend, Lew. "Lightplane Mergers: Beech, Cessna, Lear Didn't Get Together," *Wichita Eagle-Beacon*, February 10, 1990, pp. 1F and 8F.

Trimble, William F. "The Collapse of a Dream: Lightplane Ownership and General Aviation in the United States after World War II," in William F. Trimble (ed.) *Pioneers and Operations*, vol. 2: *From Airships to Airbus: The History of Civil and Commercial Aviation*, Smithsonian Institution Press, Washington, D.C., 1995, pp. 128–145.

Trubey, J. Scott. "Jet Maker Focusing on Sound Barrier," *Atlanta Journal-Constitution*, January 4, 2015, D1, 4.

Truitt, L. J., and S. E. Tarry. "The Rise and Fall of General Aviation: Product Liability, Market Structure, and Technological Innovation," *Transportation Journal*, Summer 1995, pp. 52–70.

Velocci, Anthony L., Jr. "Raytheon Aircraft, Still Troubled, Showing Signs of Turnaround," *Aviation Week & Space Technology*, August 16, 2002, p. 1.

Vidal, Eugene L. "Low-Priced Airplane," *Aviation*, February 1934, pp. 40–41.

Wallace, Lane. "Van's Air Force," *Sport Aviation*, June 2012, pp. 28–36.

Warwick, Graham. "Eclipse Redux," *Aviation Week & Space Technology*, June 18, 2012, pp. 43–44.

Weiner, Eric. "For Now, the Ultimate Status Symbol Still Sells," *The New York Times*, September 30, 1990, p. F4.

West, Ted. "Why Wichita," *Flying*, September 1997, p. 254.

Whittier, Bob. "Light Plane Heritage," *EAA Experimenter*, December 1993, pp. 29–54.

"Why Beech Is Floating on Cloud 9," *Business Week*, March 19, 1990, pp. 128–129.

Wilke, John R. "Beech's Sleekly Styled Starship Fails to Take Off with Corporate Customers," *The Wall Street Journal*, September 29, 1993, pp. B1 and B8.

Wilkinson, Kim M. "History of the Piper Aircraft Corporation," *Lock Haven Express*, July 14–18, 1987.

Williams, Nicholas M. "The Aero Commander 520," *American Aviation Historical Society Journal*, vol. 35, Spring 1990, pp. 18–37.

Wilson, Kenneth D., and Thomas E. Lowe. "Lloyd C. Stearman, 1898–1975," *American Aviation Historical Society Journal*, vol. 36, Summer 1991, pp. 82–93.

"Without Cash, Piper May Have Trouble Keeping Its Nose Up," *Business Week*, March 5, 1990, p. 32.

Books

Austin, Edward T. *Rohr: The Story of a Corporation*, Rohr Corporation, Chula Vista, CA, 1969.

Bednarek, Janet R. Daly and Michael H. Bednarek. *Dreams of Flight: General Aviation in the United States*, Texas A&M University Press, College Station, TX, 2003.

Bilstein, Roger. *Flight in America*, Johns Hopkins University Press, Baltimore, 1984, revised edition 1993.

———. *Flight Patterns*, University of Georgia Press, Athens, GA, 1983.

———, and Jon Miller. *Aviation in Texas*, Texas Monthly Press, Austin, 1985.

Cessna Aircraft Company. *An Eye to the Sky*, Cessna Aircraft Company, 1962.

Corn, Joseph J. *The Winged Gospel: America's Romance with Aviation*, Oxford University Press, New York, 1983.

Cunningham, William G. *The Aircraft Industry: A Study of Industrial Location*, Lorrin L. Morrison, Los Angeles, 1951.

Ethell, Jeffrey L. *NASA and General Aviation*, NASA, Washington, D.C., 1986.

Fairchild Hiller Corporation. *Yesterday, Today, and Tomorrow: Fifty Years of Fairchild Aviation*, Fairchild Hiller Corporation, Germantown, MD, 1970.

Francis, Devon. *Mr. Piper and His Cubs*, Iowa State University Press, Ames, 1973.

General Aviation Manufacturers Association. *The General Aviation Story*, GAMA, Washington, D.C., 1974.

Gunston, Bill. *One of A Kind: The Story of Grumman*, Grumman Corporation, Bethpage, NY, 1988.

Hallion, Richard P. *Designers and Test Pilots*, the *Epic of Flight* series, Time, New York, 1983.

Harding, William Barclay. *The Aviation Industry*, Charles D. Barney, New York, 1937.

Horgan, James J. *City of Flight: The History of Aviation in St. Louis*, Patrice Press, Gerald, MO, 1984.

Lambermont, Paul, with Anthony Pirie. *Helicopters and Autogiros of the World*, rev. ed., A. S. Barnes and Co., New York, 1970.

Loening, Grover C. *Takeoff into Greatness: How American Aviation Grew So Big So Fast,* Putnam, New York, 1968.
McDaniel, William H. *The History of Beech,* Beech Aircraft Corporation, Wichita, 1982.
National Advisory Committee for Aeronautics. *NASA-Industry Conference on Personal Aircraft Research,* NACA Langley Memorial Aeronautical Laboratories, Langley Field, VA, September 20, 1946.
Peek, Chet. *The Pietenpohl Story,* Three Peaks Publishing, Norman, OK, 2006.
_____. *Taylorcraft: The Taylorcraft Story,* SunShine House, Terre Haute, IN, 1992.
_____, with George Goodhead. *The Spartan Story,* Three Peaks Publishing, Norman, OK, 1994.
Petersen, Carl J. *The CallAir Affair: An Aeronautical History* (privately published by the author), 1989.
Phillips, Edward H. *Beechcraft: Pursuit of Perfection,* Flying Books, Eagan, MN, 1992.
_____. *Cessna: A Master's Expression,* Flying Books, Eagan, MN, 1985.
_____. *Travel Air: Wings Over the Prairie,* Flying Books, Eagan, MN, 1982.
Rasche, Richard. *Stormy Genius,* Houghton Mifflin, Boston, 1985.
Rowe, Frank Joseph, and Craig Miner. *Borne on the South Wind: A History of Kansas Aviation,* The Wichita Eagle and Beacon Publishing Co., Wichita, 1994.
Smith, Frank Kingston. *Legacy of Wings: The Story of Harold F. Pitcairn,* J. Aronson, New York, 1981.
Spencer, Jay P. *Vertical Challenge: The Hiller Aircraft Story.* Seattle: University of Washington Press, 1992.
Swick, John C. *The Luscombe Story: Every Cloud Has a Silvaire Lining,* SunShine House, Terre Haute, IN, 1987.
Thruelson, Richard. *The Grumman Story,* Praeger, New York, 1976.
Trimble, William F. *High Frontier: A History of Aeronautics in Pennsylvania,* University of Pittsburgh Press, Pittsburgh, 1982.
Underwood, John. *The Stinsons,* The Heritage Press, Glendale, CA, 1969.
Wagner, William. *Ryan, the Aviator,* McGraw-Hill Book Co., New York, 1971.
Woods, George Bryant. *The Aircraft Manufacturing Industry: Present and Future Prospects,* White, Weld, New York, 1946.
Wright, Bill. *Rearwin: A Story of Men, Planes, and Aircraft Manufacturing During the Great Depression,* Sunflower University Press, Manhattan, KS, 1997.

Annuals and Directories

Aerospace Industries Association. *Aircraft Year Book* and *Aerospace Year Book,* Aerospace Industries Association, Washington, D.C. (various editions).
_____. *Aviation Facts and Figures* and *Aerospace Facts and Figures,* Aerospace Industries Association, Washington, D. C. (various editions).
Experimental Aircraft Association. *Report to Homebuilders 2011.* Oshkosh, WI: Experimental Aircraft Association, 2012.
General Aviation Manufacturers Association. *Annual Industry Review: 1997 Outlook and Agenda,* GAMA, Washington, D. C., 1997.
_____. *General Aviation Statistical Databook,* GAMA, Washington, D. C. (various editions).
_____. *General Aviation Statistical Databook & 2015 Industry Outlook,* GAMA, Washington, D. C., 2015.
Jane's All the World's Aircraft. Sampson, Low, Marston and Co., London (various editions).
Marcovski, Michael A. *ARV—The Encyclopedia of Aircraft Recreational Vehicles,* Aviation Publishers, Hummelstown, PA, 1984.
Simpson, R. W. *Airlife's General Aviation.* Shrewsbury, England: Airlife Publishing, 1991.
Wanttaja, Ron. *Kitplane Construction,* 2d ed. McGraw-Hill, New York, 1996.
World Aviation Annual 1948. Aviation Research Institute, Washington, D.C., 1948.

Documentary Collections

Walter H. and Olive Ann Beech Papers. Ablah Library, Wichita State University, Wichita, KS.
Clayton J. Brukner Collection. Wright State University Archives and Special Collections, Dayton, OH.
International Cyclopedia of Aviation Biography. Wright State University Archives and Special Collections, Wright State University, Dayton, OH.

Index

A500 JetCruzer 178
Ace Aircraft Co. 33, 81
Adam, Rick 181
Adam A700 AdamJet 181
Adam Aircraft Industries 181, 220
Adam M-309/Carbon Aero/A500 181
ADS-B 197
Advance Aircraft Co. (*see* WACO) 8
Advanced Aerodynamics and Structures, Inc. 178
Aerial Service Corp. (Mercury Aircraft) 7, 17
Aerial service sector 7
Aerion Corp. 184, 207
Aeritalia (Italy) 134
Aero Design aircraft: 500/500A Shrike Commander/L-26A Esquire 83, 107, 135, 680F/L Grand Commander 83; Commander 100/Darter Commander (*see* Volaircraft) 93, 107; Commander 111/112/114/Alpine 108, 157; Commander 200 (*see* Meyers) 93, 107; Commander 560/560A 83; Commander 680 Super 83; Commander 720 Alti-Cruiser 83; Commander 840/900/980/1000 series (*see* Gulfstream) 108, 135; Commander/Gran Turismo Commander 108; Commander/Turbo Commander 681B/685/690B 108, 135; Courser Commander 107; L-3085/Commander 520 74, 75, 83; Lark Commander 107; (Rockwell) Jet Commander (*see also* IAI) 12, 101, 107; Sparrow/Quail/Snipe Commander (*see* Call, Rockwell) 108; Thrush Commander 108; Turbo Commander/Turbo II 83, 107
Aero Design and Engineering Co./Aero Commander, Inc. 74, 75, 83, 166; Aero Commander Division-Rockwell/Rockwell Aero Commander 107, 153
Aero Designs, Inc. 142, 189
Aero Designs Pulsar XP 189
Aerocar Aerocar I 62
Aerocar Aero-Plane 95, 144
Aerocar, Inc. 62
Aeromarine Co. 8

Aeronautical Chamber of Commerce (ACC) 6, 54
Aeronautical Corp. of America (Aeronca) 22, 34, 48, 51, 53, 60, 75
Aeronautical Research & Development Corp. (ARDC) 122
Aeronca aircraft: Aeronca C-2/C-3 22, 23, 37; Aeronca C-4 22; Arrow 60; (Bellanca) Citabria (*see* Champion) 158; (Bellanca) Scout/Champ/Decathlon 158; Chief/L-3 Grasshopper 51; Model 7/7A Champion/L-16 60; Model 11 Super Chief (postwar) 60; Model 15 Sedan 60, 63; Model 40 Chief /L-3 51; Model 65 Super Chief 51; Model K/Scout 37; Model L 37
Aerospatiale (France) 154, 156
Aerovochody (Czech Rep.) 217
AFA (Switzerland) P-16 101
AGA Corp. (*see* Pitcairn) 38
AGATE Program 170, 174, 188
Ag-Cat Corp. 159
Agusta/Agusta Westland (Italy) 70, 216
Air Commerce Act of 1926 7
Air Force, U.S. 83, 155, 160, 166
Air Medical Group Holdings 193
Air Products Co. 85
Air Tractor, Inc. 108, 159, 214; Air Tractor AT-402, AT-502 184; Air Tractor AT-802/802U/802F/ Fire Boss 214
Air Traffic Control (ATC) 105
Air Transportation Center for Excellence for General Aviation Research (CGAR) 174
Airbus (Eurocopter) 216
Aircooled Motors Corp. (*see* Franklin) 26, 58
Aircraft Industries Assn./Aerospace Industries Assn. (AIA) 54, 75, 105
Aircraft Investor Resources, Inc. (*see* Epic) 187
Aircraft Kit Industry Assn. (AKIA) 214
Aircraft Manufacturing and Development (AMD) 192
Aircraft Mechanics, Inc. 24
Aircraft Owners and Pilots Assn. (AOPA) 46, 54, 106, 172
AiRover Aircraft (*see* Lockheed) 43

Index

AiRover Starliner 43
Akron Aircraft Co. 45
Albert, Carl 134
Alexander, J. Don 11
Alexander Aircraft Corp. 11, 24
Alexander Bullet 11
Alexander Eaglerock 11
Alexander Industries 11
Alexandria Aircraft (see Bellanca) 187
Allen, John F., Jr. 86
Allen Holding Finance 178
Allied Aero Industries 86
AlliedSignal 166
Allison 250 engine 120, 122, 168
Alon Air Coupe/Cadet (see also ERCO) 86, 110; A-2 Air Coupe 110; Alon A-4 86
Alon, Inc. 86
American Autogyro 186
American Aviation A-1 Yankee (see Grumman) 119
American Aviation Corp. 85, 117, 119
American Capital Strategies 176
American Cement Corp. 110
American Champion (see also Aeronca, Bellanca) 158, 187, 214; American Champion Citation/Decathlon/Scout/Champ 187
American Eagle A-129 24
American Eagle Aircraft Corp. 23, 24
American Eagle Eaglet 25
American Eagle-Lincoln Co. 24
American Electronic Laboratories (A.E.L. Inc.) 110
American General Aircraft Corp. 157
American General Tiger (see GAAC) 157
American Jet Industries, Inc. (AJI) 94, 120
American Navion Society 86
Amis brothers 74
Anderson, Ben M. 62
Anderson, Herb 142
Anderson-Greenwood AG-14 62
Anderson-Greenwood & Co. 62, 117, 133
Arcapita 180
Arcier, Francis J. 41
Army, U.S. (Army Aviation) 87, 89, 90, 97, 116
Army Air Corps 47
Army Air Forces, U.S. (USAAF) 47
Army Air Service, Engineering Division 13
Association of Trial Lawyers of America (ATLA) 149
Atlas Aircraft Corp. 60
Atlas H-10 60
Augur, Charles H. 17
Autogiro Company of America (ACA) 27
Autogiro development 26
Aviat Aircraft, Inc. 142, 186, 214, 221
Aviat Husky 141, 186
Aviation Corporation (AVCO) 14, 26, 28, 166
Aviation Innovation, Reform, and Reauthorization (AIRR) Act 197
Aviation Manufacturing Corp. (Div. AVCO) 29

AVIC (China) 203, 208
Avid Aircraft 189
Avions Max Holste (Reims Aviation) 89
Ayres, Fred 159
Ayres Corp. 108, 134, 159, 184
Ayres LM 200 Loadmaster 159, 184
Ayres Thrush Commander (see Rockwell) 134

BAe 125–800 (see de Havilland) 162
BAe 1000 162
BAe Jetstream 134
Bailey, F. Lee 122, 145
Baldwin (Ordnance) factory 21
Ballistic Recovery System (BRS) (see Cirrus) 180
Bangor Punta Corp. 111, 113, 130
Barents, Brian 184
Barkley, Archibald S. 41
Barkley-Grow Aircraft Co. 41
Barkley-Grow T8P-1 41
Barnstorming era 6
Bass, Robert 207
Baumann, J.B. 62
Baumann Aircraft Corp. 62, 95
Baumann B-250/B-290 Brigadier 62, 69
Bays, Larry 184
Bede, James R. 119, 137, 215
Bede aircraft: BD-1 119, 137; BD-4/6 137; BD-5 Micro 137; BD-10 144; BD-12/14 144
Bede Aviation Corp. 119
Bedecorp LLC 190
Beech, Olive Ann (Mrs. Walter H.) 10, 30, 48, 64, 92, 114, 130, 155
Beech, R.K. 10
Beech, Walter H. 9, 15, 29, 30, 44, 47, 48, 53, 65
Beech aircraft: AT-10 Wichita 48; Beech Mark II/T-6A Texan 166; Beech Premier I 164; Beechcraft Hawker BH-125 125 (see de Havilland); Beechjet 400A/400T/T-1A Jayhawk 131, 154, 155, 160, 165, 203 (see Mitsubishi); Debonair 115; Duke 115, 131; E-18S "Super 18"/H-18 Super-Liner 63, 91, 115; Jet Mentor 90; King Air 250 203; King Air MC-12W Liberty 203; Model 17 Staggerwing 30, 38, 63; Model 18/C-45/AT-7/AT-11 "Twin Beech" 38, 48, 90; Model 34 "Twin Quad" 63, 103; Model 35/36 Bonanza 63, 90, 93, 131, 155, 180, 203; Model 50/L-23 Twin Bonanza 63, 69, 75, 90, 91; Model 55/58 Baron 90, 155, 180; Model 65/80 Queen Air/L-23F 90, 111, 115; Model 76 Duchess 115, 131; Model 77 Skipper 115; Model 90 King Air/King Air 100 90, 115, 131, 132, 154; Model 95 Travel Air 90, 91, 115; Model 99/99A/B99/C99 91, 111, 115, 131; Model 1900C/D 131, 154, 155, 157, 180; Musketeer/Sundowner/Sport 90, 115, 131; (Raytheon) Mark II/T-6A 166 (see Pilatus); Sierra 115, 131; Starship 2000 132, 149, 154, 162, 203; Super King Air (to King Air)

Index

200/300/350 115, 131, 132, 154, 155, 162, 165, 180, 203; T-34 Mentor 65, 66, 73, 90; T-34C Turbo Mentor 116; T-36A 66, 79; U-8F Seminole 90; XA-38 Grizzly 48
Beech Aircraft Corp. 34, 38, 47, 48, 53, 62, 75, 86, 100, 102, 105, 111, 127, 130, 153, 154, 166, 221
Beechcraft Hawker Corp. 125
Beechcraft, Inc. (new) 203
Bell Aerospace Corp. 97
Bell/Agusta BA 609 193
Bell Aircraft Corp./Bell Helicopter Textron 146, 192
Bell Helicopter Canada 146
Bell helicopters: Model 42 70; Model 47/H-13 69, 97; Model 47J/47-2A Ranger 97, 120, 122; Model 206A JetRanger 97, 116, 122, 146, 192, 215, 217; Model 206B JetRanger III/206L LongRanger/TH-67 Creek/206LT 122, 146, 168; Model 212 (Twin Two-Twelve) 122, 146; Model 222 146; Model 230 146, 168; Model 407 168, 216; Model 412 122; Model 412/412EP 122, 146, 192; Model 422 122; Model 427 192; Model 429 192, 193, 216; Model 430 168, 192; Model 505 JetRangerX 217; Model 525 Relentless 216; XV-15 193
Bellanca, August T. 85, 117
Bellanca, Giuseppe M. 21, 24, 85
Bellanca 14-19 Cruisair/Cruisemaster/Model 260C (*see* Downer, Miller) 41, 61, 85, 117
Bellanca Aircraft Corp./Bellanca, Inc. 21, 34, 50, 166
Bellanca Aircraft Corp. of America 117
Bellanca Aircraft Engineering, Inc. 85
Bellanca Aircruiser 41
Bellanca Aries T-250 133
Bellanca CH-300 Pacemaker 21, 41
Bellanca Sales Corp. 117
Bellanca Skyrocket 21, 41
Bellanca Skyrocket II 117
Bellanca Viking 260/300/Super Viking 117, 133, 158
Bennett Aircraft Corp. (*see* Globe) 44
Bergey, Karl 88
Berkshire Hathaway 172
Berliner, Harry A. 40
Berliner-Joyce Co. 40
Bleck, Max M. 113, 130, 155
Block Aircraft Registration Request (BARR) 173
Blue, Linden 131
BMW Rolls-Royce 163
Boeing B-17 99
Boeing B-29 49
Boeing B-47 63
Boeing Business Jets (BBJ) 183, 221; BBJ1/BBJ2/BBJ3 211; Boeing 747 211; Boeing 747-8 211, 221; Boeing 757 211; Boeing 767 211; Boeing 777 211; Boeing 787 211
Boeing Co. 10, 98, 174

Boeing 737 164
Boeing-Stearman Div. 42
Bogardus, George 79
Boisture, Bill 179, 202
Bollinger, Lynn L. 72, 118
Bombardier 5000/6000 207
Bombardier, Inc. (*see* Learjet) 161, 163, 211, 220
Bowers, Peter 187
Brantly, Newby O. 71, 102
Brantly B-1/ B-2/B-2A/B-2B 71, 97, 122, 145
Brantly Helicopter Corp. 102, 122
Brantly-Hynes Helicopter, Inc. (*see* Hynes) 122, 145
Brantly International 168
Brantly Model 305 122, 145
Brantly Operators, Inc. 122
Bravo Investments B.V. 145
British Aerospace Corp. (BAe) 134, 162, 179
Brown, Willis C. 25
Brukner, Clayton J. 8, 41, 86, 106
Buffett, Warren 172
Buhl, Lawrence D. 14
Buhl-Verville Aircraft Co. 14
Buhl-Verville Airster 14
Bureau of Air Commerce 7, 33, 40, 45, 79
Burke, W.A. 9
Burns, Edward C. 114, 131
Bush flying 8
Butler Aviation International 110

Call, Ivan 44
Call, Reuel T. 44
Call, Spencer 44
Call Aircraft Co./CallAir, Inc. 44, 84, 142
Call Model A 44
CallAir A-2/A-3/A-4 61, 84
CallAir A-5/A-6 84
CallAir A-9 84, 108
Camair 480 73
Cameron Iron Works 73
Caminez Engine Co. (Ranger Engine Div.-Fairchild) 26
Canadair Challenger 125, 160, 161
Canadair Global Express 164
Cavalier Mustang I (*see* Piper) 112
Central States Aero Corp. 24
Central States Monocoupe 24
Cessna, Clyde V. 10, 15, 38, 88
Cessna, Eldon 30, 40
Cessna aircraft: 400 Series (401/402/411/411A/421) 90, 111, 116; 414/414A Chancellor 116, 167; 421 Golden Eagle 116, 167; 680A Latitude 200; AA 15; AW 15; C-34 38; C-37/C-38 Airmaster 38; C-106 Loadmaster 49; Caravan/U-27A 132, 153, 154, 186; CH-1/YH-41 (*see* Seibel) 71, 97; Citation III/VI/VII 132, 161; Citation M2 200, 201; Citation Mustang 177, 182; Citation Sovereign/Sovereign+ 177, 200, 201; Citation V/Ultra/Bravo/UC-35A 161; Citation X/Ten 161, 177,

240 Index

179, 200, 201; CitationJet CJ1+ /CJ2/Encore 161, 200; CitationJet CJ2/CJ3/Bravo/CJ1+/CJ4 177; Columbus 200, 201; Comet 15; Conquest I/II 117, 153; Corvalis/T240/TTx 202 (*also* LC 40 Columbia) 188; CW-6 15; DC-6 15; Denali 201; Fanjet 500/Citation I/ Citation II/ T-47A/Citation SII series 117, 125, 153, 155, 160, 161, 165; Hemisphere 201; L-19/O-1 Bird Dog 63, 72, 89, 97; Longitude 200, 202; Model 150/152 86, 89, 116, 119, 153, 175; Model 162 SkyCatcher 175, 177, 199, 201; Model 170 63; Model 172/Skyhawk/175 Skylark 88, 89, 116, 153, 167, 169, 172, 177, 201, 221; Model 172F/T-41A/B 89, 116; Model 177 Cardinal/RG 117, 177; Model 180 63, 88, 132; Model 180 AgWagon 90; Model 182 Skylane 89, 153, 167, 177, 201, 221; Model 185 Skywagon (U-17A) 89; Model 190/195 63; Model 205A/206 Super Skywagon/Stationair 88, 89, 167, 177, 201, 221; Model 208 Caravan/ Grand Caravan 154, 159, 167, 201; Model 210 Centurion 89; Model 310/L-27A/U-3A 63, 69, 75, 89, 132; Model 320 Skyknight 90, 116; Model 336/337/O-2A/O-2B Skymaster 90, 116, 132; Model 340 116; Model 620 89; Models 120/140 60, 62, 63, 89; Mustang 201, 209; New Generation Piston (NGP) 177; T-37/A-37 63, 89, 100, 116; T50/AT-8/AT-17/UC-78 Bobcat 38, 49; T303 Crusader 132; Titan 117; XLS/XLS+ 200
Cessna Aircraft Corp. 30, 34, 47, 48, 53, 54, 62, 75, 86, 100, 105, 127, 154, 161, 214, 221
Cessna C.V. Aircraft Corp. 30
Cessna-Roos Co. 15
Champion Aircraft Corp. (*see* Aeronca/Bellanca) 54, 59, 60, 85, 117, 134
Champion Citabria 134
Champion Lancer 85
Champion 7/Traveler 85
Champion Traveller 85
Champion Tri-Traveller 85
Changhe (China) 217
Chen, Jerry 199
Chicago Tribune 99
China Aviation General Aircraft Co. (CAIGA) 187, 202, 203, 208 (*see also* AVIC); CAIGA TP150 project 202
Chris-Craft, Inc. 111, 113
Christen Eagle/II 138, 142, 186, 190
Christen Industries 142
Christensen, Frank 138, 142, 190
Christensen, Jack 96, 122
Chrysler Corp. 66, 135, 166
Cierva, Juan de la 27
Cierva C-8 27
Cirrus Design Corp. 140, 175, 180, 208, 221
Cirrus Design SR-20/SR-22 141, 169, 180, 202
Cirrus Design SR20/T-53A 169, 180, 209; SJ50 (VLJ) 180, 209
Cirrus Design ST-50 140

Cirrus Design VK-30 140
Citabria 85
Civil Aeronautics Administration (CAA) 33, 45, 46, 54, 56, 76, 79, 136
Civil Aeronautics Board (CAB) 45
Civil Air Patrol 47, 185
Civil Air Regulations (CARs) 80
Civilian Pilot Training Program (CPTP) 46
Classic Aircraft Corp. 187
Clinton, Pres. Bill 166
Coast Guard, U.S. 8
Cohen, Frank 51
Collier Trophy 27
Colonial Aircraft Corp. 72, 92
Colonial C-1 Skimmer 72, 92
Columbia Aircraft Corp. 21, 60
Commander Aircraft Co. 157, 187
Commerce, Dept. of, U.S. 40, 54, 56
Commonwealth Aircraft Corp. (*see* Rearwin) 51, 60
Commonwealth Skyranger 185 61
Commonwealth Trimmer 60
Condit, Phil 184
Congress Financial Corp. 178
Conrad, Max 69
Consolidated Aeronautics (*see* Lake) 92, 119
Consolidated-Vultee Aircraft Corp. (Convair) 57, 58
Continental Motors 67
Continental Motors Corp. 25, 156, 175
Convair 340 99
Convair Model 106 Skycoach 57
Convair Model 111 Air-Car 57
Convair Model 116 57
Convair Model 118 ConVAirCar 57, 62
Coolidge, Pres. Calvin 7
Corben, O.G. 33, 81
Corben Baby Ace 33, 81
Cord, E.L. 14, 26, 29
Cord Corp. 14, 29
Corporate Aircraft Owners Assn. 77
Corporate Angel Network 160
Couvelaire, Alexandre 133
Cox, Charles 18, 157
Cox-Clemin Aircraft Corp. 18
Craig Air Force Base, AL 31
Cromer, Robert 133
Crossfield, Scott 197
Cuauhtemoc M-1 (*see* Maule) 119
CubCrafters, Inc. 186, 214
Culver, K.K. 44
Culver Aircraft Corp. 44, 46, 52, 60, 72
Culver Cadet 44
Culver Model V 60, 86
Cunningham, James, Son & Co. 25
Cunningham-Hall Aircraft Corp. 25, 60
Cunningham-Hall PT-6 25
Curtiss, Glenn H. 13
Curtiss Aeroplane and Motor Co. 28, 29
Curtiss aircraft and engines: CE-19/AT-9 Jeep

Index

41; Challenger 30; Challenger engine 6, 29; Condor 32; CW-1 Junior 29; CW-19/-19L/-19W Coupe 32; CW-25 Coupe 41; JN-4 Jenny 6; Kingbird 29; Model 19R 19, 32; OX-5 engine 29; Robin 29; Speedwing 30; Tanager 19; Thrush 29
Curtiss-Robertson Mfg. Corp. (Curtiss-Wright Airplane Co.) 29
Curtiss-Wright Corp. 10, 29, 34, 112
Custer, W.R. 95, 117
Custer CCW-5 95, 117, 149
Custer Channel Wing Corp. 95, 117

Daimler Benz 170
Daland, Elliott 5, 28
Damon, Ralph 29
Dart Manufacturing Corp. 43
Dart Model G (see Culver) 43
Dassault (France) 176, 220
Dassault Falcon 125
Dauby Equipment Co. 73
Day, Charles H. 17
Defense Plant Corp. (DPC) 72
de Havilland Canada Beaver 132, 186
de Havilland Canada Co. 161
de Havilland Canada Otter 132, 186
de Havilland DH-125/BAe 125 125, 178 (see also BAe, Beech)
de Havilland Moth 30
Deitz, Conrad 22
Delta Air Lines 6, 219
Denney Aerocraft Co. 142
Denney KitFox 142
Denver, John 197
Depew, Richard H. 35
Detroit Aircraft Corp. 14, 28, 30
Detroit Board of Commerce 14
Diamond T-52A (Austria) 209
Doolittle, James H. "Jimmy" 20
Dornier Luftfahrt 170
Douglas A-20 Havoc 74
Douglas A-26 48, 49
Douglas Aircraft Co. 43, 57, 58, 74
Douglas B-23 99
Douglas Cloudster 57
Douglas DC-3/C-47 57, 99
Douglas Dolphin 8
Douglas PD-808 103
Douglass, Stone 156
Downer, Jay K. 85
Downer Aircraft Industries (see Northern Aircraft) 85
Downer Bellanca 260A (Miller Bellanca 260A) 85
DuPont family 21

Earhart, Amelia 27
Eclipse Aerospace 210
Eclipse Aviation Corp. 220
Eclipse 500/EA700/Canada 210

Eisenhower, Pres. Dwight 48, 83
Electric Autolite Corp/ELTRA 97
Elias Aircraft and Mfg. Co. 16
Elias, G, and Brother, Inc. 16
Emanuel, Victor 42
Embraer (Brazil) 113, 175, 176, 203, 220
Embry-Riddle Aeronautical University 174
Emivest (Dubai) 209
Emivest SK30/SJ20–2/SJ30x/SJ30-I 209
Emory, Waldo D. 25
ENAER (Chile) Pillan (see Piper) 156
Engineering & Research Corp. (ERCO) 40, 47
Engineering Technology and Investment Research Center (ETIRC) 182
Enstrom, R.J. 95, 122, 145, 194
Enstrom F-28 97
Enstrom Helicopters 95, 168, 217
Enstrom Model 480 217
Enstrom TH-28 145
Enstrom TH-180/280FX/ Shark 217
Epic Aircraft 175, 202
Epic E1000 187, 202
ERCO W-1A Ercoupe 40, 57, 60, 75, 85, 159 (see also Alon Inc.)
Ernest, Scott 201, 203
Esculier, Jacques 133
Esenwein, August 68
Europa Aviation 140
Europa Aviation Europa 140
Executive Jet Aviation 103, 172, 179
Exeter Partners 176
Experimental Aircraft Assn. (EAA) 80, 106, 137, 144, 149, 189

Fairchild, Sherman M. 6, 15, 29, 31, 58, 106
Fairchild Aircraft Corp. 15, 31
Fairchild Aircraft Corp. (see Swearingen) 134, 157, 170
Fairchild aircraft: A-10 Thunderbolt II 113; AT-21 Gunner 50; F-22 31; F-24 43, 59, 73; F-45 43; F-47 58; Fairchild Hiller FH-1100 98; FC-1 15; KR-21 15; M185 project 100; (Pilatus) Turbo-Porter/Heli-Porter 95; PT-19/PT-23 51; T-31 65
Fairchild Airplane Manufacturing Corp. 15
Fairchild Aviation Corp. 14, 29
Fairchild Dornier 170, 187
Fairchild Dornier Model 226 170
Fairchild Dornier Model 326 170
Fairchild Engine & Airplane Corp. 26, 43, 49, 58
Fairchild Hiller Corp./Fairchild Industries 97, 122
Fairchild Personal Planes Div. 58
Fairchild Ranger Aircraft Engine Div. 26
Farnborough F1 Kestrel 209
Federal Aviation Administration (FAA) 103, 104, 112, 136, 147, 149, 169, 174, 197
Federal Bureau of Investigation 50
Federal Express Corp. (FEDEX) 154, 159, 184

242 Index

Fieseler Storch 48
Finletter Commission 56
Fish and Wildlife Service, U.S. 186
Fisher Advanced Composites Components 175
Fisher Body Corp. 13
Fleetwings (*see* Kaiser) 57
Fletcher, Wendell 72, 94
Fletcher Aviation Corp./Flair Aviation Co. 93
Fletcher FBT-2 72
Fletcher FD-24 Utility 94
Fletcher FD-25 Defender 72, 93
Fletcher FL-23 72
Flyers Service, Inc. 85
Ford, Pres. Gerald R. 115
Ford, Henry 36
Ford, James B. 37
Ford AT-4 Trimotor 14
Ford Motor Co. 20
Foreign Military Sales Program (FMS) 132
Fornaire F-1 Aircoupe (*see* Ercoupe) 85
Forney Manufacturing Co. 85
Forstmann, Theodore 163
Forstmann Little Co. 135, 155, 163
Franklin Automobile Corp. 26
Frati, Stelio 142
Frati Falco F.8L 142
Friedlander, Carl 37
Friedlander, Walter J. 37
Fulton Airphibian 62
Funk, Howard 45
Funk, Joe 45
Funk Aircraft Co. 45
Funk Model B 45, 61

Galaxy Aerospace 183
Garmin GPS 171
Garrett AiResearch TFE 731-3 engine 125
Garrett AiResearch TPE 331 engine 83, 117
Gates, Bill 181
Gates, Charles C. 102
Gates, Ivan 17
Gates Aviation Corp. 103
Gates-Day Aircraft Co. 16
Gates-Day D-23/24/25 17
Gates-Day NT-1 17
Gates Flying Circus 16
Gates Learjet Corp. (*see* Lear) 103, 125, 127, 162
Gates Rubber Co. 102
Gaty, John P. 64, 92
Geisse, John H. 54
General Aircraft Corp. 118
General Atomics 131
General Aviation Co. 13
General Aviation Manufacturers Assn. (GAMA) 105, 115, 147, 149, 170, 172, 218
General Aviation Revitalization Act (GARA) 166, 170

General Dynamics Corp. 90, 116, 132, 153, 154, 165, 166
General Electric Catalyst engine 201
General Electric CJ-610 engine 100, 101, 103, 125
General Electric Passport engine 207
Getty, J. Paul 51, 60
G.I. Bill 54
Gilberti, Jack 82
Gilmore Oil Co. 21
Globe Aircraft Corp. 44, 73
Globe GC-1 Swift 44, 59, 73, 142, 156, 186
GMF Investments 134
Goodyear Corp. 57
Goodyear GA-2 57
Greenwood, Marvin 62
Groen, Jay 186
Groen Brothers 185
Groen Brothers Sparrowhawk 185
Gross, Robert E. 13, 42
Grow, Harold H. 41
Grumman Aerospace Corp. (*see* American Jet Industries) 134, 135
Grumman aircraft: G-21 Goose 42; G-44 Widgeon 42, 57; G-63 Kitten 57; G-65 Tadpole 57; G-72 Kitten II 57; G-73 Mallard 57; G-159 Gulfstream I 100; G-164 Ag-Cat (*see* Schweizer) 92, 145, 159; Grumman American AA-5B/Tiger 119, 157; Grumman American GA-7 Cougar 119, 157; Grumman American Tr2 119; Grumman American Traveler AA- 5A/Cheetah 119; Grumman American Yankee/Trainer 119; Gulfstream II 101, 103, 119, 125, 183; Gulfstream III 125 (*see also* Gulfstream Corp.)
Grumman American Aviation Corp. 120, 157
Grumman Corp. 42, 92, 111, 114, 163, 214
GS Capital Partners 179
Guggenheim, Daniel 19
Guggenheim, Daniel, Fund 19
Gulf Oil Corp. 20
Gulfstream Aerospace 157, 163, 165, 179, 183, 205, 207
Gulfstream Aerospace Gulfstream IV 135, 160
Gulfstream Aerospace Gulfstream V 163, 165
Gulfstream aircraft: G200/G250/G280 183; G650 183, 205; G500/G600 205; GIV/G450/GV/G550 135, 205
Gulfstream Galaxy 200 179

HA420 HondaJet 210
Hall, Randolph 25
Hall, T.P. 57
Hamilton, Tom 139
Hammond, Dean B. 30, 40
Hammond Aircraft Corp. 31
Hammond Model Y/Y-1 (*see* Stearman-Hammond) 33, 40
Harlow, Max 45, 60
Harlow Engineering Group 45, 52

Index 243

Harlow PJC-2/UC-80 45
Harned, Malcolm S. 117
Harvard Business School 72
Hawker Beechcraft aircraft: Hawker Beechjet 174; Hawker 400/400A/400XP 178, 179; Premier (BH 200) 178, 180, 203, 209; T-6B/AT-6 203
Hawker Beechcraft Corp. 178, 202, 203
Hawker Beechcraft Defense Co. 203, 204
Hawker Siddeley, Ltd.: Horizon 1000/Hawker 4000 179, 202, 203; HS 125/750/850/900/900 XP/1000 178
Hawks, Frank 20
Hayden, Stone and Co. 10
Heath, Edward A. 18
Heath Aircraft Co. 18
Heath Parasol 18, 24
Hedrick, Frank 65, 92, 102. 114, 130, 155
Heintz, Chris 192
Heintz, Christopher 192
Helicopter Council, AIA 54
Helicopter development 68–71
Helio Aircraft Co./Corp. 72, 92, 118
Helio Courier/Super Courier, U-10A 72, 92
Helio Courier II 92
Helio Helioplane 72
Helio Stallion 92
Helio U-5A 92
Helms, J. Lynn 112, 129
HF120 engine 210
Higdon, Lee O. 86
Hiller, Jeffrey 168
Hiller, Stanley, Jr. 70, 97, 122, 194
Hiller Aircraft Co. 70
Hiller Aircraft Corp. 97
Hiller Aviation Corp. 122, 145
Hiller FH-1100 97, 122, 145
Hiller Helicopters Co. 71
Hiller HJ-1 Hornet 71
Hiller J5 70
Hiller Model 360/UH-12/Model 12 70, 71, 112, 168; military H-23 97
Hiller UH-4 70
Hiller XH-44 70
Hillman, Douglas 145
Hirsh, Jim 214
Holmes, D. Brainerd 131
Homeland Security, Dept of, U.S. 173
Honda Aero Engines 210
Honda Aircraft Co. 210
Honeywell Corp. 163, 172, 218
Hoover, Secretary of Commerce Herbert 7
Horn, Stuart 142
Howard, Ben O. 7, 44
Howard, H.L. 73
Howard, Mulligan 44
Howard Aircraft Corp. 44, 46
Howard DGA series/UC-70/DG-13 44, 51
Hseuh, Thomas 181
Huff Daland Corp. 6, 28

Huff Daland Dusters 6
Huff Daland (Keystone) Air Yacht 8
Hughes, Howard 45, 97
Hughes 520N (Notar) (*see* McDonnell Douglas) 147
Hughes Model 269 (Model 200) 97
Hughes Model 300/330 (*see* Schweizer) 146
Hughes Model 500/OH-6A 97, 122, 146
Hughes Tool Co. 97
Hunsaker, Jerome 18
Hynes, Michael K. 122
Hynes Helicopters, Inc./Hynes Aviation Industries 145

IAI Astrajet (*see* Aero Jet Commander) 108, 160
IAI Westwind 125
Icon A5 215
Icon Aircraft 215
Impremis 176
Innes, Walter P. 10
Integrated Resources/Integrated Acquisition, Inc. 136, 160
Intermountain Manufacturing Co. (IMCO) 84
International Aircraft Manufacturing, Inc. (Inter–Air) 85
Interstate Aircraft Corp. 45
Interstate S-1A/B Cadet/Super Cadet/L-6/L-8 45, 84
Iomax Corp. 185, 214
Israeli Aircraft Industries (IAI) 108, 125
Israviation Co. 140
Italian Air Force 103

Jacob, Edwin T. 81
Jacobs, Al 26
Jacobs Aircraft Engine Corp. 26
Jaffe Group 162
Jamouneau, Walter 23, 66, 67, 111, 130
Jensen, Volmer 140
Jilin Hansing Group (China) 140
Joint Primary Aircraft Training System (JPATS) competition 166
Jones, A.R., Oil Company 25
Jones, Bert 25
Junkin, Ellwood James "Sam" 8

Kaiser Industries 57, 70
Kaman, Charles 168, 217
Kaman Corp. 168
Kaman K-MAX 168, 194
Kamen, Dean 145
Kellett, Rodney G. 28
Kellett, W. Wallace 28
Kellett Autogiro Co. 28
Ken-Royce Engines (*see* Rearwin) 24
Kennedy, John F., Jr. 197
Kenner Motors, Inc.. 26
Kettler, Dick 187

Index

Keys, Clement 15
Keystone Aircraft Co. (*see* Huff Daland) 8
Kimura, James 168
Kitfox Aircraft LLC 191
Klapmeier, Alan 141, 180, 209, 210
Klapmeier, Dale 180, 209
Klemin, Alexander 18
Klotz, Leopold 36, 50, 62
Koppen, Otto 72
Koppen-Bollinger Aircraft Corp. 72 (*see also* Helio)
Korean War 58, 63, 70
Kreider, Ammon H. 15
Kreider-Reisner Aircraft Co. (*see* Fairchild) 15, 31, 95
Kreider-Reisner Challenger C-6 (Fairchild KR-21) 15

LaHood, Secretary Ray 173
Laird, Charles 9
Laird, E.M. "Matty" 9, 10, 12, 24, 127
Laird Aircraft Corp. (Whipporwill) 9
Laird, E.M. Co. 8, 10
Laird New Swallow 9
Laird Swallow 11
Lake Aircraft Corp/Lake Amphibians, Inc. (*see* Colonial) 92, 119, 133
Lake LA-4 (*see* Colonial) 133
Lake Renegade 133
Lake SeaFury 133
Lake Turbo 270 Renegade 133
Lambert Aircraft Corp. 24, 43
Lambert Monosport 43
Lancair ES 140, 177
Lancair Evolution 188, 214
Lancair International 140
Lancair LC 40 Columbia (*see* Cessna) 140, 178
Lancair Mako 214
Landgraf, Fred 24
LanShe Aerospace 186
Larson, Agnew E. 27
Lear, William P. 99, 101, 125, 161, 221
Lear aircraft: Lear Fan 2100 136; Learjet (SAAC-23) Model 23/24 101, 125; Model 25 102; Model 31 136, 160; Model 40/45 161, 164, 170, 183; Model 85 176, 211; Models 28/29/Longhorn 125, 136; Models 35/36/C-21A 136, 155, 160, 161; Models 55/60/60XR 125, 136, 160, 161, 183; Models 70, 75 211
Lear Fan, Inc. 136
Lear Fan 2100 149
Lear, Inc. 99
Lear Jet Industries, Inc./Learjet Corp. (*see* Gates) 101, 153, 155, 165, 174
Lear Learstar 99
Lear Siegler Corp. 130, 155
Learjet Corp. (new) 136
Learstar 600 (see Canadair) 161
LeBlond Engine Co. 25
Lend-Lease Act 48

LePage, W. Lawrence 28
Let Kunovice (Poland) 184
Levine, Charles 21
Lewis, David S. 133
Liberty aircraft 191
Liberty engine 8
Light Observation Helicopter (LOH) competition 97, 98
Light Sport Aircraft (LSA) category 175, 196, 199, 201, 221
Lincoln-Page Aircraft Co. 24
Lindbergh, Charles A. 19
Lindblad, Herbert P. 92
Lindsay, David B. 112
Lockheed aircraft: Big Dipper 57; Cheyenne helicopter 120; JetStar/C-140/JetStar II 100, 125; LASA-60 95; Little Dipper 57; Model 18 Lodestar 99; Saturn 57, 103
Lockheed Aircraft Corp. 28, 40, 42, 57, 58
Lockheed Azcarate Co. 95
Lockheed-Kaiser Co. (Argentina) 95
Lockheed Martin Corp. 203
Loening Air Yacht 8
Loening Co. 8
LoPresti, Leroy P. 110, 119, 133, 156, 192, 221
LoPresti Aircraft Engineering Co. 156
LoPresti Piper Aircraft Co. (*see* Piper) 156
LoPresti Piper SwiftFury (*see* Globe) 156
Loughead (later Lockheed) brothers 5
Loughead S-1 5
LTV Corp. 133
Ludington brothers 28
Lunkin family 22
Luscombe, Don A. 24, 36, 37, 86
Luscombe Airplane Corp 34, 36, 49, 61
Luscombe Holding Co. 62, 73, 75 (*see also* Temco)
Luscombe Model 8 Silvaire 59, 61, 73
Luscombe Model 90 36
Luscombe Phantom 36
Luscombe Sedan 61
L-W-F Co. 8
Lycoming Manufacturing Corp. (div. AVCO/div. Textron). 26, 166, 168

Macchi SpA (Italy) 95
MacCracken, William P. 7
Macready, Lt. J.A. 6
Mangum, John 84
Manning, Lucious 14
Manufacturers Aircraft Assn. (MAA) 6
Manufacturers Trust Co. 66
Marine Corps, U.S. 89
Martin, Glenn L., Co. 58
Martin B-26 99
Maryland Pressed Steel Co. 21
Massachusetts Institute of Technology (MIT) 7, 18, 72
Massey, Otis T. 86
Maule, Belford D. 94, 119, 159

Index

Maule, June 185
Maule Aircraft Corp./Maule Air, Inc. 94, 134, 185
Maule Bee Dee 94
Maule Comet 159
Maule M-4 Rocket/Jetesen II 94, 119, 185
Maule M-5 Lunar Rocket 119, 159
Maule M-7, MX-7 134, 159, 185
Mauro, Ben J. 59, 92
McBean, John 214
McCauley Propellers 89, 117
McCormick, Col. Robert R. 99
McCulloch, Robert 73
McDonnell Douglas Corp. 98
McDonnell Douglas Explorer (NOTAR) 169
McDonnell Douglas F-4 116
McDonnell Douglas Helicopter Systems 169
McDonnell Douglas Helicopters (see Hughes, MD Helicopters) 146, 169, 193
McDonnell Douglas MD500 169
McDonnell Douglas MD 520 (NOTAR) 169
McDonnell Douglas MD 530 169
McDonnell Douglas MD 600 169
McDonnell Model 119/Model 220 100
Mehlhaff, Jerry 158
Meijing Group (China) 199
Menasco Co. 43
Mercury Aircraft Co. 17, 62
Mergen, Joseph J. 112
Metal Aircraft Corp. 22
Metalcraft Technologies (MTI) (see MSC Aerospace, Syberjet Aircraft) 209
Mexican Air Force 119
Meyer, Corwin "Corky" 119
Meyer, Russell W. 117, 119, 133, 153, 154, 167
Meyers, A.H. 45
Meyers, Charles W. 8
Meyers Aircraft Co. 45, 93
Meyers MAC 125/145/145T 61, 93
Meyers OTW-160 45
Meyers 200 (see Aero Commander) 93, 107
MICCO Meyers 200 186
Mid–Continent Aircraft Corp. (see Spartan Aircraft) 25
Mid–Continent C-3 25
Mid–States Manufacturing Corp. 72
Millar, M. Stuart 149, 155
Miller Flying Service (see Bellanca) 85
Mitchell, Gen. Billy 7
Mitsubishi Corp. 83, 110
Mitsubishi MU-2 83, 131
Mitsubishi MU 300 Diamond/Diamond II (see Beech) 125, 131, 179
Moellendick, Jacob 9, 10
Monnet, Jeremy 214
Mono Aircraft Inc. 24
Monocoupe Aircraft Corp./Monocoupe Engine and Aircraft Corp. 24, 46, 60
Monocoupe Meteor (Saturn Meteor II) 93
Monocoupe Model 90 24, 44

Monocoupe Monocoach 44
Monocoupe 110 186
Mooney, Al 12, 44, 72, 82, 133
Mooney, Art 83
Mooney Aerospace 178
Mooney aircraft: Acclaim 199; M-4 14; M10T/M10J 199; M-18 Mite 72, 80, 83; M-20/Master/M-22 Mustang/ 72, 82, 83, 87; M-21 Ranger 83; Models 201/231 110; MSE, M-20R Ovation 154, 199
Mooney Aircraft Corp. 72, 75, 82, 105, 110, 154, 166, 178
Mooney Aviation Company 199
Mooney Holding Co. 133
Mooney International Corporation 199
Morane-Saulnier MS-760 Paris 100, 174
Morgan, John E.P. 48
Morrow Board (President's Aircraft Board) 7
Moth Aircraft Corp. 30

National Advisory Committee for Aeronautics (NACA)/National Aeronautics and Space Admin. (NASA) 6, 56, 77, 101, 105, 174, 119, 170
National Aerospace System (NAS) 174
National Business Aircraft Assn. (NBAA) 77, 106, 170, 172, 197, 218
Navion Aircraft Co./Navion Aircraft Corp./Navion Rangemaster Aircraft Co. 86
Navion Rangemaster 86, 118
Navy, U.S. 87, 92, 106, 166
Neico Aviation 140
Neico Lancair 140
Neico LC40 140
Neico 360/ES/Super ES 140
Nesmith, Robert 81
Nesmith Cougar 81
NetJets, Inc. 219
The New Piper Aircraft, Inc. (see Piper) 157
New Standard Aircraft Co. 17
New York Aero Club 6
New York Police Dept. 70
Newco Pac, Inc. 157
NGATS (NextGen) 174
North American Aviation, Inc. (NAA) 40, 73, 89
North American Navion/L-17 54, 58 (see also Ryan)
North American P-51 Mustang 58, 81, 112
North American Rockwell Corp. (NAR)/Rockwell International 107, 125
North American Sabreliner/T-39 (see Rockwell) 100, 108, 125, 135, 160, 165
Northern Aircraft, Inc. 85
Northern Aircraft, Inc. (see Bellanca) 61
Northrop, John 5
Northrop Division, Douglas 43, 45

Odom, William P. 63
Ohio, State Experimental Station of 6

246　Index

ONE Aviation 210
Onex (Canada) 179
Osborn, Earl D. 10

Pacific Airmotive Corp. (PacAero) 122
Pan American Airways (Pan Am) 124
Parks Aircraft (div. Detroit Aircraft) 30
Patriarch Partners 193, 217
Paulson, Allen 120, 135, 163
Peiper, Paul 182
Pelton, Jack 200
Peregrine Flight International 144
Petroleum Helicopters, Inc. (PHI) 122, 146
Pew Oil. Co. 74
Piaggio P. 180 162
Piaggio SpA (Italy) 103
Pietenpohl, Bernard H. 32, 144
Pietenpohl Air Camper 32
Pilatus Co. (Switzerland) 166
Pilatus PC-9 (see Beech) 166
Pilatus PC-12 201
Pilatus Porter (see Fairchild) 95
Piper, Howard (Pug) 88, 111, 114
Piper, Thomas (Tony) 69, 88, 111
Piper, William T., Sr. 22, 23, 34, 35, 48, 66, 67, 68, 112
Piper, W.T., Jr. 67, 88, 111, 134, 147
Piper aircraft: Aerostar series (see Aerostar [Ted] Smith) 131; J-2/J-3 Cub/L-4 Grasshopper 35, 49, 59, 89 (see also Taylor); J-4 Coupe 36; J-5B Cruiser 36, 66; PA-6 SkySedan 66; PA-8 Skycycle 66; PA-10 66; PA-11 Cub Special 66, 68; PA-12 Super Cruiser 66; PA-14 Family Cruiser 66; PA-15/PA-17 Vagabond 67, 72; PA-16 Clipper/PA-20 Pacer 63, 68; PA-18 Super Cub/L-18/L-21 54, 68, 81, 87, 88, 111, 113, 130, 155; PA-22 Colt 86; PA-22 Tri-Pacer 68, 87; PA-23 Apache 69, 86; PA-23-250/235 Aztec/Aztec F 86, 113, 130; PA-24 Comanche 86, 88; PA-25/36 Pawnee/Pawnee II/ 88, 112; PA-28 Cherokee/Arrow/Warrior/Archer/Dakota 86, 88, 111, 112, 113, 157, 199; PA-28-161 Cadet 155, 156; PA-30/PA-39 Twin Comanche 88, 111; PA-31 Navajo 88, 111, 157; PA-31-350 Chieftain 112; PA-31T Cheyenne I/II 112; PA-32 Cherokee Six/Lance 2/Turbo Lance 2 88, 113; PA-32 Saratoga 113, 157; PA-34 Seneca/Seneca IV/V 112, 156, 157, 177; PA-35 Pocono 111; PA-38 Tomahawk 113, 130; PA-42 Cheyenne III/IIIA 113, 156, 157; PA-44 Seminole 130, 199; PA-46 Malibu/Malibu Mirage/M350 130, 155, 156, 177; PA-46 Matrix 177; PA-46 Meridian/M600/M500 177; PA-47 PiperJet (Altaire) 198, 199; PA-48 Enforcer (see Cavalier Mustang) 112; Pawnee Brave 130; Piper Sport 199; Skycoupe 66; T1020/T1040 130
Piper Aircraft Corp. 34, 36, 54, 62, 66, 75, 86, 105, 149, 153, 154, 155, 157, 176, 214, 221 (see also The New Piper Aircraft Corp.)

Piper Engineering Center 88
Pitcairn, Harold 26, 28, 62, 98
Pitcairn aircraft: Mailwing 27; PA-7S 27; PA-18 27; PA-19 27; PA-32 27; PA-33 38; PA-34 38; PCA-1 27
Pitcairn Aircraft Co. 27, 28
Pitcairn Autogiro Co. 28
Pitcairn Aviation 26
Pitcairn-Cierva Autogiro Co. (Autogiro Corp. of America) 27
Pitcairn-Larsen Autogiro Co. 38
Pitts, Curtis 81, 142, 192
Pitts S-1 Special 81, 186
Porterfield, E.E. "Ed" 23, 32
Porterfield Aircraft Corp. 32
Porterfield Model 35–70 32
Pratt & Whitney Canada PT6A engine 115, 215
Pratt & Whitney Corp. 155
Pratt & Whitney JT12 engine 100
Pratt & Whitney R-985 engine 26
Pratt & Whitney Wasp 26
Precision Aerospace Corp. 157
Priestly-Hunt Aircraft Corp. 86
Private Aircraft Council, AIA 54
Product Liability Crisis 127, 147–149
Pulsar Aircraft Corp. 142, 189
Purex Corp. 122
PZL (Poland) 113

Quest Aircraft 186, 214
Quest Kodiak 186, 214

Raburn, Vern 181, 182
Rachal, Hal F. 83
Ranger engine (see Fairchild) 28
Rans, Inc. 144, 190
Rans S-7 Courier 144
Raytheon Aircraft Co. (see Beech) 130, 163, 178
Raytheon Corp. 155, 162, 163
Reagan Administration 165
Rearwin, R.A. 24, 51, 106
Rearwin Aircraft and Engines, Inc. 25, 44, 47
Rearwin Airplanes, Inc. 24, 25
Rearwin (Commonwealth) Skyranger 44
Rearwin Junior 25
Rearwin Model 7000 44
Rearwin Model 8135 Cloudster 44
Rearwin Models 6000/6000M Speedster 25, 44
Rearwin Sportster 25
Reconstruction Finance Corp. (RFC) 48, 59, 62, 67
Reims Aviation (Cessna) 154
Reisner, Lewis 15, 41
Republic Aviation Corp. 58
Republic RC-3 Seabee 58
Republic Steel Corp. 110, 133
Riley, Jack 73

Index 247

Riley (Temco) Twin-Navion 73
Rivard, Armand 119, 133
Robertson, Frank H. 28
Robertson, Maj. William B. 28, 29, 50
Robertson Aircraft Corp. 28
Robinson, Franklin D. 122, 215, 221
Robinson, Kurt 216
Robinson Helicopter Co. 122, 145, 168, 194
Robinson R22 122, 145
Robinson R44 145
Robinson R66 215
Roche, Jean A. 22, 37
Rockwell Aero Commander Div. (*see* Aero Commander) 93, 103, 107
Rockwell International (*see* NAR) 135, 166
Rockwell-Standard Corp (*see* North American) 83, 85, 93, 107, 166
Rogerson Aircraft Corp/Rogerson-Hiller Corp. 145, 168
Rohr Aircraft Corp. 57
Rolls-Royce Dart engine 100
Rolls-Royce Tay engine 103, 135
Romeo Charlie Co. 155
Ronald Reagan National Airport 173
Roos, Victor H. 9, 15, 21, 24, 88
Roos, Victor H. Aircraft Co. 24
Roos-Bellanca Co. (Omaha Aircraft) 21
Roosevelt, Pres. Franklin D. 8
Rotax engine 139, 144
Royal Canadian Air Force 49
Royal Navy 48
Russ, Nash 59
Rutan, Burt 132, 152, 165, 181, 221
Rutan, Dick 152, 181
Rutan Aircraft Co. 142
Rutan LongEZ 142
Rutan Vari-Eze 142
Rutan Voyager 152
Ryan, T. Claude 45
Ryan Aeronautical Corp. 28, 45, 58
Ryan S-C 46
Ryan SC-145 46
Ryan School of Aeronautics 45
Ryan Speedster 31
Ryan "Spirit of St. Louis" 45
Ryan S-T 45

Sabreliner Corp. 135, 160
Safe Airplane Competition 19, 25
Safire Aircraft SA-26 182
Sampson, Alden, II 8
Sanwa Bank 134
Sarena, Vivek 199
Sargent, E.J. 94
Sargent-Fletcher Co. 94
Saturn Aircraft Co. 93
Scaled Composites, Inc. 132, 141, 165
Schlitter, Randy 144, 190
Schweizer Aircraft Corp. (*see* Sikorsky) 92, 117, 145, 159, 168, 194, 217

Securities and Exchange Commission (SEC) 95
Seibel, Charles M. 71
Seibel Helicopters 71
Seibel S-3 71
Sequoia Aircraft Corp. 142, 191
Sequoia Falco 191
Sequoia 300/302 142
Setuchi Holdings (Japan) 214
Setzer, Ted 139
Shell Oil Co. 20
Shenyang Aircraft 177
Short, Mac 10, 13, 42, 43
Short Brothers PLC 161, 170
Short-Takeoff-and-Landing (STOL) 19, 72, 92, 94, 119
Shriver, William C. 66, 67, 68
Shuster, James E. 179
Siegel, Herbert J. 11
Sierra Nevada Corp. 203
Sikorsky, Igor 15
Sikorsky Corp. (div. Lockheed) 192, 210; *see also* PZL Mielec
Sikorsky S-51 70
Sikorsky S-55 70
Sikorsky S-76, S-76C++/S-76D 122, 146, 168, 170, 193, 217
Sikorsky S-92/VH-92 193, 217
Sikorsky S-300/S-400 217
Silvaire Aircraft Co. (*see* Luscombe, Temco) 86
Sino Aerospace (Taiwan) 162
Sino-Swearingen Aircraft Corp. 180
Skelly, W.G. "Bill" 25, 37
Skystar Aircraft Corp. 142, 191
Skystar KitFox 142
Small Aircraft Transportation System (SATS) 119, 174
Small Airplane Revitalization Act, 2013 221
Smith, Ted, Aircraft Co./Aircraft Corp./Aerostar Corp. 94, 113
Smith, Ted, and Assoc. 110
Smith, Theodore R. "Ted" 73, 94, 110
SNECMA Silvercrest engine 201, 207
Snow, Leland 93, 108, 214
Snow Aeronautical Corp. 93
Snow S-2B 93
Socata (div. Aerospatiale) 154, 157
Socata Tampico 157
Socata TB 187
Socata Tobago 157
Socata Trinidad 157
Sonex Corp. 192
Spartan Aircraft Corp. 47, 51, 60
Spartan C2/C3.C3–225.C2–60/C2/65 25
Spartan C4/C5 25
Spartan NS-1/NP-1 38
Spartan School of Aeronautics 25
Spartan 7X 38
Spartan 7X Executive 38, 43, 60

248　Index

Sperry, Lawrence　5
Sperry M-1A Messenger　5
Spirit Aerosystems　171
Standard J-1　17
Stearman, Lloyd J.　9, 12, 28, 30, 40, 106
Stearman Aircraft, Inc.　12
Stearman Aircraft Corp.　13
Stearman (Boeing) trainer　84
Stearman C-1/C-2/C-3　13
Stearman Division (Boeing)　10, 28
Stearman-Hammond Aircraft Corp.　40
Stearman-Hammond Model Y-125　40, 61
Stimson, Henry (Secretary)　48
Stinson, Eddie　14, 29
Stinson Aircraft Corp. (div. AVCO)　29, 41, 47
Stinson Airplane Co./Stinson Syndicate　14
Stinson Div. (Consolidated Vultee)　14, 48, 67, 75
Stinson L-1 Vigilant　48
Stinson L-5 Sentinel　48
Stinson Model 10/10A Voyager/L-9　41, 48, 59, 67
Stinson Reliant/AT-19　41, 48
Stinson 6000 (Corman 3000)　14
Stinson S.M. 1 Detroiter　14, 20
Stinson S.M. 2 Junior　14
Stits, Ray　80, 142
Stits Aircraft　80
Stits Flut-R-Bug　80
Stits Playboy　80
Stits SkyBaby　80
Stoddard-Hamilton Aircraft, Inc.　139
Stoddard-Hamilton GlasAir　139, 169
Stoddard-Hamilton GlaStar　140
Stoddard-Hamilton Sportsman 2+2　140
Stoddard-Hamilton II/III/Super II　140
Sukhoi design bureau (Russia)　163
Suma, Chuck　157
Superior Aircraft Co.　86
Superior Aviation Beijing (China)　203
Superior Satellite (*see* Culver)　86
Swallow Airplane Mfg. Co. (*see* Laird)　9, 30, 45
Swearinen Metro III/C-26　134
Swearingen, Edward J.　94, 161
Swearingen Aircraft Co.　94, 112, 118, 134, 161, 180
Swearingen Merlin III/Merlin IIIB　118
Swearingen SA-26/SA-26TT Merlin/Merlin I/Merlin II　94, 118
Swearingen SA-30 Gulfjet/SJ30/SJ30-2　161, 162, 180
Swearingen SA-32T　161
Swearingen SA-226 Merlin IV/Metro (*see* Fairchild)　118, 157, 165
Swiss American Aviation Corp.　101

Taft, Sen. Robert A.　27
Taiwan Aerospace　181, 209
Tanker Transport Training System (TTTS) competition　155, 160, 161, 166
Taylor, C. Gilbert　22, 34, 49, 59, 92, 158
Taylor, Gordon　22
Taylor, John W.R.　149
Taylor, M.B. "Molt" (*see* Aerocar)　62, 95, 118
Taylor Aircraft Corp.　22, 35 (*see also* Piper)
Taylor Bros. Aircraft Co.　22
Taylor-Young Airplane Co.　35
Taylorcraft Aeroplanes Ltd.　35
Taylorcraft aircraft: Chummy 22; E-2 Cub (*see* Piper) 22; L-2 Grasshopper 49; Model 15 Tourist 59; Model 19/F-19 Sportsman/F-21 59, 118; Model 50 50; Model A 35; Zephyr 92
Taylorcraft Aviation Corp.　34, 35, 48, 54, 59, 118, 134
Taylorcraft, Inc.　59, 158
TBM 700 (Switzerland)　154, 209
(Ted) Smith Aerostar 600/601B/602P/700P series　94
Teledyne Continental engines (*see* Continental)　156
Temco Aircraft Corp.　73, 86
Temco T-35 Buckaroo　73
Texaco Corp.　20
Texas Engineering & Manufacturing Co. (TEMCO)　73
Textron AirLand Co.　204
Textron Aviation　203
Textron, Inc.　97, 163, 165, 178, 221
Textron Scorpion　205
Thomas Brothers Co./Thomas-Morse Corp.　13, 25, 27
Thomas W.T.　13, 25
Thorp, John　88, 94
Thrush Aircraft　184
Thrush Model 400　184
Thrush Model 510　184
Thrush Model 710　184
Thurston, David B.　72, 92, 144
Thurston TA-16 Trojan　144
Tilton, Lynn　193
Trans-Florida Aviation　112
Transportation, Dept. of, U.S.　173
Transportation Security Administration (TSA)　173
Travel Air Co.　10, 30
Travel Air 5000/6000 series　10
Travel Air Model 16 Sport　30
Travel Air Mystery S　19, 29
Travel Air 2000/3000/4000 series　10
Trimmer, Gilbert　60
Trimmer C-170　60
Tucker Corp.　58
Turner, Roscoe　20, 32

United Aircraft and Transport Corp. (UATC)/United Aircraft Corp. (UAC)/United Technologies (UT)　13, 28, 112
United Helicopters, Inc. (*see* Hiller)　70
Unmanned Aerial Vehicles (UAVs)　214
Utility Airplane Council　75, 105

Index

Valmet (Finland) 154
Van Grunsven, Richard 144, 190, 214, 221
Van's aircraft: RV-1 to RV-14 190; RV-3 144
Vega Airplane Co. (*see* Lockheed) 43
Verville, A.V. 14, 106
Verville Air Coach 14
Verville Aircraft Co. 14
Verville PT-10 14
Very Light Jet (VLJ) category 174, 181
Vidal, Eugene L. 33
Viking Aviation (*see* Bellanca) 133
Visionaire Corp. 165
Visionaire Vantage 165, 181
Volair 1050 (*see* Aero Commander) 93, 107
Volaircraft, Inc. 93
Volkswagen engine 81
Volmer Aircraft 140
Volmer VJ-22 140
Vought A-7 Corsair II 113
Vought Aircraft 135
Vultee Corp. (div. AVCO) 29, 41
Vultee-Stinson (div. AVCO) 42

WACO aircraft: Aristocraft 60; C Series 41; CG-3 Glider 50; CG-4A Glider 49, 50; CSO 41; E Series 41; Model F 41; N Series 41; S Series 41; YFM-5 187
WACO Aircraft Corp. 8, 9, 34, 41, 47, 60, 75, 86 (*see also* Advance, Weaver)
Waco Classic Aircraft Corp. 187
Wallace, Dwane 39, 53, 63, 89, 90, 117
Wallace, Dwight 39, 63, 64, 132
Walsh, James C. 131
War Production Board (WPB) 53
Ward, J. Carlton 58
Warner Aircraft Corp. 26
Warner Scarab/Super Scarab engines 26, 39
Waterman, Waldo 33
Waterman Arrowbile 62
Waterman Arrowplane 33

Weaver, George E. "Buck" 8
Weaver Aircraft Co. (*see* Advance, WACO) 8
Wegner, Arthur E. 155, 163
Weick, Fred A. 40, 88, 159
Weick W-1 (*see* ERCO) 40
Welch, Jack (GE) 184
Wells, T.A. "Ted" 30, 39, 64
White, Malcolm 142
Wichita Aircraft Co. 9
Wichita Division 178
Wichita University 39
Williams, Al 20
Williams EJ22 engine 181
Williams FJ 33 211
Williams/Rolls FJ44 engine 162, 179
Wing, George 94
Wing Aircraft Company 94
Wing Derringer 94
Wittman, Steve 81, 169
Wittman W-8/W-10 Whirlwind 81
Wolsey & Co. 135
World War I 5, 13
World War II 79, 80, 86, 99, 163
Wright, Theodore P. 75
Wright Aeronautical Co. 10, 21, 29
Wright-Bellanca monoplane 21
Wright brothers 18
Wright R3350 engine 49
Wright Whirlwind engine 26, 30
WTA, Inc. 130
Wyandotte Pup 32

Yankey, Charles 10, 44, 60, 64, 72, 82
Yeager, Jeana 152
Young, Arthur 168
Young, W.C. 35

Zenith aircraft: CH650 191; CH701 44, 191; CH750 191; CH801 191
Zenith Aircraft Co. 144, 191

www.ingramcontent.com/pod-product-compliance
Lightning Source LLC
Chambersburg PA
CBHW032036300426
44117CB00009B/1082